Technical Assistance in Theory and Practice

PRAEGER SPECIAL STUDIES IN
INTERNATIONAL ECONOMICS AND DEVELOPMENT

Technical Assistance in Theory and Practice

THE CASE OF IRAN

Jahangir Amuzegar

FREDERICK A. PRAEGER, Publishers
New York • Washington • London

The purpose of the Praeger Special Studies is to make specialized research monographs in U.S. and international economics and politics available to the academic, business, and government communities. For further information, write to the Special Projects Division, Frederick A. Praeger, Publishers, 111 Fourth Avenue, New York, N.Y. 10003.

FREDERICK A. PRAEGER, PUBLISHERS
111 Fourth Avenue, New York, N.Y. 10003, U.S.A.
77-79 Charlotte Street, London W.1, England

Published in the United States of America in 1966
by Frederick A. Praeger, Inc., Publishers

Second printing, 1967

Library of Congress Catalog Card Number: 65-27476

Printed in the United States of America

ACKNOWLEDGMENT

I wish to express my debts of gratitude to those who have helped bring this study to fruition.

My first word of thanks is owed to my former professors at the University of California at Los Angeles who, in addition to educating me in the field of economics, guided the development of my doctoral dissertation on the subject of technical assistance.

Long discussions of the subject held with my former colleagues in the course of my university teaching in the United States have been a rich source of inspiration and assistance to me. I owe these benefactors (too many to mention, and too difficult to associate with any single idea or contribution) a large intellectual debt.

I also wish to thank my many friends at the Agency for International Development in Washington and the U.S. AID Mission to Iran for having placed (or caused to be placed) at my disposal a good deal of statistical data and unclassified materials on Point IV. Without their valuable cooperation and assistance, the preparation of this study would have been virtually impossible.

My sincerest expression of debt also goes to a host of interviewees among the Mission staff, the Iranian government officials and others (too numerous to acknowledge and perhaps too happy to remain anonymous) who have selflessly helped me with their treasured information and thoughtful comments.

A good part of this study was prepared during a leave of absence from my teaching duties at Occidental College, under a Research Professorship from the Brookings Institution granted by the Ford Foundation. I am grateful to them all. Needless to say, they bear no responsibility for the views expressed here, or for their publication in the present volume.

The contents of this study are my own private research and views, and should in no manner be taken to reflect the views of my Government or those of my present Office.

Washington, July, 1965
J.A.

CONTENTS

PART III

THE WELCOME MAT

PART IV

THE ORDER, THE ORGANIZATION AND THE ORGANIZATION MEN

Technical Assistance in Theory and Practice

INTRODUCTION

As the Fourth Point in his Inaugural Address of January 20, 1949, President Harry S. Truman announced a "bold new program" of technical assistance to the underdeveloped world. The purpose of the program, later called Point IV, was to help the people of underprivileged areas help themselves to attain a better and fuller life through advanced technology.

Although the willingness of advanced nations to share the fruits of their knowledge, skill and experience with developing countries had already been expressed in the charters of the Atlantic Alliance and the United Nations, the President's proposal evoked a great deal of acclaim and enthusiasm both in the United States and abroad, and was hailed as new, positive, and effective American foreign economic policy. Praising it himself, President Truman proclaimed that for the first time in history, humanity possessed the skill and knowledge to relieve human suffering.[1] Point Four was to symbolize this skill and knowledge.

Four and a half years after the Presidential address, Paul Kennedy of the New York Times summed up the results of the program in a bold sentence. "Point Four," he wrote from the Middle East, "has done more to change attitudes toward the United States than the entire expenditure of life and treasure on the Korean peninsula."[2] Two weeks later came a strong rebuttal in no uncertain terms: "On the contrary," opined a seasoned student of the area, "it may be said that no policy of the United States in living memory has done more to create suspicions and resentment in Asia and the Middle East than Point Four."[3]

For a number of years the program continued to attract the enthusiastic admiration of its friends along with the relentless abuses of its foes. Toward the end of the decade, however, the wave of interest and enthusiasm about the "new" venture gradually receded and settled. And the ensuing discussions about the significance of technical assistance in coping with humanity's age-old ills took a more serious and sober look.[4]

1

The purpose of this study, a decade and a half after the Point Four enunciation, is to explore the possibilities and limitations of foreign technical assistance in promoting the socio-economic aspirations of the emerging nations from the standpoint of <u>their</u> interests and <u>their</u> needs. [5] The United States bilateral technical assistance program in Iran during 1950-1965 has been chosen as a case.

In selecting the United States Point IV program as an example of foreign technical assistance, and Iran as a model of an aid-receiving country, two basic considerations have been the deciding factor. The U.S. Point IV has been the fore-runner of the largest and the most comprehensive of all technical aid programs, and the United States is considered to be the best purveyor of the techniques and technicians needed by developing countries. [6] Iran, too, has been the first bene-ficiary of Point IV aid, and host to one of the largest technical assistance missions under the Mutual Security program, representing, in the opinion of some U.S. officials, the "show-place" of Point IV operations with respect to the "success of the program," "morale of the mission," and over-all effective-ness in "reaching the people." [7]

The present study will attempt to provide a systematic analysis of Point IV operations in Iran with a view to finding some meaningful theoretical and practical lessons from this "new" international venture. Inasmuch as Iran presents many of the problems of the emerging nations and shares many of their technological interests and needs, the study's major find-ings may also be of some value in the more general discussion of the transfer of technology from advanced nations to the underdeveloped world.

This inquiry will be limited to selected theoretical and practical considerations regarding three major aspects of the problem: (1) Iran's need for foreign technical assistance and her preparedness to receive such aid from the United States; (2) America's supply of technical assistants and her ability to meet Iranian requirements; and (3) Point IV's specific role in implementing a rational transfer of U.S. techniques and tech-nicians to the Iranian economy. Accordingly, Part I will first discuss the program and its activities in Iran, and then present a framework for analyzing program achievements. Part II will be devoted to a discussion of objectives, plans, and priorities in the program. Iran's ability and willingness to receive Point IV aid will be discussed in Part III. America's ability and readiness to help Iran will be taken up in Part IV. Part V will sum up the results and the lessons learned.

The U.S. agency in charge of Point IV operations in Iran during the 1950-1965 period has at various times been called U.S. Technical Cooperation/Iran, U.S. Operations Mission/Iran, and finally U.S. Aid Mission/Iran. For the sake of brevity, the term "Mission" is used herein for the entire period. The origin, development, activities and organization of the Mission will be discussed in the appropriate Chapters.

In preparing this study, use was made of available materials on the subject in the United States and in Iran. Interviews were conducted with American personnel, Iranian officials and other experienced and interested parties. On occasions, the investigation was supplemented by a number of field trips to the sites of some of the Mission's "showcase" projects. Observations were also made of the Mission activities and operations in the various ministries and agencies of the Iranian government.

The materials used in the study are based on a good deal of unpublished notes, memoranda, reports and brochures in the Mission's unclassified files both in Washington and Tehran; they also include some documents in the Iranian government's open files. No access was possible to the U.S. Mission's extensive "classified" records, which reportedly include information of significant research value. The secrecy and caution shown by some AID officials in refusing to divulge information even of no particular security importance have undoubtedly detracted from the import of this research; but this has been unavoidable.

Extensive use has been made of several hundreds of unpublished completion-of-tour reports (CTR) written by U.S. technicians and assistants in Iran. Included in the materials used is also a "limited distribution" study by the Mission, called the Review of U.S. Technical Assistance and Economic Aid to Iran, in a mimeographed form originally prepared as a reply to an investigating Congressional Committee and apparently destined for publication.

The collection of data for the preparation of this study has not been easy. Partly because of the strained political situation in Iran during most of the early period, and partly due to the Iranians' characteristic revulsion to formal indiscretion, no independent, evaluative analysis or examination of Point IV operations in Iran has been published in Persian. Almost all the news items (and many of the write-ups) concerning Point IV activities in the country in Persian newspapers were supplied to them by the Mission's Information Office. No reference is made to these items here.

Several difficulties were also encountered in conducting the interviews. In view of the author's Iranian nationality and his obvious allegiance to his country, most of the Point IV staff were understandably reluctant to open their hearts, and to deviate from the organization's "official line." Some of them promised to discuss the problems after they left the agency. Only a few (and notably the academicians among the Mission staff) consented to a deeper probing of the issues involved, and an impassioned discussion of these issues. On the Iranian side, too, the author's long sojourn in the United States and his associations with American universities, made the over-suspicious Iranians a bit reluctant to be perfectly frank. There was also reluctance on the part of many informed Iranians to having their "private views" publicized one way or the other.

Although due care has been taken to be as impartial as possible by collecting facts, figures and observations from different sources in order to support the study's major contentions, the findings of this study are likely to displease many Iranians and a good number of Americans. Undoubtedly, many Iranian chauvinists, who wish never to see unkind remarks about their country or culture in print, may be annoyed to find certain unembellished discussions of Iran's trials and tribulations. Many of the Point IV careerists, too, who regard any (and particularly Iranian) criticisms of their program as a sign of misinformation, if not downright ingratitude, may find some of the comments here perhaps harsh and unappreciative.

Yet, neither has the author intended to be uncomplimentary to his beloved country; nor has he meant to underrate the United States' valuable efforts to help his countrymen. If he has been critical at one point or another, it is because he has tried to be impartial. The comments received from readers of this study in manuscript form already indicate that the author's recognition of the Iranian problems (e.g., insufficient receptivity to the American type of technical assistance) is likely to be concurred with by the majority of the Mission assistants.

And what is said about Point IV (e.g., insufficient ability to solve the Iranian problems) is likely to be agreed to by the majority of Iranian observers. But the likelihood of a concensus on both sides about mutual inadequacies and limitations may, alas, still remain as distant as the two countries' distant lands and distant cultures.

References

1. "Text of the President's Inaugural Address," New York Times, January 21, 1949, p. 4.

2. Paul P. Kennedy, "Concept and Scope of Point 4 Viewed as Undergoing Shift," New York Times, September 24, 1953, p. 12.

3. Elgin Groseclose, "Point Four Aid Discussed," New York Times, October 5, 1953, p. 26.

4. See E. Larrabee, "Changing American Attitude Toward Point IV," Confluence (January, 1960).

5. The significance of the program from the standpoint of American interests and American politico-strategic or socio-economic objectives is not discussed here, and requires a separate study in itself.

6. Elaborating on the fourth point of his Inaugural Address of January 1949, President Truman maintained that a "careful examination of the existing information concerning the underprivileged countries shows particular need for technicians and experts with U.S. training." (Italics not in the original.)

7. See the testimonies of Norman Paul and Henry Byroade on the Mutual Security Act of 1954, Hearings before the Committee on Foreign Affairs, House of Representatives, 83rd Cong., 2nd Sess., (Washington, 1954), pp. 489-490.

PART I
THE HELPING HAND

CHAPTER 1 THE POINT IV STORY

In a changing society it is the race between the old problems solved and the new problems created that determines the pace of progress and the effectiveness of a given policy or program toward that progress.

This Chapter presents a summary of Point IV programs, projects, and activities in Iran during the 1950-1965 period carried out by the United States Operations Mission to Iran (and its predecessor agencies) in charge of US-Iran technical cooperation. While the discussion involves the major types of work accomplished by the Mission in their relation to the magnitude of the problems faced, it will not be a detailed and comprehensive catalog of all Point IV activities in the country. In discussing the Mission's achievements and impacts in each field of activity, too, a detailed chronicle of the individual projects, their provisions or their results is avoided. Full details on these and other Point IV activities may be found in the Mission's reports, brochures, and documents noted in this study. [1] The intention here is to pinpoint major accomplishments.

Most of the information regarding the scope, progress and impact of the projects is taken from various documents supplied by the Mission, and taken for the most part in their face value. In most cases no other alternative has been available. Since almost all the news items printed in Iran concerning Point IV work have been in one way or the other supplied by the Mission's information office, a reference to them has been considered repetitious and unnecessary.

ACCOMPLISHMENTS BY FIELDS OF ACTIVITY

As can be expected, the success of the Point IV program in Iran has not been the same in every field, but rather uneven.

In the field of Agriculture the Mission program, in cooperation with the Ministry of Agriculture and its affiliated Bongahs,
the Agricultural Bank, the Bank Omran, and the Karaj Agricultural College, was concentrated on six principal lines
of action: development of basic agricultural practices,
mostly through extension work; improvement of plant science;
livestock improvement and disease control; forestry and
conservation; improvement of water resources and facilities;
and "land reform," including agricultural credit and cooperative management.

The Mission's success in these lines was varied. In the
areas of livestock improvement, forest and range management,
and improvement of irrigation practices, the Mission's achievements do not seem commensurate with the expended money and
effort. In undertaking new research (particularly in seed
improvement), however, the results were worth the effort,
although, again, a better coordination with other projects and
programs would have brought more productive results.

A bigger and more remarkable contribution was the introduction of an almost revolutionary concept of agricultural
learning through practice. Agricultural education in Iran
before 1950 was modelled after the old systems where the
place of learning was separate from the place of work; men
of learning were also separated from the practitioners of
knowledge by social status, outlook and mental capacity.
Almost totally divorced from the practical application of their
knowledge, most of the graduates used to become desk-
conscious employees of the Ministry of Agriculture, leaving
farm practices to millions of illiterate peasants who had to
learn from each other. Thus, in many areas of Iranian agriculture, the common practice did not go far beyond what
Iranian peasants knew some 2500 years ago.

A Utah State Agricultural College team, contracted by the
Mission, was successful in making significant inroads into the
whole way of thinking about the College, its responsibility and
its place in the agricultural life of Iran. A new four-year
curriculum with separate fields of specialization was established; a demonstration farm was spruced up; several new
dormitories, a functional laboratory and a usable library were
built and equipped; and a number of the College's faculty were
sent to the United States for study and observation.

Another "cultural shock" in the Iranian agricultural com-munity was brought about by the introduction to Iran of the essentially American concepts of agricultural extension and 4-H Clubs.   The Service and the Clubs were designed to bridge the gap between the illiterate practitioners in the field and the non-practicing scientists at the Agricultural College and the Ministry.   Prior to the introduction of the extension service, the average peasant's contact with the Ministry of Agriculture staff was, in the words of a Mission advisor, limited mostly to the latter's exercise of sovereignty, i.e., their tax collection and police function. [2]   Agricultural ex-tension began to emphasize a new aspect of this relationship: the guidance function, and the concept of the "government for the benefit of the people." The significance of this function in the Iranian setting was particularly profound because the pre-valence of illiteracy among Iranian peasants, and their in-ability to make use of published material, made the extension agents' "word of mouth" the best method of giving them know-how, self reliance and courage.

The agricultural program was bolstered by the dispatch of some 270 Iranian agricultural specialists to the United States for study and observation.   The whole scheme is still young and has a long and tortuous way to go. And due to the existence of formidable obstacles in its way (e.g., old-timers' resistance, paucity of real local research in the Ministry or the College, inadequate coordination among the agencies concerned, and the inadequacy of financial support), it is still regarded by some cynics as too sophisticated a program for Iran.   There is also a possibility that a lot may happen to change the program's orientation and effectiveness before the Service's present 1200 agents reach the goal of 6,000, (two for each 1,000 families in Iran as against three for each 1,000 families in the United States), or the present 500 4-H Clubs approaches U.S. proportions.   But a cornerstone is laid and the building on it is going up now.

In the field of Public Health, the program was designed to provide both technical and financial assistance for the im-provement of general health and sanitary conditions in Iran. The principal activities centered around the development of public health facilities, mobile health units, health centers and laboratories; endemic disease control (e.g., malaria eradica-tion); and environmental sanitation, including health education (e.g., sanitary water works and deep water wells, public baths and sanitary privies, schools for nursing, sanitary science, and medical laboratory science).

The most noteworthy (and a widely publicized) achievement in this field was the control of malaria, a most devastating health hazard in some heavily populated parts of Iran. Originally started in the late 1940's by the Iranian government and the World Health Organization, the project was given a big boost by the Mission's contribution of sizeable amounts of DDT and the necessary trained personnel. With continued help from WHO, the Near East Foundation, and UNICEF, the Mission teams sprayed some 16,000 villages four years reportedly bringing malaria incidence in Iran from an alarming average rate of 67 per cent to an insignificant and tolerable 5.2%. Although a new species of DDT-resisting mosquito has developed recently threatening these and other areas, the situation can never be the same again.

A less conspicuous achievement, but one of much greater originality and wider impact, was the propagation of the concept of public health and disease prevention, as contrasted with the familiar notion of cure. Prior to Point IV assistance, the Ministry of Health's budget for public health activities was no more than 10% of the total; organization, methods and supplies were inadequate, and almost none of the professional staff had formal public health training. Continued large sums had to be spent on combating the recurrent epidemics with little funds, personnel or interest available to survey and control the outbreak of communicable diseases.

By establishing a public health cooperative and by giving it good support in terms of personnel, supplies and authority, the Mission managed to establish a nucleus of small but appreciative native staff, and helped them make some significant and lasting contributions to the whole area of public health. Despite some early handicaps (unfamiliarity with village folkways, haphazard allocation of funds, mal-distribution of sanitary supplies) the concept of public hygiene began to spread fast. Good in-service training of Ministry employees and successful publicity in getting villagers acquainted with public health measures (sanitary toilets, unpolluted water, innoculation) brought noteworthy results. Some skeptical villagers who at the beginning had to be bribed to accept free toilet slabs, water pumps, or preventive shots, were later willing to accept them and pay a share of their costs.

Despite some post-Integration set-backs (and some doubts on the part of a Mission advisor [3] about people's sufficient knowledge for healthy life, adequate motivation to change their unhealthy living patterns, enough confidence to cooperate with health agencies, and minimum stimulus to initiate health activities), the concept of public health has been accepted by enough Ministry leaders to make it stick. The Mission's handwriting on the village mud walls (such as "innoculated against smallpox," "DDT'd against Malaria") has left its in-delible mark even if it is for no other reason than the villagers' inability to whitewash them! The departments of public health and environmental sanitation, too, continue to be part and parcel of the Ministry of Health because the incumbents' bureaucratic magic for survival is powerful enough to ward off the evil eye.

In Education, the Mission program was designed to pro-vide additional school facilities, more and better trained teachers, better reading material, and a revised curriculum. In implementing the program, intensive teacher training courses were established, and a number of Iranian nationals were sent abroad. Elementary schools in the rural areas were built, repaired or equipped. Books, pamphlets, charts, maps and other educational supplies were distributed to schools. School curricula were changed to include fundamental education, vocational (agricultural and industrial) education, home economics and physical education. Through a contract with the Syracuse University Film Unit, a number of motion pictures in support of the Mission's agriculture and health activities were prepared and shown in the villages.

The most outstanding achievements here were changes in the psychology of teaching, school-community relations, teachers' outlook and school administration. Point IV assist-ance made many Iranian teachers realize that interest in the capabilities, aptitudes, emotions, and individual problems of their students was no less important than interest in the subject matter which was so close to their hearts. By using real-life experiments along with academic subjects, the youngsters were taught to regard the school not as separate, but as an integral part of their later living -- a somewhat new concept in Iran, where schools were regarded as a kind of purgatory, the redemption from which should be relished with absolving merriment.

Keeping up with the progress of science through reading and research was emphasized by requiring special examinations

for promotion -- an almost revolutionary step in an environment where even university teachers were sometimes lecturing
out of their thirty-year-old notebooks, and had to show no
other qualification for promotion than seniority. A significant
change was made in the system of administrative supervision,
where ministry inspectors no longer served as investigators
and fault-finders, but as guides to better teaching and administering schools. Good progress was also noticeable in
making elementary textbooks more interesting and readable.

Compared with the number and magnitude of the unsolved
problems in the Iranian public education (e.g., ever-increasing
demand by an awakened and rising population to get into
school; acute shortage of school buildings, teachers and supplies; a lack of private support for financing higher education;
and the continuing dilemma within the Ministry of Education
about the contents of curricula and stages of education) the
Mission's efforts were probably a drop in a vast ocean. But no
matter how small the relative magnitude of these efforts may
seem, their impact on those who came into contact with them
was deep-rooted and irreversible.

The experience of some of the Mission's keener observers
is a good indication of this impact. The impression that these
technicians got early in their tour was very different from
what they noticed later. At first, the people had the feeling
that the lack of funds was the most serious if not the only
restraining influence in the development of educational opportunities. Accordingly, there was a tremendous demand for
material objects, and a dearth of inquiries related to professional activities. At the close of their tours, however, they
noticed a large number of people who had come to realize
that money was only one of the problems along with several
others, and who developed a profound interest in ideas and
institutions. [4]

In the field of Public Administration, the Mission established six main projects aimed at strengthening the organization, personnel and procedures of the GOI ministries, improving the quality of public statistics, establishing an Institute
for Administrative Affairs, reorganizing municipal management, and assisting the Iranian Plan Organization in its
administrative reforms.

As early as 1954, advice and assistance were given to
the Ministry of Finance for the establishment of program

budgeting. Special efforts were made in 1955 to introduce the American technique of position classification. Plans were made in 1955 to conduct and publish a national census, develop a statistical program and improve the statistical system. A municipal management association was formed. A special law for creating the positions of stable undersecretaries was passed in 1959, and a High Council was created to provide stability and continuity within the Iranian administration.

As can be expected in a delicate and sensitive area such as Public Administration, the results were not as noticeable as those in agriculture, education and health. Of the special legislation prepared for the establishment of a high council of administrative undersecretaries, government reorganization, income tax reform, municipal administration, the civil service commission, and the independent audit agency, only the first was passed. [5]

Of the new institutions that were set up, the High Council of the Undersecretaries and the Municipal Association gradually lost their original impetus and orientation; and until 1964 when a new Budget Bureau was established, performance budgeting became simply a name (or misnomer) for the traditional budgets. The Position Classification Survey was continued for a year after its U.S. financial support ended, was later transferred into a moribund agency for a while, and then virtually abandoned. The Public Statistics Project finished its first phase of operation by publishing the first national census of Iran. Later on, its budget was reduced; some of its employees shifted to other agencies, and its initial glamour was lost.

The Institute for Administrative Affairs, started in 1955 through a contract with the University of Southern California, went through a long period of near-fatal crises, and after some behind-the-scenes bickering among the "old guard" (who wished it to be a part of the University of Tehran School of Law) and the "young Turks" (who wished to set it up outside the University system) was finally established in the Law School. Transferred into a newly-established School of Business and Public Administration in 1964 as part of the Tehran University, the Institute still has a long way from becoming an efficient American-type institution of higher learning. But it is a going concern with a staff, a curriculum and a library of its own, offering specialized courses to social science students.

Managerial assistance to the Plan Organization was offered through a third-party contract, because the Plan management was reportedly "reluctant" to accept the Mission's
advice in its operating and administrative problems. [6] The
contract was signed in 1957 with Washington's newly-established
Governmental Affairs Institute, and hailed by the Plan management at the time as the forerunner of sweeping administrative
reforms not only in the Plan Organization but in the whole
administrative machinery of the Iranian government. The
group, consisting of eight men recruited by the Institute in the
open market, undertook the task of reorganizing the Plan
Organization and began its work in the areas of organization
and methods, budgeting, finance, and personnel management.
In the first phase of its task, it took the group a good three and
a half years just to get a reorganization chart approved by the
Plan management, with very little substantive change over the
existing one. In the area of methods and procedures, the
suggested reporting forms were favorably received but did not
get widespread acceptance. Filing, record keeping and office
procedures were relatively more successful. In the budgeting
and finance phase of the project, the group's simple manual
on finance was fairly well accepted and implemented. In
personnel management the personnel manual, position classification procedure and salary schedules suggested by the
group were not implemented. In manpower development, a
very good start was made in collecting data on Iran's manpower resources and requirements published by the Institute
and the Plan Organization. [7]

Altogether, the Mission's public administration activities
achieved some of its more mechanical goals in matters of
form, style and method, but could do little to improve the
substance of administration. But this type of operation was
naturally subject to rapidly diminishing returns. There was
only so much that could be done within the narrow framework
of the administrative status quo. [8]

Community Development was another field where Mission
efforts again revolved around the purely mechanical aspects
of the problem. The original Project 30 (Crown Land Distribution) was established in 1952 to provide "supervision,
training and guidance" to the beneficiaries of Crown Lands
who were "actively engaged in tilling the soil." The Mission's
role in the project, however, was largely limited to financial
support. The Chief of the Mission's Community Development

Division apparently did not approve of the policy and methods followed in land distribution.   While he agreed that in the absence of proper resettlement programs, additional lands, and non-agricultural employment opportunities for the excess farmers it was impossible to follow any other methods, he still questioned the wisdom of parcelling the available land equally among the operating peasants regardless of the size of holdings. [9] Another Mission advisor two years later observed that the land division had often been economically unsound with units too small or too poor to provide minimum credit requirements, and no organization or plan to give technical assistance to the new landowners. [10]   And the Near East Foundation team that had the responsibility of administering the project agreed that inadequate surveying of land, insufficient consideration of the economic size of individual holdings, uneven capabilities of farmers for making proper use of the land, the difficulty of new landowners to accept responsibility for decision-making, lack of educational or organizational programs prior to distribution, and the absence of efficient credit organizations left the program accomplishments "a good deal to be desired." [11]

The Community Development Project went into operation in 1954, a year after it was signed, and eventually absorbed other related projects.   This was an omnibus scheme dealing with projects as concrete as slabs for village latrines, and as abstract as democracy in village councils.   Hundreds of small village units (baths, mosques, schools, mortuaries, water systems, roads, bridges, clinics, adult literacy classes in fundamental education, and village councils) were established.

On the credit side of the program, apart from physical improvements, particular mention ought to be made of the introduction of the spirit of self-reliance and cooperation into Iranian village thinking and practice.   Feeder roads, bridges, water works and other village units that were built on a "do-it-yourself" basis and through the villages' own cooperative effort, were good omens for a democratic awakening of many dormant souls.

Due to the essentially institutional nature of the project, however, significant deficiencies have been reported in its execution and effectiveness.   A Mission advisor, assigned to make an evaluation of the program and the Near East Foundation's role in it, concluded that the project's organization was encumbered by too widely-spread activities, inexperienced personnel, lack of proper training and organization programs in the village, cumbersome administrative practices, general lack of public and government interest and support, and lack of clear understanding of the function of community development. The Near East Foundation that was contracted to administer the program, too, was found to be spreading its professional resources too thinly, carrying out a number of non-related activities, and employing far too many advisors in relation to the stage of program development. [12] Observations made by others in the field also show that many of the village installations were not properly appreciated, used or maintained. Too many village councils reportedly fumbled, and few of the "loans" made to these councils were ever paid back.

The field of Industry and Engineering (including transportation and communications) had by far the largest number of projects. The Mission's contribution was mostly financial assistance for the expansion of Iran's industrial capacity. The major share of aid for the improvement of Iran's transportation and communication systems also took the form of financial aid. In the words of the Chief of the Division's Transport and Communications Branch, during the seven and a half years in which he was in Iran, "remarkable progress" was made in certain phases of the program, but these accomplishments in his opinion were "mostly in physical improvements." The major job yet to be done, he added, was "to develop the organizations and training of Iranian nationals for carrying out an integrated transportation and communications system in Iran." [13]

The technical assistance offered by the Industry Division was mainly through the consulting and industrial management services of George Fry & Associates of Chicago. The Fry group was hired by the Mission through a $1,175,000 contract in 1954 to help the Plan Organization reorganize, streamline and prepare its money-losing factories for sale to private enterprise. The group had the additional charge of attracting foreign private investment into Iran for new enterprises. In the four years of operation under Project 79, the group's nine technicians established a reasonably practical cost-accounting system for the sugar and cement companies and an accounting management audit system in the textile mills. Appraisals were made of approximately fifty government plants; a number of analyses and reports were prepared about the regulations of foreign investment in Iran, and Iran's industrial needs.

Yet, despite the relatively high calibre of the group membership, their lasting achievements do not seem to loom large. Sugar company reorganization and management practices suggested by the group (and accepted at first) were not continued later because of a change in the directorship of these companies. The group's recommendations to reduce the number of excess workers in the textile and cement factories were found impractical and unacceptable by the Plan Organization. Only two small plants were finally sold, and their sale had nothing to do with the Fry services.

After the termination of the original contract in 1959, the Mission re-hired the group through a new two-year, $375,000 contract under Project 109 to assist the Ministry of Industry's newly-established Industrial Development Center in its program of technical assistance to private industry and, again, for the attraction of foreign private capital. [14] In the new capacity, the group became involved in some demoralizing friction with the Center's Iranian management regarding budgetary support, transportation facilities, quality of counterparts and over-all cooperation. It also came into conflict with the Mission's own Industry Division staff regarding jurisdictional responsibility. [15] In the meantime, a number of brochures and industry guides were prepared and distributed among private investors, and some technical advice on accounting and office management was offered. These achievements, however, did not keep the Ministry from complaining that "no positive results" were achieved in getting "small loans from foreign sources to assist in the development of small and medium industry." [16]

In the relatively minor fields of Point IV activity, the Mission had its most outstanding, although least publicized, success in its Project 33 (Public Safety). The project, manned from the very beginning by people who knew their profession well, succeeded in the nearly complete overhaul of the operational techniques in the Police Department. The Police Academy and the In-Service Police School were aided through the establishment of a revised three-year curriculum, a professional faculty, and a police library. Police communications were improved through the installation of a modern radio network, and an automatic telephone exchange on patrol cars. A modern identification bureau, complete with national fingerprint file, a photo section, and a scientific crime laboratory was instituted. The Tehran traffic was brought under partial control through an effective traffic education program, intersection control, street marking, and proper accident report and analysis.

In the field of Labor, the Mission's work (Project 41) was in labor training, establishing labor standards, improving management-labor relations, and employment security. Under this project a national employment service was established in the Ministry of Labor. Skill-improvement and on-the-job training classes were set up; regulations and procedures of factory inspection and labor law enforcement were prepared; labor relations conferences and seminars were conducted for both labor and management; and recreational facilities were provided for Isfahan workers. Yet, here again, no substantive aid seems to have been received in the delicate areas of labor legislation, management-labor relations and industrial democracy.

POINT IV BENEFICIARIES

The discussion of Point IV achievements in Iran will not be complete without reference to the beneficiaries of the program.

In its first Annual Report put out in 1952, the Mission claimed that "In all cases its projects had been designed with the objectives of assuring that the benefits will flow to the people of the rural areas who comprise over 80% of Iran's population." Seven years later, in the course of the Senate Foreign Relations Committee hearings on the Mutual Security Act of 1959, Senator Hubert Humphrey of Minnesota sounded as though he had some doubts about the fulfillment of the Mission objectives:

> My observations, based partly on the comments people visiting the area have made to me, is that in Iran the rich in the country are getting richer, and the poor are not getting much better off. This is not the observation of any one person. This is the usual observation. [17]

Despite such observations, the fact that the masses of cultivators and laborers were helped by the Point IV assistance (or total U.S. aid, for that matter) is hard to deny, although the extent of these benefits cannot be accurately ascertained. Those directly involved in Mission activities, i.e., those who were helped with improved seed, healthier poultry or live-stock, a few new tools, some medical treatment or preventive innoculations, and a token of new village facilities undoubtedly improved their lot. They did receive something which they would not have received without Point IV aid. Their number may not have been large in comparison to those who needed similar assistance; in relation to their needs, too, the amount of aid they received may not have been substantial. But in the absence of reliable statistical data to the contrary, it would be difficult to say they were not better off. Needless to say, a part of the assistance that was meant for the peasants, or offered for their benefit, helped the landlords too, and per-haps even more.   But that does not alter the fact that the latter had no monopoly in receiving aid.

The chief beneficiary of the Point IV program in Iran, however, seems to have been the Iranian government itself; in a sense, the country as a whole. In addition to the Mission's financial assistance to the Plan Organization and the other state agencies, the Iranian government managed to meet some of its most urgent foreign exchange needs during the oil crisis. Thanks also to the Mission's foreign exchange resources, the Iranian government was able during this foreign exchange crisis to help some 900 Iranian students in the United States with limited amounts of "cheap" dollars needed to continue their studies in America. Without this assistance many of the students would have had no other alternative but to leave their studies unfinished and return to Iran empty handed.

Another main beneficiary of Point IV in Iran was the Mis-sion's large local staff -- a variety of employees from janitors, drivers and office clerks to various technicians, engineers, doctors and lawyers.   Outstanding among the professional personnel, also, was a group of American-trained Iranians who, by virtue of their qualifications, knowledge of English, familiarity with the United States, and connection with one another, were given priority to work for the Mission. These and other Point IV employees received good salaries, favor-able treatment and a number of enviable privileges. In view of the reduced government activities and rising unemployment following the oil nationalization, job opportunities for most of these people were few indeed. In the absence of such income and employment possibilities, almost all of these people would have added to the Iranian government's already unbearably large body of civil servants, or joined the country's unemployed and intrigue-bound intellectuals.

Next to this group was a large number of Iranian nationals sent abroad, mostly to the United States, as Point IV trainees for periods varying from three months to a year. These individuals, chosen from among Point IV's own employees, government officials and private citizens, were enabled to travel abroad, see new things and new places, broaden their experience, improve their training, and occasionally also receive higher educational degrees. Without Point IV most of these people would have had no chance for free travel and/or education outside of Iran.

The last group of beneficiaries were private industrialists who received technical assistance and guidance from a Mission-financed team of management consultants in the Industrial Guidance Center, as well as the Mission-backed loans from the Industrial Guarantee Fund. But in both cases the benefits were perhaps not very large.

NEW PROBLEMS RAISED AND NET RESULTS

Disregarding the political, social, and moral issues involved, the short-term economic benefits derived from Point IV should be weighed against at least two "cost" considerations. The first set of offsetting "costs" in the Point IV case involved budgetary and balance-of-payments difficulties which developed as a result of (a) the local government's commitment to pay its fair share of the program's cost; (b) increased national propensity to import; and (c) misdirected investments. The second set of "costs" involved the disrupting impact on joint projects of the sudden cessation of U.S. grants and gifts.

The Iranian government's inability to fully pay its share of the program's outlay and its obligation to pay arrears in subsequent years were constant drags on the perennially deficit-ridden public budget. The balance-of-payments problems of the mid-1950's which necessitated an austerity-oriented Economic Stabilization Program in 1960 were also

traceable, partly at least, to the "demonstration effects" of
Point IV activities.   The major residential housing recession
in the city of Tehran, starting in 1959 and continuing well into
the 1960's, was also partly caused by excessive and miscalculated local investments in modern quarters, presumably, to
take care of the Mission technicians' increasing demand for
American-type houses.   The demoralizing effect on the joint
projects of the sudden and drastic reduction of U.S. technical
aid after the Integration is also on the debit side of the program.   The unfavorable impact of Integration on many young
and burgeoning projects was much greater than the amount of
aid withheld.   In many cases the people's desire and enthusiasm for furthering project goals were so suddenly lost, or the
projects' momentum was so notably reduced, that the situation
could not be brought back to normal without an expenditure of
money and effort greater than that which was required at first.

A similar type of argument can be presented about the
political benefits of the program for Iran. Some of the Mission's more outspoken interviewees seemed to believe that the
very presence of American technicians in different parts of
Iran was valuable enough to the country to outweigh all other
considerations.   By being present and involved in far-flung
development activities in various parts of the country, so the
argument ran, U.S. technicians could give moral support to,
and put necessary confidence in, the Iranian leadership to solve
their development problems.   And, most important of all, as
long as they were physically present on location there would
be an assurance that activities from the rival camp could not
fill the existing socio-political vacuum and sabotage local
development efforts.

This argument may have validity under certain circumstances.   But in the Iranian case, it does not seem to go very
far. While the significance of American moral support to many
resistance-generating projects cannot be denied, it should
also be remembered that the very presence of too many
Americans spread over a country had its own discernible
politico-economic disadvantages. Senator William Fulbright
of Arkansas, Chairman of the Senate Foreign Relations Committee, seems to have no doubts about these disadvantages:

        The United States maintains aid programs in
    about 90 countries. Many are token programs

designed to maintain an American 'presence'
which I take to be a euphemism for the exertion
of one form or another of political leverage.
It is an open question whether an American aid
'presence' gains any more leverage than it gives.
There is often far more to be gained by a conspicuous American 'absence' from a country than
by an American 'presence.' [18]

In the case of Iran, too, the American "presence" was not
without cost. [19]

A quantitative analysis of the foregoing costs and benefits
is not possible. But a qualitative evaluation by His Majesty
the Shah is available:

Naturally some of the technical assistance
directors in Iran have been less imaginative and
effective than others, and the same has applied to
their subordinates, a few of whom have had to be
sent home. Inevitably some of the projects have
been less wisely conceived than others, and a few
have had to be abandoned as ill-advised. But
taken as a whole, the work in Iran has provided
us with never-failing aid and inspiration in our
successful efforts to build a better nation.

I am happy to recognize that Point Four has
helped us towards the achievements that I described in the chapters on agriculture and education. In the field of public health, their medical
and nursing technicians have joined hands with
our own experts to work with missionary zeal in
the most far-away places.

These few illustrations of Point Four assistance by no means exhaust the list, nor do they
convey what the work has meant to us. For example, the programme has helped us expand our
industry and improve our transport and communications. It has sent hundreds of Persians
abroad for study and observation in their chosen
fields. It has financed the production of over a
hundred technical assistance films for teaching

first principles in such fields as agriculture and public health; and these have had a tremendous popular impact, especially in the villages.[20]

* * *

The forthcoming "vivisection" of the Point IV program in Iran is not designed or intended to reflect upon any particular project, program or policy. Nor is it meant to blame what is found imperfect or deficient on any one person, agency or country. The intention is to examine the facts in order to discover the defective factors; to dissect the parts to be able to build a better whole; to see what actually happened in the past in order to uncover the right paths (and to avoid blind alleys) in the future.

References

1. For a more recent sample of these documents, see High-lights of the Aid Program in Iran (Tehran: USAID/I, January, 1964).

2. See W. E. Carroll, "Agriculture," in the Review of the U. S. Technical Assistance and Economic Aid to Iran, 1951-1957 (Tehran: USOM/I, 1957?). Mimeographed with no pagination. (Hereafter called RUSTEAI.)

3. G. W. McDonald, "Health," in RUSTEAI, n. p. (Italics not in the original.)

4. See R. M. Goff, CTR, August 15, 1956, p. 2; and J. A. Fitz, CTR, August 30, 1960, p. 4. Curiously enough, in later years when Iran had to foot the entire program's bill, it was invariably the U. S. advisors who complained about the lack of adequate and timely budgets and funds. See, for example, D. K. Brumbaugh, CTR, May 20, 1963, p. 5, and J. C. Ballard, CTR, June 25, 1964, p. 7.

5. Upon the Mission's advice, the Iranian government finally agreed in 1956 to establish in each ministry the position of a permanent administrative undersecretary to be appointed by the Council of Ministers for five years, and subject to no change by the incoming ministers. This was obviously a right move in the direction of greater administrative stability. But the success was only partial as none of the "permanent" undersecretaries appointed in the summer of 1958 for five years was in office by 1960.

6. See Norman Armour, "Greece, Turkey, and Iran," Report to the Special Committee to Study the Foreign Aid Program, Senate Document #52, 85th Cong., 1st Sess. (Washington, 1957), p. 1220.

7. National Manpower Resources and Requirement Survey, Iran, 1958 (Tehran: GAI, July, 1959); Industrial Vocational Training in Iran (Tehran: Plan Organization, 1959); and High-Level Manpower Development in Iran (Tehran: GOI, May, 1960).

8. Mission advisors apparently busied themselves mostly with the mechanical aspects of administration, e. g., position classification, office procedures, correspondence control, budget presentation, and the like. As the mechanics of management, however, involved more efficient operation (e. g., fewer workers for a given job), the Mission recommendations sometimes aggravated the problem of surplus employees and thus could not be put into practice.

9. For details concerning Project 30 and the difficulties involved in it, see H. C. Larsen, CTR, January 5, 1955.

10. Cf. Lucy Adams, CTR, September 5, 1956.

11. "Near East Foundation Program in Iran," in RUSTEAI, n. p.

12. Paul Phillips, CTR, August 8, 1957, p. 2. See also Harlan Cleveland et al, The Overseas Americans (New York: Mc Graw-Hill Co., 1960), p. 158.

13. R. O. Gustafson, CTR, December 10, 1959, p. 9.

14. Although the contract was only for two years, the group's planned schedule called for four years, six months of which were to be devoted again to "orientation"; another six months were set aside to "develop" experience for project base; and the last two years (not covered by the contract) for completing the "full scope of contract responsibilities." See George Fry & Assoc., 3rd Quarterly Report, April, 1960, p. 2.

15. See USOM/I Projects Status Report to ICA/W, June 16, 1959, p. 6.

16. Letter of the Minister of Industry to USOM/I, May 3, 1960.

17. Mutual Security Act of 1959, Hearings before the Senate Committee on Foreign Relations, May 13, 1959, 86th Cong., 1st Sess. (Washington, 1959), p. 608 ff. For a similar point of view see Peggy and Pierre Streit, "Close-Up of the Foreign Aid Dilemma," New York Times Magazine (April

13, 1958), p. 6 ff., and L. M. Winsot, "Mid-East Aid," Letters to the Editor, Wall Street Journal, December 15, 1958.

18. "Foreign Aid? Yes, But With A New Approach, " New York Times Magazine (March 21, 1965), p. 105.

19. See Norman Armour, op. cit., p. 1220.

20. H. I. M. Mohammed Reza Shah Pahlavi, Shahinshah of Iran, Mission for My Country (London: Hutchinson & Co., 1961), pp. 300-303. For an outsider's evaluation of the program, see C. Skrine, "New Trends in Iran, "Royal Central Asian Journal (April, 1955).

CHAPTER 2

A FRAMEWORK FOR ANALYSIS

The effectiveness of a program of foreign technical assist-ance should be measured by the number of solutions it may find to the problems which the aid-receiver cannot solve easily or independently.

The U.S. bilateral technical assistance program in Iran, commonly known as "Point IV," has been a part, and only a small part, of the total American aid to Iran. Under the Mutual Security Act of 1954 [1] and its amendments the United States has made available to the government and the economy of Iran three major types of assistance: (1) military; (2) eco-nomic (including technical); and (3) special assistance. Under the Agricultural Trade Development and Assistance Act of 1954 [2] and its amendments, also, the U.S. has provided Iran with American surplus agricultural commodities. Table I shows total U.S. aid to Iran during 1950-1965.

The military assistance program has included military equipment, advisory and training personnel, and funds as well as technical services for military installations. Economic assistance has been offered in the form of defense support, development loans, and technical aid. Defense support has been extended through commodity, financial, or other forms of assistance to relieve the local economic burdens caused by the country's military alliance with the United States. Under the general umbrella of defense support, grants have been given for financing Iranian general budgetary deficits; Mutual Security Loans have been made to assist economic projects mutually agreed upon by the two governments. [3] Development loans have been made available through the Development Loan Fund for road construction and industrial development.

Under the rubric of Special Assistance, grants were given to the Iranian government in the critical period

28

immediately after the fall of the Mossadegh Government in August, 1953, to meet some essential public expenditures and to finance some 45 "emergency" public works projects in various parts of the country. [4]

Under Title I of the PL 480 (the agricultural assistance program) surplus farm commodities have been sold to the Iranian government agencies against local currency to be earmarked for common defense expenditures, or for joint development projects. The bulk of this assistance has been allocated for loans to the Iranian Plan Organization; the rest has been used to make a few small "Cooley loans" to American business firms in Iran. Under Title II of the same Law, bread grains and surplus foodstuff have been donated for the relief of flood and earthquake victims in the country directly or through such agencies as CARE, UNICEF and others. Under Title III, a small amount of U.S. surplus agricultural commodities has been bartered for Iranian mineral raw materials. Under Title IV, wheat and corn have been sold to Iran against long-term loans payable in dollars.

In addition to these grants and loans, a relatively small assistance has also been extended for the guaranty of some U.S. private investments in Iran against the risks of currency inconvertibility, nationalization or war. The Export-Import Bank of Washington has also made several separate loans to finance American made capital equipment imported to Iran mostly for the dieselization of the Iranian State Railways, and for road maintenance projects.

The U.S. Technical Assistance, which serves as the focal point of this study, encompasses programs and activities envisioned in President Truman's Inaugural Address of 1949, his Message to Congress in June 1949, the Act for International Development of 1950, [5] and its amendments in subsequent years. Under this category of aid, the U.S. government has furnished Iran: (1) the services of several hundred technical assistants; (2) training opportunities for several hundred Iranian nationals; (3) various types of demonstration equipment along with various quantities of agricultural and industrial supplies; and (4) cash grants for payment of foreign or domestic requirements of technical cooperation projects.

As can be seen in Table I, the $116.2 million total U.S. technical assistance discussed here is a relatively small percentage of total U.S. contributions: about eight percent of the total aid and slightly more than 14% of the economic aid. The purview of this study is thus limited to only a small and specialized portion of U.S. aid to Iran and does not include the whole gamut of American assistance. The conclusions reached here, too, relate only to the technical component of the U.S. aid and may not necessarily be valid for the American assistance in general, and military assistance in particular.

Even the United States technical assistance program has passed through four different phases or periods during the last decade and a half, and the over-all evaluation of this study may not be equally applicable to each period. The first period began with the signing of a Memorandum of Understanding between the United States and Iran on October 20, 1950, [6] and laid the groundwork for the Exchange of Notes between the Technical Cooperation for Iran (TCI) and the Iranian Prime Minister on January 19-20, 1952. [7] The "joint" activities and operations of the two cooperating governments in subsequent years were integrated into the Iranian's own administration in 1956, and the United States Mission was officially transformed into an advisory agency. [8] The financial contributions of the new agency to the costs of the program under a Special Activities Account were gradually decreased until 1960 when the total costs of local operations were borne by the Iranian government. Since 1961, U.S. technical assistance to Iran has been offered under a new agreement signed at Tehran, December 21, 1961. The technical component of the new agreement has been mostly limited to financing the salaries of U.S. advisors and training expenses of Iranian participants. [9]

TECHNICAL ASSISTANCE: MEANING AND USAGE

While the significance of foreign technical assistance in promoting economic growth is generally recognized and widely discussed, commensurate attention has not been paid to its precise relation to the process of development, and the manner in which it can be optimally effective in this process. This section attempts to provide tentative answers to both of these questions.

Foreign technical assistance, strictly speaking, refers to any external efforts in the form of advice, demonstration or performance which are (1) beyond the indigenous capabilities of the recipient itself, and (2) designed to improve certain specific techniques of planning, communication, control, or operation. Such an assistance may apply to the whole complex of an aid-receiving society or it may be limited to a small segment of it. It may, on one extreme, cover long-term expert assistance at the highest level and for the whole structure of government planning. At the other extreme, it may simply consist of a one-shot assistance for the rearrangement of the host country's national anthem or the design of its flag.

In its broadest application, foreign technical assistance is not limited to the economic field. Such other social goals as domestic political development, cultural refinement, religious enlightenment, or military modernization, may all lend themselves to technical assistance from abroad. Political development may involve promotion of democratic institutions, pluralism or the rule of law. Cultural refinement may include furtherance of progressive attitude or artistic endeavors. Religious enlightenment may take the form of ecumenical universalism or reduction of superstition. Military modernization may come about through better combat readiness or training in guerrilla warfare.

Nor is the need for foreign technical assistance confined to the so-called underdeveloped countries. Any country in any stage of development may need some kind of technical aid from abroad. In fact it is an erroneous notion both theoretically and empirically to limit technical assistance to less-developed nations. Theoretically, the possibility of exchange or offer of technical assistance may loom much larger among technically advanced nations than among countries with widely different states of technological development. Empirically, too, there has been clear evidence in the postwar recovery of Western Europe to show vividly that the benefits of U.S. technical (apart from financial) assistance under the Marshall Plan have by no means been less important than the benefits accrued to underdeveloped nations of Asia and Latin America through the Point IV program.

Foreign technical assistance in the sense discussed here has two major tasks: (1) the discovery of problems that are unknown or unfamiliar to the recipient; and (2) the supply of solutions that are beyond the latter's technological or material capacity to provide for itself. These tasks together involve four basic _processes_ in the give-and-take of assistance: (a) an examination of the symptoms for the diagnosis of the problems; (b) devising and prescription of new solutions with demonstration of their applicability; (c) training and supervision in the local use of prescribed remedies or techniques; and (d) provision for an assimilated continuation of the adopted techniques and practices in a routine fashion without further need for foreign training and/or supervision. Foreign technical assistants, in other words, are expected to serve as problem-finders, advisors, trainers and persuaders. [10]

Technical aid may be oriented toward three distinct but interrelated _aspects_ of economic growth: (1) techniques of planning, operation and production; (2) institutional framework and organizational structure; and (3) cultural values and attitudes. The first category includes (a) innovations in traditional methods of production and/or operation, (b) introduction of new and locally rational techniques, and (c) provision of catalytic or bottleneck-reducing resources from abroad. The second category involves improvements in such economically significant institutions as credit availability, tax exemptions, foreign investment guarantees and the like. The third category covers (a) progressive changes in the people's attitudes toward work, saving and risk-taking, (b) their "will to progress," and (c) their confidence in their own ability to lift themselves up. [11]

In both of its tasks and in all aspects of growth, foreign technical aid can be offered at the various _levels_ of the country's socio-economic structure: from the decision-making levels down to the various echelons of operation and execution. Problem finding and diagnosis, for example, may be applied to a very small and purely technical problem (e.g., determining the characteristics of a native plant disease); or, they may be put to work to analyze a highly important aspect of social life (e.g., conspicuous consumption and low propensity to save). Pure advice can be offered at the ministry level, or at the levels of provincial administration, municipalities or village councils. Training and demonstration can be conducted in the skills of operations at the operational level or in the skills of decision-making at the policy level. Participation in actual operations and diplomacy in getting people ready to accept change can take place at almost all levels of operation or decision-making, i.e., from conducting a research experiment in a central university to building dams or school houses in remote parts of the country. [12]

CRITERIA FOR EXAMINATION

The adoption of standards in terms of which the economic worth of a technical assistance program can be properly determined is, to be sure, not easy. [13] The impact of technical assistance projects (particularly those dealing with institutions, values and attitudes) is generally indirect, sometimes invisible, and often slow. The choice of the evaluative criteria is thus inevitably biased by the researcher's own predilections. And the findings are often neither quantitatively measurable nor presentable. The task of evaluation becomes particularly difficult when the objectives of the program are many and varied, and the priority among different objectives cannot be determined by only one hierarchy. Under such conditions almost everything that can be said about the program may prove to be true.

On more than one occasion, for example, American officials, Congressional survey teams, and the Mission staff, have attempted to measure the value of U.S. technical assistance to Iran on the grounds of ensuing domestic political stability, orientation toward the free world, decline of local communist activities, and military alliance with the United States. A former Mission Director, Mr. William E. Warne, once expressed the belief that American "bread cast upon the troubled waters of Iran" was being returned tenfold to the American taxpayers. [14] In a later address he declared:

> The Technical Assistance and Economic Aid programs in Iran have done just exactly what they were designed to do, namely they have been influential in keeping Iran an independent nation and Iran has continued to be oriented to the free world. [15]

Evaluations such as these are proper mostly from the political or strategic viewpoints of the donor. Maintenance of political stability in a troubled area, orientation of a developing nation toward the West, and support of friendly local elements in a strategic country may all be worthy goals and worthy deeds. But the goals and deeds that this study is prepared to discuss and examine are different.

The objective of this study is to determine the possibilities and limitations of the U.S. bilateral technical assistance program from the standpoint of continued and sustained economic growth in Iran. To the extent that the aid efforts, directly or incidentally, have hit at the roots of the elements inimical to growth, or brought about marvels that can expedite progress, their contributions are also taken into account. But in the context of this study, Mission achievements are not judged from the standpoint of political or tactical interests of the United States. This latter problem deserves a study by itself.

The intention of this study is to describe instead of prescribe; to examine rather than evaluate; to judge but not to censure; to offer critique and not criticism. Within the framework of such objective search and impartial research, this study will present ten basic criteria or hypotheses[16] of optimum effectiveness in terms of which achievements and limitations of the program can be examined. These criteria or hypotheses seek to establish certain minimum requirements for an ideal bilateral assistance program, and seek to determine the extent to which the United States Point IV program has actually fulfilled these requirements.

The first element or criterion of effectiveness is consistency which hypothesizes: (a) the clarity and coherence of the program objectives; (b) rational selection and coordination of methods used to attain these objectives; (c) the existence of a clear and well-established plan within which project priorities are reasonably delineated; and (d) the program's correspondence to the host country's total development effort. The second element or criterion is receptivity which divides itself into two hypotheses: (a) local understanding and appreciation of technical needs and the means for their satisfaction and (b) the environmental capability for using foreign efforts in these directions. The third element is transferability of advanced technical know-how based on three hypotheses: (a) the ability of an advanced nation, economically, politically, and culturally to offer needed technical aid; (b) the existence of a proper organization for implementing such aid;

and (c) the quality and fitness of foreign technical assistants in this bilateral effort. And the last element is assimilation whose relevant hypothesis is the suitability of imported techniques and know-how to the local setting, or the ultimate adaptability of the foreign program to the host country's own development efforts.

Within the framework of these elements or criteria of optimum effectiveness, foreign technical assistance can be considered a contributor to the economic growth of the less developed countries if it can give favorable answers to each and every one of the following questions:

Is the foreign technical assistance program offered to a developing country explicitly designed to attain specific, feasible objectives?

Are the basic policies employed to attain these objectives internally and externally consistent?

Are the specific programs suggested by these policies arranged in a proper order of priority?

Are these projects rationally related to the recipient country's own program of economic development?

Is such a close relationship as does exist between foreign technical assistance and the country's own development plan properly understood by the planners and developers in the host country?

Is the advanced country capable of offering the needed technical assistance to the developing nation?

Is the organization for imparting the needed assistance suitable to the effective implementation of such aid?

Do foreign technical assistants in such an organization fit their tasks in the host country?

Will the program actually lead to an eventual integration with the host country's own development activities?

In the following chapters, an attempt will be made to examine some of the answers to each of these questions.

TABLE I

Summary of U. S. Aid to Iran, 1950-1965
Obligations and Authorizations
(Millions of Dollars)

Program and Agency	Cumulative Aid Through Fiscal Year 1965
Agency for International Development:	
Technical Aid Grants	116. 2
Support Assistance and Special Grants	265. 9
Development Loans	139. 2
Support Assistance Loans	79. 0
Food for Peace (PL 480)	
Title I. Local Currency Sales:	
Grants for Common Defense	5. 9
Loans to Private Industry	4. 8
Loans to the Government	36. 4
Title II. Emergency Relief	39. 1
Title III. Voluntary Relief	21. 4
Title IV. Dollar Credit Sales:	
Government to Government	11. 8
Private Sales	3. 7
Export-Import Bank Loans	97. 3
Military Grants [1]/	677. 3
Total Economic Grants and Loans	820. 7
Total Economic and Military Aid	1498. 0

Source: Figures supplied by the Agency for International Development and USAID/Iran

---

[1]/ Through Fiscal Year 1964.

References

1. Public Law 535, 81st Cong., 2nd Sess.

2. Public Law 480, 83rd Cong., 2nd Sess.

3. U. S. dollars under this category of aid have been used to finance essentail imports or exchanged for local currency to be used as "counterpart funds" for financing local costs of approved projects.

4. The list of these projects and their functions may be found in the USOM/I, Annual Report, June 30, 1956.

5. Title IV of Act to Provide Foreign Economic Assistance, Public Law 535, 81st Cong., 2nd Sess.

6. For the text of the Memorandum, see Appendix A.

7. For the text of the Notes, see Appendix B.

8. For the conduct of the program under "integration" see Ch. 12.

9. The text of this Agreement is shown in Appendix C.

10. See Ch. 4.

11. See Ch. 7.

12. See Ch. 12.

13. See Walter R. Sharp, International Technical Assistance: Program and Organization (Chicago: Public Administration Service, 1952), p. 52; T. C. Blaisdell, "Problems of Evaluating the Effectiveness of Development Measures, Economic Development and Cultural Change (January, 1954).

14. 23rd Weekly Report of TCI Director to ICA, Washington, January 17, 1953, p. 6.

15. William E. Warne, Presentation of the Mission Program in Iran, address at the NEA Regional Conference of FAO, December 12, 1953 (Tehran: TCI, 1953?), p. 1. See also "U. S. Official Says Iran Needs Help," New York Times, January 1, 1958, p. 1.

16. The term "hypothesis" is used here in its common meaning as a "theory, proposition, or supposition tentatively accepted to explain certain facts or to provide a basis for further investigation." Thus the "hypotheses" of the following chapters will be presented not as controversial assumptions needing substantial proof, but as commonly-held presumptions subject to more detailed confirmation.

PART II

THE POLITICAL ECONOMY
OF
AID

CHAPTER 3

A PROGRAM OF ALL THINGS TO ALL MEN

The effectiveness of foreign technical assistance depends, above all, on: (1) the selective clarity of the objectives for which the aid is offered, and (2) the internal consistency among these objectives.

The successful give-and-take of foreign technical assistance, for any objective and between any two nations, requires that the aid program be clear and consistent in the selection of its goal or goals. If a particular program of aid has more than one objective (as has been the case with Point IV), these objectives should be mutually reinforcing, or reasonably compatible with each other. And if reasonable consistency among the objectives cannot be assured, then there should be only one hierarchy (or one system of transcendence) under which basic functional or temporal emphases on the conflicting goals can be ascertained.

A review of the Point IV program in its original world-wide presentation in 1949 fails to reveal any such degree of clarity or consistency among its objectives. As has been pointed out on another occasion, [1] Point IV has been a program of all things to all men.

The background of the program is all too familiar to require detailed presentation. The scourge of the Second World War brought scores of nations into closer contact with each other. Many of the less fortunate members of the world community along with their more prosperous neighbors rallied under a common banner, and fought against a common enemy. Once victory was assured, however, this common struggle of both the rich and the poor ended up with a different impact on each group. While the Allied victory heralded the end of fighting for the exhausted rich, it marked the beginning of a new strife for the uneasy poor -- a fight against poverty, disease and ignorance.

In the eyes of Point IV pioneers the underdeveloped areas of the world, with an overwhelming majority of their population stirred and awakened [2] by their increased contacts with the outside world, were ripe for social revolution. [3] Restless and dissatisfied with their economic life, and increasingly conscious of their miserable lot, these people were getting more and more impatient for a change. [4]

The Soviet Union was offering them encouragement toward an overthrow of the existing political and social order in favor of establishing a Soviet-type government and a monolithlic economy. [5] The United States, however, although in sympathy with their aspirations, [6] was believed to lack a positive, constructive, and concrete program for them. [7] The basic postwar goal of the United States foreign policy was the attainment of a just and lasting peace in a free, expanding and prosperous world economy. [8] This policy was regarded fundamentally as not one of preserving the status quo, but nevertheless opposed to violent revolution.

POINT IV'S PHILOSOPHY AND OBJECTIVES

As there was widespread fear in the Western world that prevailing dissatisfaction and restlessness among the people of underdeveloped areas might induce them to accept ideologies or systems that would promise them greater economic and material security, it was believed that something better had to be shown them by the West, and shown them fast, so as to keep them from losing hope in the West [9]. It was argued that the security [10] and prosperity [11] of the United States were closely bound to the security and economic progress of the underdeveloped world. [12] The United States would have strong allies in the cause of peace, liberty, representative government and private enterprise; she would be able to develop and maintain a steady source of strategic raw materials as imports, prosperous markets for her exports [13], and profitable outlets for her surplus investible funds [14]; and she could also help others to share the benefits of political liberty, individual dignity, economic progress and the fullness of life. [15]

In the minds of the framers of Point IV, these interests and objectives could best be served by a program of technical assistance accompanied by creative foreign investments.

Such a program was believed to enable the developing countries to obtain their aspirations for a better life while staying out of the reach of communism. Economic and social progress in these countries was, in turn, believed to advance the cause of democracy, mutually beneficial trade and greater political stability for the entire community of free nations. [16]

It was to further these interests and objectives that the "bold new program" of American technical assistance was announced. The purpose of this program, according to President Truman, was to help the people of underdeveloped countries to help themselves toward attaining a better and fuller life. Said the President, in part:

> We must embark on a bold new program for making the benefits of our scientific advances and industrial progress available for the improvement and growth of underdeveloped areas.

> For the first time in history, humanity possesses the knowledge and the skill to relieve the suffering of these people.

> The United States is pre-eminent among nations in the development of industrial and scientific techniques.

> We should make available to peace-loving peoples the benefits of our store of technical knowledge in order to help them realize their aspirations for a better life. And, in cooperation with other nations, we should foster capital investment in areas needing development.

> Our aim should be to help the free peoples of the world, through their own efforts, to produce more food, more clothing, more materials for housing, and more mechanical power to lighten their burdens.

> The old imperialism--exploitation for foreigh profit--has no place in our plans. What we envisage is a program of development based on the concepts of democratic fair dealing.

All countries, including our own, will
greatly benefit from a constructive program for
the better use of the world's human and natural
resources.

Greater production is the key to prosperity
and peace. And the key to greater production is
a wider and more vigorous application of modern
scientific and technical knowledge.

Democracy alone can supply the vitalizing
force to stir the peoples of the world into tri-
umphant action, not only against their human
oppressors, but also against their ancient
enemies--hunger, misery, and despair.[17]

Later, in his message to Congress on June 24, 1949,
the President asked for specific legislation to put his Point
IV program into action. The President's proposal was enacted
on June 5, 1950, under the "Act for International Development". [18] This Act declared it to be the policy of the United
States

. . . to encourage the flow of technical knowledge and
capital to countries which provide conditions
under which such technical assistance and capital
can effectively and constructively contribute to
raising standards of living.

U.S. interest in the program was declared in Section 402 of
the Act to fall in "the freedom and in the economic and social
progress of all peoples" which could, in turn, promote democratic ways of life, international trade, understanding, good
will and peace. [19]

In 1951, a year after its passage, the Act for International
Development was amended by placing American military, economic and technical assistance under a unified program.
Under Section 2 of the Mutual Security Act of 1951, the purpose
of the Point IV Act was amended as follows:

The Congress declares it to be the purpose of
this Act to maintain the security and to promote
the foreign policy of the United States by author-
izing military, economic, and technical assistance

to friendly countries to strengthen the mutual
security and individual and collective defense
of the free world, to develop their resources in
the interest of their security and independence
and the national interest of the United States and
to facilitate the effective participation of these
countries in the United Nations system of collective security. [20]

The emphasis was thus noticeably shifted from "raising
standards of living and creating new sources of wealth"
to the "individual and collective defense of the free world,
security and independence of friendly countries and the national
interest of the United States." The conflicts among the
program objectives began to come into the open.

As the eligibility for assistance became clearly contingent upon direct contribution to American security, the nature
of the program became more complex. Instead of such innocuous provisions of the original Act as giving the program
full publicity, coordinating various technical schemes in the
country, and cooperating with other beneficiaries of Point IV,
the new Act tied American aid to serious political and strategic
commitments. According to Section 511 (b) of the Act, no
economic or technical assistance was to be supplied to any
nation unless the President found that the supplying of such
assistance would strengthen the security of the United States
and promote world peace. [21]

A year later, the U. S. policy of containing communism
was reiterated in the Mutual Security Act of 1952, which made
it clear that "no country shall receive any assistance hereunder unless it takes decisive action to marshal its resources
collectively and participate in programs which promote collective security in the appropriate areas." [22] The Mutual
Security Acts and foreign aid legislation of subsequent years
followed this provision and, explicitly or by implication,
made the communist threat a requirement for receiving American aid.

Although as a result of extensive criticisms in and out of
Congress, the "prerequisites" were subsequently softened in
the Mutual Security Act of 1954, it was clear that the Point
IV program tried to bring about a curious miscegenation of

selfishness and altruism. [23]   A study devoted entirely to an
analysis of the development of the Point IV idea seems to
show that the program at its birth, if not in its conception,
was politically intentioned although its methods of application
were economic:

> President Truman set forth the concept that the
> United States develop the backward areas of the
> world as a step in the effort to contain commu-
> nism. Later, during the evolution of the Point IV
> program and its legislation, it was recognized that
> other ends could also be sought through the
> development of the backward nations, which, if
> achieved, would contribute to the attainment of
> some other objectives of the United States. [24]

As pointed out on another occasion, these other objectives of
the program were not only conflicting with each other, but
also inconsistent in themselves. [25]

POINT IV OBJECTIVES IN IRAN

Against the background of this complexity, conflicts of
standards and lack of clear purpose, Point IV's major difficulties in Iran should not be surprising or unexpected. A
cursory review of the Irano-American relations during the
1940's and the Iranian situation in 1950 will show how the serious
conflicts among Point IV objectives plagued the program in
Iran.

The U.S. technical assistance to Iran was effectuated
under a "Memorandum of Understanding" signed on October 19,
1950, between the governments of the United States and Iran,
establishing the first Point IV program in the world under
the Act for International Development. Although the Memorandum was silent with respect to the exact aims of the
United States in offering technical and economic assistance
to Iran, it was clear that America's concern about the welfare
of the people in Iran was the same as her interests in similar
strategic areas of the globe.

Ideologically, the United States wished to keep Iran in
the Western camp by insuring its political stability through
economic aid. Economically, the goal was to keep Iranian
oil flowing to Western markets, and to have part of its ac-
cruing income spent in the West and in the United States.

Socio-politically, the aim was to cement Irano-American relations badly needed in a divided world and particularly in a trouble spot close to the Soviet Union. The material progress of Iran could also benefit the United States (in the same principal ways as other underdeveloped countries) by providing America with an expanded export market, a cheap source of raw materials, and outlets for investing excess savings.

The evidence shows, however, that at the time Point IV aid was given to Iran, the economic gains for the United States were not important enough to justify the cost of the program to the American taxpayer.   Iran's trade with the United States at the time constituted a very insignificant part of the total American foreign commerce, and in all probability was to remain so, despite possible rises in the level of the Iranian national real income. [26] As a source of raw materials Iran had little to offer: apart from petroleum, the country had no important strategic material the United States badly needed.   As far as oil was concerned, the American government seemed more concerned with keeping the Iranian petroleum resources out of Soviet hands than with developing these resources for herself.   And she already had some interests in it anyway. [27]   Outside the petroleum field, Iran did not seem to provide a vast outlet for America's "surplus" investible funds.

It can thus be argued that as far as the United States was concerned, the essential point in its program of technical and economic aid to Iran was at the time more political and strategic than commercial and economic. [28]   Economic development was considered desirable for its expected political stability, rise in the national level of living, and resistance to the danger of communism.

Presenting the administration's argument before the Committee on Foreign Affairs of the United States House of Representatives, Mr. Jonathan Bingham said in 1952:

> In some areas, along the periphery of the communist powers, the urgency of the situation is particularly acute.   In these areas, notably

> in. . . Iran, our program must be so devised as
> to achieve a fundamental improvement in the
> basic condition of the people's lives within a mat-
> ter of a very few years. . . This does represent
> an increase in intensity and in quantity of the
> program, brought about by the increased tensions
> in the world in the last two years. [29]

On another occasion, the former Deputy Administrator
of Technical Cooperation Administration pointed out that
although the United States did not approve of the Iranian government's stand on the Anglo-Iranian oil dispute, the Point IV
program was expanded in Iran in order to avoid leaving the
people with the "feeling that they had been utterly abandoned
by the West, and that they had no hope of making any progress
except through moving in the direction of communism." [30]

A U.S. technician in the field corroborates with this view
by saying:

> During the entire first year of my stay in Iran,
> political interest was constantly vying with project
> interests.   That was inevitable since the pro-
> gress of our projects was so closely integrated
> with the political situations under which we had
> to work. [31]

The same point was time and time again made by U.S. officials'
testimonies before Congressional committees.   In one of
these testimonies, an administration official boldly admitted
that what the United States was after in Iran was not to build
a dam, or do this or that; it was a campaign in the cold
war. [32]

CONFLICTS AMONG OBJECTIVES

In view of the fact that the basic American objectives --
of containing the Iranian Tudeh (communist) party, helping
the Iranian government attain a quick and noticeable increase
in national income, and helping to alleviate misery among the
Iranian masses -- could not be simultaneously satisfied, the
program faced serious policy dilemmas and burdensome operational paradoxes.

To the extent that Point IV was to secure immediate political and strategic gains for the United States, it was necessary for the Point IV Mission to align itself politically with the local elements friendly to the Western cause, and to support the anti-communist elements in every possible way.   Insofar, however, as the program had to satisfy increasing popular demands for a better material life, it had to cut the costs of anti-communist activities and campaigns in order to give sufficient heed to an immediate rise in the levels of consumption.   And a rapid and significant increase in the domestic levels of consumption (essential to the short-run popularity of the program) had to be reconciled both with a high rate of long-term economic growth and the desired level of military preparedness.

Another curious anomaly was apparent in the program's attempt to win favors from opposing interests within the host country.   According to a U.S. Congressional team, the Point IV program was from the beginning billed as having a "grassroots approach" and concerned with the welfare of the common people.   In hearings on the Mutual Security Act of 1954, this fact was explicitly reaffirmed when a Congressman asked an ICA official, "Are we endeavoring to reach the masses of people in our aid program in Iran?" and the reply was, "That is exactly our direction." [33]   But at the same time, it has been admitted that for its very existence and in order to operate in a foreign land, the program had to enjoy the approval and the cooperation of the elite in power. As one writer states:

> . . . The Technical Cooperation Administration was well aware of the shortcomings of the frame of reference within which it worked. . . Point IV officials have stated openly in Congressional hearings that one cannot advocate the changes which William O. Douglas envisages and still be welcomed by the governments in power. [34]

This necessary and inevitable concern with the feeling of the class in power, in the opinion of an unfriendly critic, made it indispensable for the program to make an "open alliance with the traditional colonial power and native reactionary element." [35]   While this view may be considered distorted and hostile, the fact remains that the technical

assistance program had to give favorable considerations to
the personal and often legitimate interests of, say, landed
and mercantile classes in the Iranian Majles in order to obtain their political support.   And, these considerations were
not always believed to be in the interest of the common man --
the man whose level of living was to be raised. [36]

As a program of government-to-government, too, Point
IV had to operate through the official agencies of the host
country.   If new agencies had to be created, they had to be
public institutions.   The United States could not offer direct
help to individual Iranians in private organizations without
running the risk of severe political accusations and significant
operational difficulties.   And, quite naturally, inasmuch as
the people rightly or wrongly, consciously or unconsciously
felt a gulf between their narrow, immediate interests and the
broad, long-term programs and projects of government organizations, it was impossible for the program to be popular
with all groups at the same time.

The Point IV program showed a closely connected con-
flict of standards in still another area: basic reforms.
Point IV strategists were convinced that a program of foreign
aid could not be simply concerned with the transfer of international technology and capital, but should also pay due
attention to the development of public and private institutions
and to improvements in the distribution of income. [37]   But
as will be shown in Chapter 9, the United States was not prepared to advocate and/or support many reforms she had
traditionally preached and was ideologically committed to
promote.   Apart from the necessity of securing the support
and cooperation of the powerful local elements, the American
concern in keeping socio-political stability in the area made
the Point IV program overtly aloof to hazardous reforms.
A careful student of the subject has portrayed this paradox
by saying:

> It often seems that while trying to help the
> common man through our programs of technical
> cooperation under Point IV and the like, we at
> the same time endeavor to preserve the status
> quo.
>
> We sometimes find ourselves in the incon-
> gruous role of helping the pot boil while trying
> to sit on the lid. [38]

Another important example of the incongruity in the basic concept of the program was Point IV's ardent desire for a rapid improvement in the people's standard of living and its simultaneous desire for achieving this goal through democratic means and free institutions. This was obviously neither easy nor altogether practical.

Modern economic history of the monolithic countries has shown that short-circuiting the process of economic development involves a good deal of government planning, supervision and control; and that economic growth under free market conditions (and its political counterpart, democracy) may in effect be slow, tedious and even wasteful. There are also theoretical indications that under economically backward situations (e.g., high propensity to consume, inferiority of domestic manufactures and services, and high income elasticity for foreign goods) the development process may not become self-sustaining and cumulative without government intervention and without some infringement on consumer sovereignty. [39]   In the Iranian institutional setting, with its long history of government initiative, direction and control, it was doubly hard to obtain economic progress and grassroots democracy at one and the same time. [40]

Adding to the program's conceptual and functional contradictions was also a temporal ambivalence toward quick actions that could at the same time produce lasting impacts. In an attempt to protect political and strategic interests of the United States, the program had to place its chief emphasis on short-run, tactical and expedient maneuvers the results of which could be immediately noticeable. As an aid to local developmental efforts, however, it had to follow a basically long-run process, paying due regard to a proper system of priorities and functional relationships among development projects. "The objective of the program in the early days," confided a Mission official in a private interview, "was to keep the country on an even keel. We tried to keep influential people happy, in power, and friendly to us. We tried to do things that people seemed to like and felt were good for them."

The gist of the difficulties involved in obtaining lasting results from such crash programs and ad hoc measures is summed up in a number of reports by the Mission's technical assistants:

> Due to the inevitable pressures for quick results and for showy expositions, there have been projects and activities put into practice before the theory or philosophy on which they were based had taken firm hold. The results have sometimes been . . . a beautiful temporary effect. [41]

> Because of pressures for results, activities and projects are often pushed to completion without taking the time to lay the proper groundwork for adequate village improvement. [42]

> It is my conviction that the 4-D program in the field, at village and club level, has grown and developed faster than the Extension Service's ability to serve the program adequately. [43]

As will be seen in Chapter 10, these conflicts of standards and policy ambiguities plagued the program's administration, too. The Mission was often run at the total discretion of its Director who, in turn, had to sacrifice some long-term projects in order to reach more immediate goals. And since the priority among standards that were most likely to be invoked in evaluating the program's achievements was not determined beforehand, the Director's discretion did not always coincide with those of the policy makers and program planners in Washington, or in Iran.

References

1. Jahangir Amuzegar, "Technical Assistance Diplomacy," Business Topics (Michigan State University, May, 1958).

2. Harry S. Truman, "Message to Congress, June 24, 1949," Technical Assistance, U. S. Senate Report 139, 85th Cong., 1st Sess. (Washington: GPO, 1957).

3. Cf. Averell Harriman, "The Future of Point IV: Two Views," New York Times Magazine (September 26, 1954), p. 13 ff.

4. Strengthening the Forces of Freedom, U. S. Department of
    State, General Foreign Policy Series #28 (Washington, 1950),
    p. 62.

5. "The Point IV Program," Building for Peace, U. S. Depart-
    ment of State, Economic Cooperation Series #11 (Washing-
    ton, 1949), p. 1.
6. Strengthening the Forces of Freedom, loc. cit.

7. See D. K. David, "Mobilizing Our Ideals," in E. C. Bursk
    (ed.), Thinking Ahead for Business (Cambridge: Harvard
    University Press, 1952), p. 5.

8. Our Foreign Policy, U. S. Department of State, General
    Foreign Policy Series #26 (Washington, 1950), pp. 4-5;
    Jack N. Behrman, "Foreign Aid as a Technique in Attain-
    ing U. S. International Economic Objectives," Ph. D. Dis-
    sertation, Princeton University, 1951, p. 89 ff; and William
    T. R. Fox, United States Policy in a Two-Power World
    (New Haven: Yale University Press, 1947).

9. Christian A. Herter in Congressional Record 96, Part 3,
    March 24, 1950, p. 4050.

10. Dean G. Acheson, "Aid to Underdeveloped Areas as Mea-
    sure of National Security," Department of State Bulletin
    (April 10, 1950), p. 552; and John B. Condliffe, Point IV
    and the World Economy (New York: Foreign Policy Assoc.,
    1950), pp. 11-13.

11. Partners in Progress, A Report to the President (Washing-
    ton: GPO, 1951), p. 1.

12. For a discussion of American interests in the development
    of underdeveloped areas see, among other references, B. F.
    Hoselitz, The Progress of Underdeveloped Areas (Chicago:
    University Press, 1952); Seymour E. Harris, Foreign Aid
    and Our Economy (Washington: Public Affairs Institute,
    1950); The Annals of the American Academy of Political and
    Social Science, March, 1950; The Academy of Political Sci-
    ence Proceedings, May, 1952; Eugene Staley, The Future
    of Underdeveloped Countries (New York: Harper, 1954); and
    Foreign Economic Policy and the National Security, U. S.
    Department of State, Economic Cooperation Series #29
    (Washington, 1954).

13. World Economic Progress Through Cooperative Technical
    Assistance, U. S. Department of State, Economic Coop-
    eration Series #15 (Washington, 1949), p. 1.

14. B. A. Javits, Peace by Investment (New York: Funk and Wagnalls, 1950).

15. Strengthening the Forces of Freedom, p. 62. See also Bold New Program, Series 1-8 (Washington: Public Affairs Institute, 1950) and W. R. Espy, Bold New Program (New York: Harper, 1950).

16. Point IV Background and Program (Washington: Legislative Reference Service, Library of Congress, 1949), pp. 2-5.

17. For the full text of President Truman's Inaugural Address see Technical Assistance, Senate Report 139, Washington, 1957.

18. Title IV, Public Law 535, 81st Cong., 2nd Sess.

19. Cf. G. C. McGhee, "The United States and the Underdeveloped Areas, Department of State Bulletin (June 26, 1950).

20. Public Law 165, 82nd Cong., 1st Sess.

21. Cf. Carl McGuire, "Point Four and National Power of the United States," American Journal of Economics and Sociology (April, 1952). For the early attacks on the program, see "President Truman's Global Plans," New Republic (January 31, 1949); "Truman's Colonial Experiment," Nation (February 5, 1949); "Bold New Program," and "Partners in Reaction," Nation (March 24, and June 13, 1951); and "The Fallacy of Point IV," Newsweek (July 7, 1952). For one of the latest tracts in defense of the program, see Frank M. Coffin, Witness for Aid (Boston: Houghton Mifflin Co., 1964).

22. Public Law 665, 83rd Cong., 1st Sess.

23. Where Do We Stand on Point IV?, U. S. Department of State, Economic Cooperation Series #20 (Washington, 1949), p. 862.

24. Edward M. Rickard, "An Evaluation of Point IV as Part of United States Economic Policy," Ph. D. Dissertation, University of Colorado, 1950, p. iii. For the American business community's early skepticism about the "business" nature of the program, see "Point IV, a Fantastic Utopia," Commercial and Financial Chronicle (July 28, 1949); "Truman's Point IV on Trial," and "Pro and Con of Point Four Program," Commercial and Financial Chronicle (July 28,

December 1, 1949 and March 16, 1950); <u>United Nations World</u> (May, 1949); and <u>Fortune</u> (February, 1950).

25. See Jahangir Amuzegar, "Point IV: Performance and Prospect," <u>Political Science Quarterly</u> (December, 1958).

26. Between the years 1947 and 1951 the average annual export of the United States to Iran was only one third of one per cent of the American total exports per year. The figure for import from Iran was one fourth of one per cent of the average annual imports.

27. With regard to petroleum, three factors were mainly responsible for the American attitude. First, America had by far the largest proven oil reserves in the world itself. Second, she had already sufficient oil interests in the Middle East and elsewhere to guarantee her a safe, steady and cheap supply of petroleum in time of peace. Third, it was clear that in case of a major war with the Soviet Union, the Iranian oil installations would not be immune from Soviet air attacks, and the Iranian oil would not be of great value in time of war.

28. The widespread belief in Iran that the strength of the Iranian Tudeh party had a lot to do with the initiation, operation and growth of Point IV was not totally unfounded. In the 1941-1953 period, Iran was the center of the largest, and most disciplined communist party in the Middle East. And the fact that she also received by far the biggest share of the Point IV appropriation for the area between 1950 and 1953 was not generally regarded as a mere coincidence.

29. Mutual Security Act Extension, <u>Hearings</u> before the Committee on Foreign Affairs, House of Representatives, 82nd Cong., 2nd Sess. (Washington, 1952), p. 958.

30. Jonathan B. Bingham, <u>Shirt-Sleeve Diplomacy</u> (New York: John Day, 1954), p. 180.

31. R. E. Hensley, <u>CTR</u>, September 21, 1954, p. 2.

32. Mutual Security Act of 1956, <u>Hearings</u> before the Committee on Foreign Affairs, House of Representatives, 84th Cong., 2nd Sess. (Washington, 1956), p. 46.

33. <u>Report of the Special Study Mission</u>, House of Representatives, House Report No. 2147, 84th Cong., 2nd Sess. (Washington, 1956), p. 206.

34. Walter B. Blass in <u>New York Times</u>, October 14, 1953, p. 28. The reference is to William O. Douglas, <u>Strange Lands and Friendly People</u> (New York: Harper, 1951).

35. Paul A. Baran, "Point IV - Four Years Later; I: The Rich Got Richer, " Nation (January 17, 1953), p. 45.

36. See, e. g. , J. N. Wallace, "A Talk in Iran: An Educated Iranian Questions the Value of U. S. Policy and Usefulness of Aid, " Wall Street Journal, October 24, 1959, p. 5.

37. Economic Strength for the Free World, A Report to the Director for Mutual Security by the Advisory Committee on Underdeveloped Areas (Washington, 1953), p. 9.

38. Stanley A. Cain, "Trends in International Resources Development and their Significance for the United States, " Conservation (Corvalis: Oregon State College, 1952), p. 33. See Theodore J. Kreps, "Point IV and the Domestic Economy," Annals of the American Academy of Political and Social Science (March, 1950), p. 167; and Harold R. Isaacs, Two-Thirds of the World (Washington: Public Affairs Institute, 1950), p. 41.

39. Jahangir Amuzegar, "Foreign Aid and the Negative Trade Effect in Underdeveloped Countries, " Indian Economic Journal (October, 1960).

40. A good example of the paradox of accelerated economic development under democratic institutions can be found in the objectives of Project 30, Crown Land Distribution in Iran. As a gesture toward the establishment of a large class of independent peasant-landowners, this was considered by Mission leaders as a wise and courageous social project. Yet to some Mission technicians, a mere fragmentation of large economic units into small and often uneconomic holdings with no adequate compensatory arrangements could not be expected to result in increased agricultural productivity, particularly in the first formative years of operation.

41. W. A. Cram, CTR, January 4, 1958, p. 12.

42. R. C. Gosda, CTR, February 9, 1963, p. 3.

43. Anthol Riney, CTR, April 22, 1963, p. 6.

PROPER
DIAGNOSIS AND
EFFECTIVE CURE

The success of foreign technical assistance depends, inter alia, upon its ability to diagnose hitherto unknown problems and/or prescribe hitherto unknown solutions in the process of local development.

The cooperative efforts among nations bent on raising productivity, income and standards of living cannot all be called technical. Such international economic arrangements as the European Economic Community, the Colombo Plan, the General Agreement on Tariffs and Trade, the Commonwealth Preference System all promote economic growth in one way or the other. Multi-national financial consortia or bilateral economic agreements, too, may have varying degrees of technical elements in them. But they are not programs of foreign technical assistance.

TECHNICAL VS. NON-TECHNICAL AID

An aid program that is designated as technical must be distinct from other types of aid (e.g., low-interest or interest-free loans, emergency and relief assistance, grants-in-aid and other non-technical schemes). The question is: What is really technical assistance as distinct from other kinds of aid? Does it exist by, and in, itself? Can it be distinguished from other categories?

The literature on the nature and substance of technical assistance is unfortunately one of the least rigorous and least satisfactory of the economic discussions of recent years. This unfortunate lack of rigor is further aggravated by the unduly widespread and generally non-professional treatment of the subject in popular writings. The common identification of technical assistance with the United States

Point IV program, too, has done its share in adding to the confusion.

The Inaugural Address which laid the cornerstone of U.S. bilateral technical assistance speaks very generally of "the knowledge and skill" that can relieve human sufferings and the "scientific advances and industrial progress" which should be made available by advanced countries for the growth of underdeveloped areas. The June Message defines technical assistance simply as "technical, scientific and managerial knowledge necessary to economic development," including:

> not only medical and educational knowledge, and assistance and advice in such basic fields as sanitation, communications, road building, and governmental services, but also, and perhaps most important, assistance in the survey of resources and in planning for long-range economic development.

The Act for International Development refers to technical assistance as an aid that, along with capital funds, can

> effectively and constructively contribute to raising standards of living, creating new sources of wealth, increasing productivity and expanding purchasing power. [1]

The Mutual Security Acts of 1952 and 1954 speak of technical assistance in terms of:

> programs for the international interchange of technical knowledge and skills designed to contribute to the balanced and integrated development of the economic resources and productive capacities of economically underdeveloped areas.

These activities are expected to include:

> economic, engineering, medical education, agricultural, fishery, mineral, and fiscal surveys,

demonstration training, and similar projects that
serve the purpose of promoting the development
of economic resources and productive capacities
of underdeveloped areas. [2]

In these documents and those of the United Nations
Technical Assistance Board, the criteria for distinguishing
technical assistance from other types of aid seem to follow
two rather narrow lines. If the amount of assistance is small
and consists totally of "teaching or demonstrating" and
"the equipment and commodities necessary for instruction or
demonstration purposes," [3] it can be considered technical.
If, on the other hand, the aid consists of significant outlays in
cash, credit or commodities, it should be designated as financial
or other.

As can be readily seen, these criteria, while useful as
simplified identification, are neither necessary nor sufficient
for a more rigorous definition. This Chapter intends to show
that foreign technical aid can be identified as a distinct approach to aid and that it can be offered and received separately
and independently from other categories of aid

Technical, scientific and managerial knowledge that can
be purchased in the world markets by a country's own resources
(or by using foreign grants or loans) is not here considered
as technical aid because technicians and technical experts
are no different than tools and equipment that could be purchased abroad if funds were available. Advice and equipment
that are readily purchasable abroad are in effect no more
than a substitute for financial assistance, budgetary aid, surplus commodities, or any other type of aid. The aid-giving
party can just as well make the value of technicians' time and
equipment available to the aid-receiving country and ask that
the funds thus granted be spent in the donor's labor and/or
product markets.

Conversely, there is no sufficient reason to consider
foreign cash grants or loans spent by the recipient country
for the purchase of advice or demonstration equipment, as
non-technical aid. A loan or grant which is used exclusively
for the acquisition of foreign know-how is as much technical
as if the latter were offered directly. The outward form of
aid or the process of its transfer cannot thus serve as a denominator of its true nature.

The definition suggested in this study relates to the possibility (or the elasticity) of substitution between different kinds of aid, i.e., between different policies, approaches and methods.   If the assistance can be easily substitutable by a grant or a loan, then it cannot be considered technical. A cash grant should, therefore, be considered non-technical, except in special cases when it is offered with the proviso that it should be spent on the types of outlays that are properly technical.   The technicians' advice is perhaps the closest thing to what may properly be called technical assistance.   Yet even here, the substitutability requirement must hold.

Under two types of circumstances, assistance received from abroad is of the technical (i.e., non-purchasable, non-substitutable) variety: first, the circumstances under which the problem to be solved by foreign assistance is not conceived or ill-conceived by the recipient.   An emerging country, for example, may not know the causes of its general or specific ills; or, it may attribute its plight to erroneous causes.   Development planning in such a country is like renovating a giant but faltering business enterprise: someone has to find out where things have gone wrong, and what could be done about them, before specific solutions can be found and implemented. This is the diagnostic technical assistance -- the type that can detect the real but unknown problems, the real but unknown causes.

The second type of situations under which foreign assistance can be regarded as technical, relates to circumstances where the real causes or problems are more or less known; simple and obvious remedies or solutions, too, are mostly familiar; but effective remedies or solutions are largely unknown or unavailable to the aid-receiving country. A country bent on economic development may have diagnosed its basic deficiencies, the major impediments to its economic growth, and the prerequisites for its development.   Yet it may be incapable of finding effective means of solving these problems.   Here foreign technical assistance is of a therapeutic nature.

Under the substitutability requirement, whenever basic problems and their effective and realistic solutions are known and familiar to the aid receiving country, but capital funds are the only deficient factor, foreign assistance in whatever forms that may be offered cannot be considered technical. In other words, where outside help simply adds exactly the same to the existing supply of domestic factors without offering anything new or untried, the aid is something other than technical. If an underdeveloped country knows how to build proper roads or dams or factories, a developed country can do very little in these fields by offering technical assistance. All it can do is supply additional funds, equipment and skilled labor to augment domestic efforts. In such cases, the aid offered in the form of men or machines can be readily substituted by cash: it is simply a grant-in-kind instead of a grant-in-cash.

Under certain special circumstances, however, even though the problems and their solutions are both known to the host country, it would be useful methodologically to describe some categories of foreign assistance as technical or at least quasi-technical. Here the components of foreign assistance such as commodities, equipment and technicians' time, while familiar to the host country, and theoretically purchasable in the world markets (i.e., substitutable by cash grants), may, in effect, possess a very small degree of substitution with other forms of aid. There may be instances, for example, that for political, emotional or administrative reasons a grant of cash may be used by an underdeveloped country in such a way as to deter economic development instead of expediting it. The country may, for example, use foreign grants on internationally prestigeous or domestically fashionable projects instead of using foreign resources on nationally imperative and more urgent schemes.

In these instances, the real economic need of the host country may require that the aid be offered in the form of skills and equipment instead of cash. This is the international counterpart of the national case for providing direct government services to the needy, instead of relief payments in cash, lest the recipients spend the latter in less desirable avenues. The analogy with an individual's case is that of a physician who, in addition to diagnosing the malady and prescribing medication, administers the drug himself lest the patient neglect his own interests and the "doctor's order." Quasi-technical is a term which may be used for cases where the degree of substitution with other forms of aid is very small or negligible.

Defining technical assistance this rigorously is not a matter of curiosity or useless intellectual hair-splitting; it is a matter of clearer thinking. If all technical aids were to be considered substitutable with financial assistance, or if no difference were to be made between different types of aid, the effectiveness of technical assistance would be substantially different from those discussed here. Where foreign aid is non-differentiated, or in ''liquid'' form, the appropriate criteria would be the general propriety of national economic planning, the choice of investment outlets and the country's over-all absorptive capacity. But when men, machine, and advice are provided in specific forms, additional criteria would be necessary to measure the suitability of the specific techniques, approaches and methods. Now, while some of the criteria supplied in this study may be relevant for all types of aid (and, in fact, necessary for domestic economic development with, or without foreign aid), other elements or criteria that are presented here are more closely related to technical aid and should be discussed as such.

IRAN'S NEED FOR TECHNICAL AID

The technical problems that the U.S. Mission to Iran was expected to diagnose and cure were essentially a series of long-run problems in the basic fields of development. [4] First, it was the problem of revitalizing a large agricultural sector whose techniques were often as old as recorded history, whose yield was low by any standards, [5] and whose management was largely feudal and inefficient. [6] Second, it was the problem of saving a small and struggling industrial sector whose productivity was low per man, per machine and per operating plant; whose growth was unplanned and unbalanced; and whose structure was burdened by overstaffing, badly maintained equipment and poor management. [7] Third, it was the problem of expanding and improving the transportation and communication networks that were plagued by improper maintenance and poor managerial quality. [8] Fourth, it was the problem of improving an educational system that was glaringly outmoded in its basic philosophy, curricula, methods of teaching, choice of textbooks, physical facilities and administrators. [9] Fifth, it was the problem of improving health conditions characterized by an infant mortality rate of 50%, an average life expectancy of not more than 30 years, a wide variety of prevalent diseases and frequent epidemics. [10] And finally, there was the problem of an underdeveloped administrative machinery beset by a top-heavy organizational structure, an outmoded civil service system and a largely under-utilized staff.

As basic techno-economic problems, these were familiar, elementary, and not peculiar to Iran; they were shared by most other underdeveloped countries. Nor were these problems difficult to diagnose, nor individually unresponsive to standard cures. Yet, in their total composition, and particularly in their environmental pattern, they were sui generis, needing special diagnosis and cure. Like a patient suffering from a number of familiar and individually curable, but mutually complicating ailments, Iran needed a carefully balanced prescription specifically prepared for her over-all condition, and sufficient vigilance in having the remedy applied in the prescribed manner. Piecemeal treatment, patent medicines, and the patient's own discretion could not be solely relied upon to do the work.

TYPES OF AID OFFERED BY POINT IV

The lion's share of aid offered by the United States under the rubric of technical cooperation to cure the foregoing problems consisted of outlays which, in the narrow sense of this study, could not all be called technical.

Of some 162 projects listed by the Mission in the years 1950 to the end of fiscal 1965, some 59 projects [11] had little or nothing to do with technical aid. The Mission itself lists 31 of these, initiated between 1956 and 1965 as Capital Assistance Projects, i.e., projects whose avowed objectives were to provide U.S. funds for the:

-Completion and equipping of industrial plants, irrigation facilities, or roads,
-Provision of buildings, facilities and materials for partly finished Iranian schools,
-Construction of community centers,
-Establishment of few factories, or
-Financing the purchase of foreign-made workshop, railroad, airport, or otherwise heavy construction equipment.

In most of these projects, funds granted by the Mission were
also used for the cash purchase of local materials and
supplies. The sum total for these projects should thus be
considered financial grants-in-aid.

To these should be added some 33 other projects [12]
launched ostensibly for the purpose of:

-Aiding Iranian institutions and technicians to
improve their skills through the use of better
mechanical devices and equipment,
-Building up existing facilities needed for training
and demonstration of modern methods of operation,
-Establishing repair shops to train Iranian personnel in the maintenance and repair of modern
equipment.

But in 22 of these projects, U.S. funds were again almost
totally spent for the purchase of equipment, instruments,
materials and supplies from abroad, or for defraying their
local transportation, installation and labor costs. In only a
few of these projects, where funds were spent mostly for
hiring needed technicians or for dispatching local participants
abroad, the training provided was of the technical variety.
Most of the equipment and supplies brought into the country
under these projects could be obtained by Iran itself if necessary funds were available to the Iranian government.

Of the remaining projects, 59 had relatively less to do
with the purchase of machinery or commodities, and were
more involved in the offer of advice. [13] But again, not more
than half of these would fall into the category of truly technical
assistance projects. The rest of the projects could at best
be regarded as quasi-technical, although even for this designation many of the projects would not qualify without stretching
the concept. [14]

As Hurewitz points out, in the early phase of the program,

The accelerated Point Four efforts in Iran resembled less a technical aid program than a last-
ditch holding operation, pending a settlement of
the Anglo-Iranian dispute. Because of the financial

crisis in Iran, the Technical Cooperation Administration . . . did not insist, as was its normal
practice, that the recipient government contribute
a fair share of the cost, and not all of the funds
were used solely for instruction and demonstration.   Indeed more than half was devoted to
development schemes. [15]

An estimated breakdown of actual U.S. expenditure on
Point IV projects in nine main fields of activity between
Fiscal Years 1951 and 1964 (the last year for which figures
are available) appears in Table II.   Of about $96 million
spent on all 151 projects mentioned above, approximately
$32 million (spent on some 59 projects) should be considered
as purely financial assistance.   Another estimated $28 mil-
lion (spent on the 33 projects in which technical component
was not significant) should be considered as partially financial.   Of the total project expenditures, perhaps no more
than $36 million was thus spent on the 59 projects of relatively
greater technical component and should be regarded as mostly
technical aid.   The rest of the technical assistance appropriation was for non-project expenditures.

PROBLEMS RECOGNIZED AND SOLUTIONS FOUND

The observations and recommendations made by Mission
assistants often contained accurate diagnosis of Iran's well-
known and familiar problems.   Some of the solutions offered,
too, seemed to be proper and correct remedies.   But judging
from the contents of the assistants' end-of-tour reports, the
scope, dimension and depth of the problems and solutions
embodied in these reports do not seem to rank much beyond
the findings of previous foreign technicians or substantially
different from the already familiar and the well-known.

In the four basic fields of Mission activities (agriculture,
education, health, and public administration), the problems
that the Mission advisers diagnosed were not new but the
same old and familiar ones.   In agriculture, for example,
the Mission's diagnosis of the Iranian ills was low food production, caused by poor quality seed, wasteful irrigation
practices, lack of pest control, waste of natural fertilizers,
and antiquated cultivation methods. [16] In education, the basic

TABLE II

Estimated Project Expenditures by Fields of Activity
Cumulative to June 30, 1964
(Thousands of Dollars)

Program	Technicians	Participants	Contract Teams	Commodities	Capital Projects	Other[a]	Total
Agriculture	7260	1600	1229	4576	487	1431	16683
Community Development	1356	190	1534	792	495	2158	6525
Education	4627	701	958	2221	357	421	9285
Health	4610	940	1426	190	10277	77	17520
Industry	1454	773	1669	2244	9130	313	15583
Labor	754	281	-	145	-	326	1506
Public Administration	4018	923	2479	1492	-	428	9340
Transportation & Communication	1427	525	25	3395	1461	1280	8113
General & Miscellaneous[b]	3044	3075	1272	2349	1357	428	11525
Total	28550	9008	10592	17404	23564	6962	96080[c]

Source: Figures supplied by Agency for International Development.
a) Including costs not allocable to individual projects.
b) Includes projects in communication media, banking, Ostan operations, special training, and technical support.
c) The difference between this figure and total U.S. grants for technical cooperation relates to the overhead costs of operation and the obligated but unspent funds.

difficulties were found to be a traditional, outmoded system, and lack of adequate finances. [17]   In the field of health, the problems were found to be the same as those surveyed by the Overseas Consultants in 1949 and the Rockefeller Foundation in 1952. It was also admitted that the seriousness of these problems had been recognized before Point IV aid by the local government and voluntary organizations in the field of public health. [18] In the field of public administration, the underlying problems were found to be "the lack of continuity in leadership, inadequate training of personnel, and the need to assign and accept responsibility." [19]   In the less important fields, the discovery of unrecognized or unfamiliar problems was even more limited.

Thus, while the Mission activities and the statistical data collected by the Mission staff shed considerable light on some of the known problems, or their functional interrelations, Point IV's achievements in the diagnostic type of assistance to Iran seem to have been lackluster and limited. In fact, many of the "problems" that were diagnosed by the Mission assistants (e.g., outmoded systems of operation, lack of trained personnel, limited finances) were the very folklore of underdevelopment itself, and could hardly be called problems.

A point that was often lost sight of by early Point IV pioneers, and by many more people in the United States, was the complex relationship between economic backwardness (i.e., the absence of advanced technology) on one hand, and a host of other factors (including the shortage of capital funds) on the other.   The eighty per cent of the Iranian population which the Mission found illiterate were not in this plight because nobody in Iran could sing the praise of education or recommend remedial measures.   The high degree of illiteracy was due to the fact that proper universal education was not an easy goal for a large and poor country to reach: schools had to be built and expanded; books had to be purchased and distributed at low prices; young graduates had to be induced to go to the villages by offering them better pay and improved living conditions.   And all this required money, among other things.

If health conditions were deplorable, it was not simply because nobody there knew how to spray DDT, or how to use water filters, but because public health and environmental sanitation needed public health education which required

money, organization and administrative stability. Trained
doctors had to be attracted to the villages through higher pay
and better working conditions. Clinics, hospital beds, mobile
health units and laboratory facilities had to be provided on a
larger than demonstration basis. [20]   The Ministry of Health
had to enjoy internal stability to put its program to work.

Agricultural techniques were outmoded and productivity
low, not because no one knew the advantages of better seed,
deeper plowing, more generous irrigation, use of fertilizers
and insecticides, or better crop rotation. The impediments
to agricultural efficiency were deeply rooted in the country's
socio-economic fabric and they had to be solved in a single,
coordinated manner. A mere introduction of the same advanced technology as practiced in America would not do the
trick. In one expert's opinion, actual methods of agriculture
in Iran were in fact well adapted to the peculiar characteristics
of the country, and could not be easily altered without far-
reaching changes in the other sectors of the economy. [21]

In the area of therapeutic assistance (i.e., providing
effective solutions to recognized and familiar problems),
the bulk of Point IV aid seems to have revolved around
familiar solutions to common and identified problems. Apart
from the sizable amount of off-shore commodities and equipment brought to Iran (and a number of brick-and-mortar projects which were of non-technical variety), the bulk of U.S.
technical aid simply added to the supply of existing resources.
In the fields of agriculture, education and health, existing
physical facilities such as laboratories, classrooms and clinics
were completed, remodeled or furnished. In the field of labor
a number of ordinary, low cost houses and a recreation center
were constructed. In the field of communications, the existing
radio stations were duplicated or expanded.

Under one of the projects in the field of adult education
the Mission claims to have taught 16,000 Iranian gendarmes
a six-month course in reading and writing Persian. The
justification was that these gendarmes would not be effective
in performing their duties without a rudiment of literacy.
This was obviously a correct diagnosis. But neither this
diagnosis nor its needed cure required foreign technical
assistance. These facts were already recognized and there
was no obstacle in the way of educating these gendarmes except apparently the lack of funds. All that was needed and

received was money for the employment of teachers, provision of facilities, purchase of supplies, etc.

The rationale of U.S. technical assistance for the archit-
ectural design of Iranian village schools and clinics is even
more difficult to obtain.   While Iran had a reasonably good
architecture school of its own, and a large number of foreign-
trained architects designing finest city buildings, the Mission
offered Iranian government agencies the services of an expensive team of American architects to help them design village
installations.   In view of the existence of native resources
at a much lower price, and the inevitably modest nature of
the structures that the team was asked to design, the Mission's
assistance was really nothing that was novel or badly needed.

The following expert advice of a highway maintenance technician as to the country's need is another example of the
Mission's therapeutic recommendations: legislation governing
load limits and speed; additional equipment, stations and
personnel; an adequate budget; provision of management and
training teams; standardization of equipment; and provision of
a foreign technician for each highway station at least for two
years [22] -- recommendations that were accurate and useful
but hardly in need of a highly-paid foreign adviser to discover them.

In the field of agriculture there were recommendations
such as: further decentralization of budget and finance;
better transportation; suitable office "necessary for prestige";
and close coordination among Mission divisions. [23]   These
were, again, known and familiar observations.   Yet not only
this technician, but the ones that preceded and followed him
on that project offered a repetition of the same recommendations over and over again.

In forestry, a special consultant, brought in especially
to survey the situation, admitted that he could add little to
what had been written on the general or specific aspects
of Iran's forestry problems since 1940 by eleven other
American advisors.   And the unanimous diagnosis was:
overcutting of forests due to confused ownership rights and the
financing of Forestry Bongah's operation by means of fees
for cutting permits.   The last consultant's recommendations
were the same as the ones before him: classification of
forest and range lands, reorganization of Forestry Bongah,

and provision of more foresters. [24]   As late as in 1963, a
Mission forestry advisor was still complaining about: lack
of a sufficient number of well-trained professional personnel; lack of a well-planned, coordinated forestry program; and lack of financial support by the government of
Iran. [25]

The Mission's limitations in offering needed solutions
in the tangible fields of development were matched by its
weakness in offering novel solutions in the intangible areas
of land reform, public administration, community organization
and industrial management. In the institutional framework of
development where nobody in Iran had an effective and workable
solution to some of the fundamental problems, the Mission
technicians, too, were incapable of providing effective answers. In the case of the Crown Land Distribution (Project
30), for example, the Mission's own technicians and the members of the Near East Foundation team kept complaining about
the way the project was carried out, but were apparently unable to suggest better practical solutions. In the preparation
and/or implementation of land reform legislation -- a highly
political as well as technical problem -- the Mission seemed
outwardly noncommittal and inwardly uncertain.   Although
some U.S. technicians were privately skeptical of the new
law's success, their suggestions and criticisms lacked the
profundity of a solid, sensible and workable program. [26]

In the field of public administration, the thorniest and
most baffling by far of all the Iranian administrative problems was the question of what to do with literally hundreds of
idle employees in government agencies and state companies
who regularly drew their salaries but did not report for work
or did not do much at their desks. Any simple solution was
bound to be politically sensitive, psychologically delicate, and
economically unpopular.   But this was exactly the type of
problem which required expert advice and an especially
tailored solution.   And this was a problem for which no solution was ever offered.

In community development, the delicate and highly controversial problem of political decentralization was left
dangling.   This problem, again, had no easy or identified
solution, and required the most careful political analysis
and social examination.   But the Mission understandably
shied away from making the required analyses or examinations.

In the field of industrial management, no effective and practical solution was found for the long-discussed and difficult problem of government enterprises. A special management consultant team, hired at considerable cost by the Mission to sell government-owned industrial plants, succeeded in selling only one small rice cleaning plant, and this was admittedly a real estate rather than an industrial sale, as some valuable land went with the small factory. Selling government plants (including Point IV's own capital outlays) was, of course, not easy: their original costs were high; they were more than doubly staffed; their yields did not favorably compare with market rates of interest; they were too large to be sold for cash or to any one individual capitalist; and the conditions for selling them on credit or as corporations were not favorable. [27]   But again, it was the existence of these very difficulties that caused Iran to ask for foreign advice.

Many of these problems, of course, had no solution totally satisfactory to all parties concerned.   Even if technically-compromised, and reasonably satisfactory approaches could be found, they might have been politically or otherwise unacceptable. Yet, the need for finding methods, approaches and policies that could partially satisfy most parties was there and was not sufficiently met.

In short, what Iran needed in terms of technical assistance was a number of people, who, if not versed in the "art of the impossible," would at least be capable of finding their way through such seemingly blind alleys and impassable walkways. In some of these cases, many solutions available to the country's own experts had been tried and had failed.   There was need for new approaches and untried remedies.

References

1. Technical Assistance, Senate Report No. 139, March, 1957, p. 80.

2. Ibid. , p. 91.

3. Technical Assistance and Related Programs, Senate Report No. 1956, 84th Cong. , 2nd Sess. (Washington, 1956), p. 9.

4. The problems involved in developing the Iranian economy are discussed in a comprehensive study by the Overseas Consultants, Inc., Report on Seven-Year Development Plan for the Plan Organization of the Imperial Government of Iran (New York: OCI, 1949). Volume I-V.

5. For discussions of Iran's agricultural problems at the time see Gideon Hadary, "Iran: A Survey of Agriculture, " Foreign Agriculture (September, 1949); Afif I. Tannous, "Agricultural Production and Food Consumption in Iran," Foreign Agriculture (February, 1944); A. G. Black, "Iranian Agriculture: Present and Prospective, " Journal of Farm Economics (August, 1948); C. D. Holland, "Persia's Agriculture is based on the Soil, " Great Britain and the East (May, 1950); and M. A. Djamalzadeh, "An Outline of the Social and Economic Structure of Iran, " I and II, International Labour Review (January and February, 1951).

6. For a detailed description of Iran's system of landownership and tenure before the recent land reform program, see A. K. S. Lambton, Landlord and Peasant in Persia (London: Oxford University Press, 1953). P. H. T. Beckett, "Persia's Need for Land Reform, " The Fortnightly (February, 1952); Gideon Hadary, "The Agrarian Reform Program in Iran," Middle East Journal (Spring, 1951); and Frankin S. Harris, "Landownership in Iran, "Foreign Agriculture (February, 1953).

7. For details regarding the problems of Iran's industries, see Overseas Consultants, Inc., op. cit. , Volume IV. For briefer descriptions and more information, see International Labour Review (May, 1949); N. S. Roberts, Iran: Economic and Commercial Conditions (London: H. M. Stationery Office, 1948); and Iran: Annual Economic Review for 1950, U. S. Department of Commerce, Business Information Service (May, 1951).

8. Cf. "Transport and Communications in Iraq, Iran, and Afghanistan, " Transport and Communications Review (October - December, 1950; World Trade in Commodities, U. S. Department of Commerce (December, 1949) ; and John M. Bee, "Persia's Progress Depends on Communications, " Great Britain and the East (June, 1950).

9. Cf. Overseas Consultants, Inc. , op. cit. , Vol. II; and Jahangir Amuzegar, "Point IV and Education in Iran, " School and Society (September 29, 1956).

10. Cf. E. E. Palmquist and F. F. Aldridge, "Iran's Public Health Cooperative Organization" and "Malaria Control in Iran, " Public Health Reports (October, 1954).

11. Projects 1; 2; 3; 4; 6; 7; 8; 11; 12; 13; 14; 15; 16; 17; 18; 21; 23; 25; 27; 29; 37; 46; 47; 49; 54; 55; 56; 63; 65; 66; 68; 69; 70; 71; 72; 73; 77; 80; 81; 82; 86; 87; 95; 96; 97; 98; 99; 123; 127; 128; 129; 137; 217; 218; 220; 254; 267; 268; 270.

12. Projects 5; 10; 19; 22; 24; 28; 31; 32; 33; 36; 38; 43; 51; 53; 57; 58; 59; 60; 61; 62; 64; 67; 75; 76; 84; 85; 91; 101; 104; 119; 124; 130; 501.

13. Projects 9; 30; 39; 41; 44; 45; 48; 78; 79; 88; 90; 92; 94; 102; 105; 107; 109; 110; 113; 115; 116; 118; 126; 131; 132; 133; 204; 206; 207; 208; 209; 210; 211; 212; 213; 214; 215; 216; 219; 221; 222; 223; 224; 226; 228; 229; 230; 231; 232; 233; 235; 236; 237; 238; 239; 240; 243; 262; 263.

14. Of the total 160 projects, 11 were either not activated or merged with other projects. For a brief description of most of these projects see A Review of U. S. Foreign Policy and Operations, Senate Document #78, 85th Cong., 2nd Sess. (Washington, 1957), pp. 95-138. A list of these projects appears in Appendix D.

15. Jacob C. Hurewitz, Middle East Dilemmas (New York: Harper, 1953), p. 237.

16. See Annual Report of the U. S. Operations Mission to Iran for the years 1954, 1955, and 1956 (Tehran).

17. "Education," in RUSTEAI, np.

18. "Health," in RUSTEAI, np.

19. Annual Report of the U. S. Operations Mission to Iran, June 30, 1956 (Tehran: USOM/I, 1956), p. 15.

20. "The idea that a health project should be established on a demonstration basis," writes a Mission Health Chief, "is impossible when people want and need actual service. People in Iran wanted medical care and not instruction on how to dig deep wells. Therefore, in order to start the preventive teaching program, people had to be given assistance in the relief of symptoms before they were well enough psychologically to have faith in the advantages of preventive medicine." See G. G. McDonald, "Health," in RUSTEAI, n. p.

21. Gideon Hadary, "The Agrarian Reform Problem in Iran," p. 184. See also W. B. Fisher, The Middle East: A Physical, Social and Regional Geography (London: Methuen, 1952), p. 65.

22. S. C. Stoddard, CTR, June 21, 1956, pp. 7-8.

23. G. W. Ramsay, CTR, December 30, 1958, p. 6.

24. See A. E. Dunscombe, CTR, April 15, 1959, and A. C. Hankins, CTR, November 23, 1959.

25. W. M. Sands, CTR, June 1, 1963, p. 3.

26. One of the advisors to Project 30, Crown Land Distribution, who in the course of his interview with the author was unusually critical of the project's implementation, could not suggest one single practical solution other than the land reform program had to be further studied by a "team of experts. "

27. See USOM/I, Projects Status Report to ICA/W, June 16, 1959.

CHAPTER 5   PLANNING AND PRIORITIES

Foreign technical assistance can inject the needed stimuli into a developing economy only when it is based upon a clear, well worked-out plan toward specific, preferably long-range, objectives whose priorities are mutually agreed upon by both the aid-giving and the aid-receiving parties.

Deliberate economic development is a process of rational social choice for achieving pre-determined economic objectives. The process is not self-starting, and requires a strong initial push. It also needs a period of long-term planning and continued attention to bear fruit. Since growth itself is a continuing and a time consuming process, developmental objectives would not be reached optimally unless they are ranked according to their immediacy, "sequence of emphasis" and ultimacy. Not only must ultimate long-range goals be precisely defined, but short-range program objectives and immediate project targets, too, must be determined in such a way as to bear a proper relationship to the prescribed goals.

PROGRAM PLANNING AND PROJECT PRIORITIES

The task of the planners is (1) to formulate principles upon which a firm base for a progressive economy can be built; (2) establish specific programs of action in each basic field of development; and, (3) in the light of these principles and programs, mobilize natural resources and energies in the service of detailed projects. Development principles must be formulated with regard to the country's capabilities and limitations. Specific programs must be drawn on the basis of the country's resources and basic needs in major fields of development. Project priorities must be worked out for the specific allocation of resources where they can be most profitably employed both politically and economically.

The process of development is as much the cause of broad structural and institutional changes in the economy as it is the result of these changes. Deliberate economic development thus necessitates a careful consideration of the prerequisites of economic growth as well as an intelligent prediction of its manifold implications. These considerations and predictions can rationally be made only under an organized system. Systems are based on hierarchy, inter-dependence and lines of command. An organized system of deliberate growth thus requires planned priorities, a rational choice among competing, and often mutually exclusive, development projects.

The necessity, if not the inevitability, of such a choice for the underdeveloped areas arises from four additional and interconnected realities. First, the aspirations of the underdeveloped nations for improved living and working conditions are generally far beyond their native capacities and capabilities, thus necessitating a most careful use of domestic resources. Second, the capacity of advanced nations to assist these developing nations in their development efforts is fairly limited and far below these nations' expectations, thus requiring a careful appropriation of skills and techniques most suitable to local conditions. Third, there is need, politically, socially, and morally for short-circuiting the process of development so that underdeveloped nations can narrow the gulf that now separates them from advanced nations. And, fourth, economically and administratively, there is need for coordination of foreign and domestic efforts so as to avoid both unnecessary experimentations and bottlenecked frustrations.

To ensure the efficiency of planned economic development, changes that eventually occur, and those that ought to be brought about deliberately, must be simultaneously adjusted and coordinated. The introduction of advanced know-how, machinery, and institutions must go hand in hand with favorable changes in the character and magnitude of the cooperating local elements. [1] A country today that presents the Western technological conditions of the mid-nineteenth century, cannot obviously wait for 200 years to catch up with the West. The only way to shorten this time period is to avoid the experimental trials and errors of the West and to benefit from the results of already proven technology. As a careful student of the subject has pointed out, changes in technology have to be supported by continually adjusting institutions and organizations.

But changes in organizations and institutions should go only as fast as the people's behavior, thought patterns and value systems can adjust to them. [2] Without systematic and regularized planning, a balance between these elements cannot be maintained.

As in all cases where the scale of operation makes the difference in the cost of production, so there is a minimum scale (with certain built-in indivisibility) in a program of foreign technical assistance.   And as there are economies of scale in most processes of production, so there is something called the "vectoral influence" of the assisting group in most processes of technical aid. This influence cannot be obtained without a group or a team.   Thus, while individual foreign technicians may perform their tasks skillfully and devotedly, the combined impact of the group may become undermined by lack of priority determination and the group influence.

PLANNING AND PRIORITIES IN THE IRANIAN CASE

As will be seen below, the rapidity with which the Point IV program burgeoned out in Iran made it impossible for the Mission to make necessary arrangements for program planning. The pressure of time and circumstance, too, mitigated against continuity of policy, and project coordination.

The "Memorandum of Understanding," signed at Tehran on October 19, 1950, set up a program of exchange of knowledge and skills for the purpose of improving living conditions and productivity of the rural areas in Iran. Special attention was to be given to a coordinated approach to problems of education, sanitation, and agricultural practices.

The program was to begin at the village level, and to provide for a number of demonstration and training centers to be established throughout the country. The Iranian government was to provide local personnel, land, buildings, and equipment required for the demonstration and training centers. The government of the United States was to provide the services of technicians, equipment, and apparatus not produced or manufactured in Iran. A Joint Commission was to be established in order to direct policies and procedures regarding the operation of the program. The Commission was to make recommendations in respect to the personnel and material

requirements of the program, and to harmonize Point IV
operations with other technical-aid programs carried out in
Iran by other private or public agencies. [3]

Soon after Point IV activities began, however, the dispute over the Anglo-Iranian oil agreement broke out and
culminated in the nationalization of the oil industry in Iran
and a diplomatic break with Great Britain. The rapid de-
terioration of the Iranian economic situation and the virtual
demise of the Iranian First Seven Year Plan, coupled with
constant demands from an impatient public brought new pres-
sures to bear upon the small and struggling Point IV program.

The dilemma created by the oil nationalization for the
United States government was a serious one. Washington
could not let her long-time ally down by siding with the Iranians,
nor did she wish to further reduce her popularity and prestige
in Iran by backing up the British. The result was a policy
of benevolent diplomatic mediation. As Hurewitz has pointed
out, the United States government, while expressing her desire
for an amicable solution of the dispute, tried to retain the
friendship of both disputants. On the one hand, she helped
Britain financially to offset its oil and dollar deficits while
rejecting Iran's request for substantial financial assistance. [4]
On the other hand, Point IV appropriation was markedly
expanded to help the Iranian government during its dollar
shortage and other financial difficulties. [5]

By the middle of the fall of 1951, the U. S. Congress approved total appropriation for the fiscal 1952 technical cooperation program, and $23.7 million was allotted to Iran.
The implementation of the new and expanded program would
have ordinarily required the conclusion of a new aid agreement between the two countries. However, since such an
agreement, explicitly, or by implication, would have also
"reaffirmed" the principle of U. S. aid to Iran and would
presumably have placed Iran in the American political camp
the neutrality-minded government of Dr. Mohammad Mossadegh
refused to acquiesce. The compromise was an "Exchange of
Notes" between the Iranian Prime Minister and the Director
of the United States Mission (instead of the American Ambassador as the customs and protocol would have suggested).

The Notes exchanged in January 20, 1952, replaced the
old Memorandum of Understanding and, by setting up an

"expanded" technical cooperation program and a method of operation, became the new instrumentality of U. S. aid to Iran.   Soon after the exchange of these Notes the Technical Cooperation for Iran (as the Mission was then called) began concluding a series of program and project agreements with Iranian ministries and agencies.

As the program grew month by month, however, emphasis was no longer placed exclusively on technical aid but shifted increasingly toward economic and financial aid.   The shift of emphasis was so rapid that by the middle of 1952 the original technical aid program was overshadowed by a vast economic scheme. [6] Although the economic program was often referred to by TCI officials as a "widespread program of technical assistance" [7] to justify it under the Point IV Act, the difference between the two programs was too obvious to escape notice.

The three original fields of operations were broadened to include industry, transportation and communications, natural resources development, housing and labor relations. In 1953, public works, public administration and land distribution, too, were added.   And in 1954, a full-fledged program of economic development was under way.   As the Annual Report of the Mission for 1954 states:

> The United States Technical Cooperation Program in Iran aims at assisting Iran to improve the health, education and general welfare of the people of Iran. Emphasis is placed on developing agriculture, improving basic industries, developing natural resources, expanding the transportation and communications facilities, and developing administration.

By June 30, 1954, the Mission was a vast, countrywide organization with a full-blown bureaucracy of its own, employing over 200 American technicians and close to 2000 Iranian nationals, or more than the combined personnel of Iran's own Plan Organization and three other ministries at that time.   A year later, by June, 1955, the Mission had 300 Americans and 2500 local employees taking care of over 100 regular and 45 "emergency" projects all over the country. [8]

All of this came with almost no prior planning. The flexible nature of the program objectives was further complicated by frequent changes in subsequent years. As an official statement submitted to the Foreign Affairs Committee of the United States House of Representatives states:

> The Iran program had given primary support for different objectives at different periods as in the circumstances the U.S. interest required. [9]

That is, in less than half a decade the objectives of U.S. aid to Iran changed from self-help in 1951, to ensuring government stability in 1952-1953, the economic support of the new government pending the oil settlement in 1954, the assistance to the Second Seven-Year Plan in 1955, and the support of the government that had joined the Baghdad Pact from 1956 on.

Program Planning

The testimony given by Director Warne on June 8, 1956, to a Committee of the U.S. House of Representatives, is an interesting illustration of the pressure of time and circumstances under which the program was formulated.

> MR. MOUNTAIN. Can you give us briefly the instructions that you got in Washington on the carrying out of this program?
>
> MR. WARNE. Yes, sir.
>
> Dr. Mossadegh, the Iranian Prime Minister, was in Washington part of that time, and one of my first jobs was to meet with him and to tell him that there would be allotted $23,450,000 for the Iranian program in the 1952 fiscal year. I told the Prime Minister that the program would be worked out in Iran in cooperation with his representatives. He proposed right then that we build the Karadj Dam.
>
> There was a final briefing session for me in Dr. Bennett's office.
>
> The final briefing was attended by more than a dozen people from TCA and State. One of the advisers present who, a short time earlier, had spent several months in Iran urged inclusion

of industrial-type projects in the program. Another urged the drilling of 500 deep wells. Dr. Bennett asked me to pay special attention to the Karadj Agricultural College. It was made clear to me that the rural improvement program which had already been started on a modest basis was not to be considered the whole program, but that I should develop broader activities. [10]

In the opinion of the House Government Operations Sub-committee, the sum of $23 million of technical aid to Iran which Congress appropriated in November, 1951, was not determined by prior planning and must have been arbitrarily arrived at in Washington. It apparently seemed to be the total grant the U.S. could allot to Iran at that time. [11] Of the Mission's responsibility in obtaining this allocation, the Sub-committee was even less charitable:

> Amounts requested for United States aid to Iran seem to have been picked out of the air. There is no evidence that they were based on advance study of what the Iranian economy needed, the amount it could absorb, or programs which could be intelligently administered by the United States personnel available at the time to expend the funds.
> The conduct of the United States operations mission's affairs appears to have been based on the assumption that as long as United States aid funds were spent promptly it was not a matter of great consequence as to what they were spent for. [12]

The unplanned and ad hoc nature of the Mission programs and projects is also indicated by the program leaders themselves. A chief of the Mission's Industry Division writes:-

> It is something of a misnomer to have called the various projects an industrialization program as they merely were comprised of nineteen separate projects. . . located in various sections of the country, and in some cases for purposes other than pure economic development. [13]

The following statements show the situation at the start
of the program in the field of agriculture:

There was no clear understanding in the minds
of the agricultural technicians as to what the
agricultural program should be, how it should be
developed, or how it would operate. [14]
The program was initiated during times of
extreme political stress when the greatest emphasis was placed on immediate impact. The
selection of agricultural machinery and equipment
was not always wise and appropriate. [15]

Project Priorities

The basis for the allocation of Point IV funds among
specific projects is not easy to ascertain. According to
the priorities set forth in the Act for International Development of 1950, Point IV projects were to be (1) an appropriate
part of the program reasonably designed to contribute to
the balanced and integrated development of the country, (2)
actually needed in view of similar facilities existing in the
area and otherwise economically sound, and (3) not financeable
by private capital at reasonable terms. [16]   In the Iranian
case, however, the multiplicity of project agreements signed
under the first annual appropriation, their varied scope and
magnitude, and the obvious lack of cohesion among them,
fail to indicate whether the formulation of the projects was
based on all or even any of these priorities.

Although the Mission's distributed instructions for later-
date programming procedures [17] were reasonably adequate,
there is good reason to believe that these procedures
were not strictly followed in the early period. Since time
was apparently against the Mission, and little heed could
be paid to the planning of details, Point IV projects were
drawn up with obvious haste. Of the 160 projects formulated
by the Mission throughout the country during 1950-1965,
some twenty projects in eight fields of operation were signed
up in one month, June, 1952, and 18 of these in one week before
the end of the fiscal year 1951. Among these were some technical, long-range projects such as assistance to the Karadj
Agricultural College, Preparation of Mineral Resources Development Plan, and the Development of Land and Water Use

Plans that involved years of teaching and demonstration before the country could carry them out on its own. On the other hand there were extremely short-range projects such as the Completion of the Bandar Abbas Water System, Completion of Dezful Sanitation, or Drilling of Deep Water Wells that took only a few months to finish, and which the government could do without foreign technical assistance. There were non-technical projects such as Expanding the Rey Cement Plant or the Agricultural Census that involved U.S. expenditures of less than $200,000, and there were others like the Construction of the Tehran Water Treatment Plant, or Expanding Tchitsazi Mill, to which the U.S. agreed to contribute more than $2,000,000. Projects Nos. 11 and 12 each covered more than 10 different activities, while projects Nos. 22 and 27 signed in the same day, both had to do with the drilling of a few deep wells.

Not only did these projects fall in such widely different fields of activity as housing, telecommunications, natural resources and community development, they were not interrelated either functionally or geographically even in one field. In health, for example, there was a small water treatment plant in a southwestern town, a big malaria control program in the north, and the construction of a water system for the capital city of Tehran almost totally unrelated to each other. In the field of agriculture, projects for locust control, the curriculum revision of the Agricultural College, completion of three distant dams, and the demonstration of ghanat construction were lumped together. In industry there was one cement plant and one sugar refinery in the south, one textile mill and one slaughterhouse in the north, and a plan for development of mineral resources scattered elsewhere.

As a result partly of the haste in obligating these funds, five of the projects signed in June, 1952, had to be discontinued soon after; three were merged with other projects, and one passed its completion deadline by several years and was not finished even by the end of the decade. Nine of the projects signed after 1953 were later virtually abandoned and 30 were gradually merged with others. Of the other projects that are listed in the Mission publications as "completed and successful" or "partially successful," at least five were found to be poorly designed, not operational due to lack of auxiliary factors, or otherwise suffering from "serious operating deficiencies." [18] The absence of prior planning for projects

undertaken between 1953 and 1955 fiscal years, in the opinion
of the General Accounting Office, is indicated by frequent
transfer of funds from one project to another, and the long
lapse of time between the signing of a project and its initial
execution, undue delays in the completion of projects, and
the later realization of the unsuitability of technicians and
equipment for the projects to which they were assigned. [19]

In the case of the Fars Cement Plant (No. 1), the Mission
officials admit that delays, loss of parts, and many other difficulties encountered were "a result of inadequate surveys,
lack of proper engineering, and lack of technicians to man
the job." [20]   In project No. 18, the Tehran Slaughterhouse,
five years of effort went into altering and expanding existing
facilities and operations.   Then, as a result of a U.S. Army
nutrition team's findings that meat thus provided "was not
fit for human consumption," it was decided to construct a
new slaughterhouse.   As of June, 1959, the building structure
was not yet completed, and, due to further delay in receiving
equipment, the September, 1964, completion date had to be postponed again.

The sum of $190,000 that was originally appropriated for
the preparation of a "comprehensive and detailed plan for
mineral resources development" under Project No. 20, was
never used until August, 1953, when part of it was alloted for
the purchase of equipment for the Kerman Water Supply
System.

In the case of Project No. 24 (Improvement of Post and
Telecommunications), it was admitted that the over-all plans
were not complete because the Ministry had omitted a program
of training of personnel to install and maintain the system. [21]

Funds provided in 1953 for Project No. 29 (Development
and Improvement of Highways) to assist in financing the cost
of four planned highways were diverted later in 1954 to the
purchase of steel pilings for the repair of certain bridges in
the Caspian area.   The pilings arrived in 1955 and reached
their destination in 1956 when it was discovered that the
Ministry of Roads did not have the proper equipment to
install them. [22]

In the case of Project No. 31 (Processing Dried Fruits)
there was reportedly so much delay in processing orders for

the equipment that subsequent price increases made the establishment of the plant impossible within the earmarked budget. After additional funds were budgeted and the site selected, construction could not start because no qualified technician was available. The project was finally turned over to the Plan Organization in 1955 for "implementation."

Half a million dollars worth of modern equipment was purchased between 1953 and 1958 for Project 38 (Bureau of Standards) before obtaining the professional staff, proper organization, or enactment of the required legislation. As a result, more than three quarters of the machinery provided by the Mission was still lying almost idle in subsequent years. [23]

The handlooms ordered under Project 61 (Improvement of Handloom Industry) arrived in Isfahan before the land for the Kuhpayeh plant was purchased, or invitations for bids on construction issued. Project 83 (Bonded Warehouse) was established before suitable land could be purchased for the site, and the project had to be abandoned later.

The Community Development Project No. 64 is another example of inadequate planning and the lack of priority. The project started in June, 1953, to support the newly enacted Farmer's Share Law under which 10% of the landlords' income was to be appropriated for village improvement. [24] At first the major emphasis was on a vast building program (bath houses, schools, mosques, sanitary latrines). Then the emphasis was placed on establishing village councils and cooperatives on an extensive Ostan-wide basis. Later on, attention was directed to the selection of specific areas for intensive work on the so-called "block" basis under which multipurpose village level workers (or Dehyars) were to be trained. And finally, interest was shifted toward building concrete things, such as feeder roads to be financed on a 50-50 basis with villagers and the government participating.

As a result of these frequent vacillations between the support of structures on the one hand, and institutions, on the other, the concept of community development was never really fully understood by the Iranians. A Chief of the Community Development Division admits that the multiplicity of activities labelled as community development mitigated against a sound program based upon a proper rationale. [25]

A community development specialist who arrived on the scene after the establishment of the new government in 1954, admits that on his arrival in Iran the degree of awareness of village council programs was not very high, and that while considerable sums of money had been spent, most of the expenditure had not been planned wisely. [26]

Another community development specialist, writing in August, 1960, six years after the establishment of the program, comes to the belated conclusion that:

> Since the needs are so great and our combined resources are comparatively small, it seems that the time has come for some more orderly development of the rural areas. This means a realistic assessment of all available resources, a ranking of needs, and a rational plan to eliminate overlapping and assure the most effective use of technical, natural and human resources.

Then he adds in a most candid fashion that perhaps the Iranian Plan Organization might be willing to send an economist to help his division [27] -- a sort of technical assistance in reverse.

A year later, another community development advisor has this to say:

> Still serving in Iran are American personnel in other technical areas who received their first and only concept of CD work during the crash program.
> While admitting a complete lack of expertise in such matters, this advisor cannot resist venturing the unsolicited opinion that these problems will remain unresolved until a priority list of basic changes--jointly agreed upon as necessary and accomplished one-by-one over specific periods of time--are made a condition of further and continuing aid to Iran. [28]

A Deputy Director of the Mission sums up the results of the Community Development Division in 1962:

> . . . a great deal of useful work has been done in the field of community development.

However, these efforts have been dependent on sustained external assistance and they have not been part of a well-coordinated and integrated program for rural development. Hence the Community Development program has not achieved the results which were expected considering the expenditure of technical and material resources. [29]

Of special interest also is the fate of Project 82 (Saw Mill) and 92 (Food Processing) -- the only new fields introduced by the Industry Division outside the Plan Organization's own industrial program. Ostensibly for the purpose of providing Iran with a demonstration mill to show "modern lumbering methods," a project agreement for the erection of a hardwood hand sawmill (including a power house, repair shops and seasoning yard on the Caspian forests) was signed early in 1954. Of this agreement one of Mission's own contract teams wrote three years later:

> The agreement is extremely brief and does not include normal safeguards and stipulations as to the methods of operation, timetables, progress reports, guarantees as to land acquisition, timber rights or types of operating authority or agency. At the time of the execution of this agreement, no inventory had been made to determine the type and quantity of wood, and no operators were available, and the temporary site selected was evidently the one recommended by the Agriculture Division Chief on his personal investigation. [30]

Yet, in the same year, 1954, a contract was signed with a U.S. manufacturer for the importation of over $400,000 of sawmill machinery. The equipment arrived, and a site was finally selected in 1955. But since there was no road with bridges strong enough to withstand heavy diesel generating units, the machinery could not be taken to the mill site and was unloaded on a beach near Pahlavi, some 20 miles away in the open.

In 1956 a UN expert who was brought in on the project found the equipment too fragile for the Iranian wood, and

showed dissatisfaction with the area, the site and the proposed procedure. Consequently, in May, 1957, the Mission
sought the advice and assistance of George Fry & Associates.
While the rust caused by rain and moisture was being removed from the equipment, George Fry technicians reportedly
came to the conclusion that the mill was too big for Iran and
had to be replaced by a portable sawmill. The Mission's
own technicians disagreed with the recommendation and urged
the Mission to take over direct responsibility for continued
operation. The date of completion, set for July, 1957, was
moved to 1959. Despite the Mission's insistence that timber
rights were "the single most critical operating cost item in
the entire project," no significant effort was made to acquire
these rights from the large number of small owners in the
area. There was also no indication that necessary funds
would be available for the purchase of these rights, as well
as log-handling equipment and access roads, when the mill
was ready for operation. The mill was finally made operational in 1964.

The planning story of Project No. 92 is less eventful
but equally interesting. The original purpose of this project,
signed in 1954, was an "industrial survey" to determine
the feasibility of increasing efficiency in existing Plan Organization factories by utilizing waste products (sugar molas-
ses, wood and rice wastes). No such survey was ever made,
however, and in 1955 the project's name changed to Food
Processing Services, incorporating projects Nos. 31, 56, 68
and 69, (Dried fruit, Bandar Abbas canning factory, community
canning and date curing). The project description became
"Demonstration and Training in Food Processing."

The new objective evidently was not to establish a commercial canning industry but a demonstration plant. In his
end-of-tour report, the chief of the Food Processing Branch
of the Industry Division said:

> We have discarded all plans to develop im-
> mediately a commercial type canning industry.
> Our only aim is to improve present operation
> and spread education in canning methods and the
> use of canned goods. For the most part, this will
> be done at village levels. Except for the cost
> of collapsible cans, a complete demonstration
> plant can be made for less than $25,000. [31]

Yet, only one year after this pronouncement, an expanded commercial type canning program was undertaken without further studies or surveys to determine the availability of the raw materials; the kind and cost of the finished products; the size of the market; and the methods of distribution. In the absence of such studies, a Stanford Research Institute team, later contracted by the Mission to offer the required technical assistance in demonstration and training, could not perform its duties effectively and had to leave.

The development of Project 109 (Industrial Development Center) is best described by one of its own advisors as follows:

> This project was begun in June of 1956 with little apparent thought given to the ordering and layout of the equipment or to employees' housing facilities. The first equipment orders were not placed until approximately two years later indicating poor planning and timing.
> Since due to the lack of interest and budget support from the Iranian Government the project has not progressed as it should have, it has now been closed without having put the laboratories into operation." [32]

COSTS OF NON-PLANNING

The foregoing tale of the Mission's planless development is meant only to show the fate of a technical assistance program in action. The Iranian experience in this regard emanates neither from inherent deficiencies in the nature of foreign technical assistance programs nor from the concept of the Point IV program. The lack of program planning, and the handicaps, delays, and deficiencies resulting from it relate mostly to the nature of Point IV operations. Most of the projects to which reference was made in the foregoing section were emergency or crash activities strung up to keep the Iranian economy afloat during the post-nationalization crisis and cannot really be called technical projects. They came under the technical assistance umbrella mostly because the Point IV "agreement" was the only legal instrumentality through which all economic aid to Iran could be channeled.

The projects signed in later years seem to have been formulated with less haste, greater care, and more caution.

Gradually, the procedures for the presentation of projects for Washington's approval were tightened to such an extent that beginning in 1955, under the Project Proposal and Approval (PPA) System, the Mission had to give a detailed description of the proposed project including number and functions of technicians, number and kind of participants, detailed list of commodities, project objectives, and the method of its implementation. The new procedure undoubtedly made the formal presentation of projects more precise, and induced Mission officials to press for the collection of more extensive and accurate information from the local government before agreeing to the formulation and implementation of new projects.

Yet the weight of the early projects could not be easily shrugged off. The waste or misuse of machines, equipment and supplies resulting from planless operations is recognized by the Mission itself. According to a Mission document, when the Master Joint Fund was established in 1954, the physical conditions of the property and the records could best be compared to a "dump heap." The property compound was filled with supplies and equipment, some of which had been in Iran for several years. The over-all storage facilities as well as the methods employed were inadequate. Valuable machinery as well as large quantities of fertilizers and chemicals were sometimes left in the open. [33]

The magnitude of the damage from this lack of synchronization cannot be determined easily or precisely. But a number of examples in different fields of the Mission's operations collected from the technicians' end-of-tour reports may serve as an indication of the diversity of the problem. A Mission horticulturalist complains that he often felt "in the dumps" because he could not get some minor materials that were needed in his work. [34] A technician in charge of on-the-job training for automobile repairs states that he was without a garage for several months and could not demonstrate what he was teaching. Once the garage was finally acquired, his office was moved to another building where there was no classroom. [35] A business education advisor employed to give in-service instructions in typing, shorthand and office procedure to government employees says she was for several months without the equipment, supplies and textbooks ordered from the United States and even then, without a suitable building or qualified bi-lingual counterparts. [36]

According to a Mission Sanitary engineer none of the eight water distribution systems contracted for Iranian cities in 1952 was finished by 1956, partly due to "delay in receiving necessary fittings from the Sanitary Engineering Division in Tehran."[37]   A railroad advisor blamed the inability to implement his program on the lack of training equipment that had been on order for "well over one year." [38] The work of the industrial machine shop in Tehran was reportedly held up for almost two years because a special machine which was ordered in 1957 had not arrived by the end of 1958 and which, after 10 months of search and investigation, was finally found to be resting at the receiving port all this time. [39] A foundry specialist brought to the Tehran Institute of Technology discovered that the Institute's Point IV-financed, half-finished foundry building had been designed without adequate consideration of the foundry program. [40]

Planning deficiencies of the earlier times thus continued to plague subsequent operations.   A technician from the Industry Division said in a 1960 confidential interview:

> Many of the early industrial projects to which we contributed money and manpower were politically instigated projects. And once we were committed to support them, they kept dragging on. Now there is not enough money to institute more useful projects, and nobody seems to dare to suggest that we pull out of the old ones. Even now, we give no advice to the Iranian government on the basis of an industrialization policy. We offer advice only on individual projects.

This lack of complementary relationship among the Mission projects inevitably reduced their effectiveness as part of a comprehensive program. [41]   The program in agriculture, for example, went its own way trying to increase productivity partly through mechanization and reducing the need for agricultural workers without being much concerned about how and where such a released labor force could be employed. The education program emphasized an increase in literacy and created a desire among peasants to know more and to want more, with little or no concern for the outcome of such increasing expectations. Health activities attempted to lengthen human life and to enhance the capacity to enjoy more things in life without ensuring the means to satisfy the newly-created needs.   Community development schemes stirred up village folks into greater participation in determining their destiny, with little or no real effort to change socio-economic institutions that hampered such participation.

The disadvantage of this type of operation was not so much in failing to offer coordinated advice (although the program suffered much from lack of coordination); the real shortcoming of the situation was the inability to provide the atmosphere, the thought process, the pattern of behavior necessary to change the old, and instill a new technology. Without such a climate, a lonely and teamless advisor, however competent he was, could not accomplish a great deal.

WHOM TO BLAME?

The responsibility for the lack of planning, cohesion, and consistency should not be placed on the Mission alone. As Mission officials have pointed out in defense of their position, [42] the shifting nature of program objectives and directions, the uncertainty of its appropriations, Washington's delays in the procurement of technicians and equipment, and the Iranian government's political, financial and administrative difficulties were all contributing or conditioning factors. The temporary nature of the program itself was such that no one in the Mission knew at any time how long the program was going to continue, at what speed, in what magnitude and with what emphasis. Programs and projects had to be presented to Congress and justified each year for annual appropriation. And not until the country's share of the total foreign aid appropriation was known, could the Mission decide on its own program and project allocations.   Oftentime, the country's share was not communicated to the Mission until the middle of the fiscal year.

The political urgency of getting the program under way as quickly as possible, without worrying much about its internal consistency or its external implications, was another factor. The following statement by a former Mission official seems to reflect this:

Iran has had its share of missions and surveys.   Few of their recommendations actually materialized.   They were surveys of things to be

done but seldom giving justification for the individual projects. Even surveys taking months
and years did not result in supporting data on
which a justification could be based. How then
could USOM/I have been able to provide in 1952
complete justification for projects which had to
be started quickly under a "do-something" policy?
In 1952, many projects were accepted by the
Mission more or less as "bail out" or "foot
in the door" projects. There was no opportunity,
time or technicans available to complete comprehensive surveys ordinarily necessary. [43]

Still another factor inhibiting the Mission's systematic
planning was the composition of Mission Staff and technicians.
As will be detailed in Chapter 11, the Mission assistants
were largely composed of practitioners in certain disciplines,
arts or crafts and impatient for quick and tangible results.
They had little time, or love for planning beyond their immediate horizons. In this respect they were in the company of
that successful scientist of whom a known educator said:

Rather than spend valuable time worrying
about when and how a mistake was made, his
energies were always directed at getting on with
the job. [44]

Getting on with the job and not "wasting" valuable time
in thinking and planning seems to have been the dominant
feature of the Mission's modus operandi throughout the period.
As one of the Mission's disgruntled "thinkers" put it:

There was little thinking being done at the
Mission. Very few questions were asked and
much less theoretical discussion was held. There
was no real philosophy behind the program, no
clear policy for its implementation. There was
no theory, no analytical evaluation of the accomplishments. The whole operation was purely
expediential, dealing with day-to-day problems.
There was plenty of know-how but very little
know-why.

The head of a U.S. philanthropic organization in Tehran confirmed this observation by calling the program "an unrelated, uncoordinated bunch of sincere but fragmentary efforts that could lead nowhere in particular."

Defending the Mission's position against these criticisms, a devoted Mission technician tried to put the blame on Washington and the Congress:

> It is impossible to justify a project for research and development, for thinking and theorizing, to Congress. Each division has to justify its existence by carrying on operating projects. The Mission, too, presents the divisions' operating projects as a justification for its existence. Nobody at any level -- the division, the country Mission, or the ICA/W -- wants to go out on a limb by suggesting a project whose concrete results cannot be described beforehand.

Yet, as can be seen elsewhere in this study, Congress and Washington had their own tale to tell.

Closely connected with this planless dynamism was the fourth factor - a sort of exhilarating bewilderment in the face of the country's enormous problems, and the conviction that anything constructive would help Iran no matter where it landed or how. Mission officials, anxious to please Washington and do something for Iran, simply did not think that it would really matter where they began. As one official confided: "Everything needed improvement; every sector of the economy needed assistance. We simply did not have time to worry about priorities." A junior economist of the Mission in a private interview tried to put this in crude marginal terms:

> The Iranian problems of social and economic development are so many, and the need for outside help so overwhelming, that no matter where you put an individual technician, he would be useful provided he is listened to. If the country needs 5,000 technicians and only 250 are available, it makes little difference in which field they are employed. At this stage of the game, there is no need for concern as to the criteria for the allocation of technical assistance.

In so far as these statements apply to the earlier period, they are not difficult to understand, and perhaps not even difficult to justify.   What is hard to understand or justify is the continued lack of adequate planning in later years. As late as 1964 the two industrial education advisors to Project 270 (Armed Forces Vocational Training) list the factors unfavorable to their discharge of duty as: lack of preparation for the project site; delay in providing adequate buildings; nagging logistic support for supplies; inadequate development for courses of study; [45] and ''lack of a suitable plan to provide conscripted graduates from the program with simple inexpensive tool kits or limited financing to help them put their acquired skills to use.'' [46]

The material and non-material damages to the program, due to lack of planning and priority determination, have not been light.   Material damages are too familiar and well-publicized.   They include the high cost and inefficiencies of most of the industrial schemes; the questionable economic justification of some irrigation dams; the unsuitability of a significant quantity of the imported equipment and livestock; an untold number of days of wasted technicians' time; and the questionable welfare effects of other projects. [47]

But of greater over-all importance, perhaps, was the non-material damage to the American scientific and managerial reputation in Iran, and the loss of confidence on the part of the Iranians in the advantages of foreign technical assistance. As a well-informed sutdent of Iranian problems put it, it is only during the early stages of a program that the foundation for later work must be laid, and the trust and confidence of the people whom the program intends to serve must be won. [48] In this respect, the Mission's early operations left much to be desired.

References

1. See H. W. Singer in the Yearbook of Education, 1954 (New York: World Book Co., 1954), p. 75.

2. S. K. Day, "Role of Foreign Aid," Political Quarterly (July-September, 1959).

3. One and a half million dollars of U. S. funds were allotted for the fiscal year 1951 to be used for the preliminary

program arrangements, recruitment of personnel, and purchase of supplies.

4. The Iranian request considered to be "the immediate, urgent minimum" is reported to have been for $129 million. See New York Times, August 8, 1949, p. 3.

5. Jacob C. Hurewitz, op. cit., p. 45.

6. Thirteenth Weekly Report of TCI Director to ICA/W, September 25, 1962, p. 2.

7. Twenty-fifth Weekly Report of TCI Director to ICA/W, January 31, 1953, App. 2, p. 2.

8. No specific target was set up for the desirable degree of improvement in living conditions; no definite goal was set for the rise in agricultural or industrial productivity; nor was any time limit fixed for the Point IV program to bear fruit and be assimilated.

9. Criticisms of the Foreign Aid Program, Committee on Foreign Affairs, House of Representatives (Washington: Committee Print, June 12, 1954), p. 72. (Italics not in the original.)

10. U.S. Aid Operations in Iran, Hearings before a Subcommittee of the Committee on Government Operations, House of Representatives, 84th Cong., 2nd Sess. (Washington, 1956), p. 212.

11. Ibid., p. 15.

12. U.S. Aid Operations in Iran, First Report by the Committee on Government Operations, House of Representatives, Report No. 10, 85th Cong., 1st Sess. (Washington, January 1957), p. 3.

13. R. D. Stickney, CTR, May 9, 1956, p. 2.

14. Reply to Questionnaire of Subcommittee of Government Operations Committee, House of Representatives, U.S. Congress (Tehran: USOM/I, 1957), p. 46.

15. Ibid., p. 47.

16. Section 403, Act for International Development, 1950. For a detailed discussion of these criteria, see Charles Wolf, Jr., Foreign Aid: Theory and Practice in Southern Asia (Princeton: Princeton University Press, 1960), p. 64.

17. See "Basic Operating Policies for Formulating Point IV Programs," "Functional Annual Plan of Work," and "Request and Justification" in RUSTEAI.

18. See the Comptroller General of the United States, Audit Report to the Congress of the United States: U.S. Assistance Program for Iran (Washington: General Accounting Office, 1955).

19. See "Program Planning Report" submitted by G. H. Staples of the General Accounting Office in U.S. Aid Operations in Iran, Hearings, p. 36.

20. W. F. Benning, "Industry," in RUSTEAI, n. p.

21. Because of the lack of proper planning, the equipment purchased in 1953 for the Kerman Water Supply project, for example, had to remain in storage for five years awaiting the design and construction of a water system which was not finished until 1958. The home cannery equipment ordered under Project 68 did not arrive in time for use by the home cannery technician before the end of her tour of duty. Conversely, the buildings for industrial laboratories under Project 109 were finished by 1959 while not more than 20 per cent of the equipment, and no technicians, had been made available.

22. W. F. Benning, "Industry," in RUSTEAI, n. p.

23. According to a Mission advisor attached to this project, even as late as 1959, the 'program planning' for the project had not progressed beyond its material phases (i. e., building and equipment) and no plan had been made to get the people concerned—ministry officials, on the one hand, and producers and exporters, on the other -- acquainted with the objectives of the project and its benefits to the country's economy. See T. L. Swenson, CTR, April 30, 1959, p. 3.

24. The Law was later amended to give landlords "greater voice" in the village councils.

25. C. J. Nelson, CTR, July 30, 1960, p. 7.

26. Brewster Wilson, CTR, May 8, 1956, p. 2.

27. W. J. Cousins, CTR, August 11, 1960, p. 6. (Italics added.)

28. J. L. Armon, CTR, December 18, 1961, pp. 4, 7. (Italics added.)

29. R. E. Galloway, CTR, May 28, 1962, p. 1.

30. George Fry & Assoc., Lumbering Operations in Caspian Region, USOM/I Project 82 (Tehran, 1957).

31. See B. W. Brown, CTR, December 17, 1957, p. 9.

32. J. W. Swann, CTR, September 1, 1962, pp. 4-6.

33. "Master Joint Fund Operations and Background, " in RUS-TEAI, n. p.

34. See G. H. Blackman, CTR, December 5, 1955, p. 26.

35. See R. E. Cox, CTR, January 16, 1956, pp. 4-5.

36. See M. L. Chaffin, CTR, November 7, 1957, p. 3.

37. J. J. Barry, CTR, March 12, 1960, p. 10.

38. D. S. Reid, CTR, April 16, 1959, p. 6.

39. H. J. Burgi, CTR, August 25, 1960, p. 5.

40. A. S. Goss, Jr., CTR, November 16, 1960, p. 2.

41. For indications of a continued "lack of adequate planning," see A. P. Donovan, CTR, July 29, 1963, p. 5; and W. H. Holloway, CTR, March 3, 1964, p. 11.

42. U. S. Aid Operations in Iran, Hearings, p. 793.

43. W. F. Benning, "Industry, " in RUSTEAI, n. p. (Italics not in the original.)

44. See General Electric Defense Quarterly (July-September, 1960), p. 33.

45. L. D. Hulit, CTR, July 7, 1964, p. 5.

46. H. J. Opperman, CTR, May 13, 1964, p. 5.

47. See Examination of Economic and Technical Assistance Program for Iran, Fiscal Years 1956-1960 (Washington: General Accounting Office, 1961).

48. Harold Allen, Rural Reconstruction in Action (Ithaca: Cornell University Press, 1953), p. 1.

CHAPTER

6

TECHNICAL AID AND THE DOMESTIC PLAN

The effectiveness of a program of foreign technical assist-ance for economic development depends on (1) the wisdom and propriety of the economic development plan it is to assist, and (2) the program's rational correspondence to the entire do-mestic development effort.

No program of foreign technical aid, of course, can ever assume the full task of economic development. Technical assistance can at best be only a part, and sometimes not even a significant part, of the total development endeavor.

Since foreign technical assistance can only serve as a means to a broader and more comprehensive end of economic expansion, its value depends on its supplemental correspon-dence to the total effort toward that end. Technical aid would be of little value in itself if the economic development plan to which it applies is unwisely thought out, poorly established, or improperly executed. [1] In fact, as has been repeatedly pointed out, in the absence of a comprehensive and well-worked plan, the limited scale and the gradual approach of demonstration and pilot projects may result in greater frus-tration and more disappointment [2] and may do more harm than good. [3]

But the prior existence of a systematic plan is, to be sure, only a necessary condition. It is also imperative that: (1) the technical assistance scheme correspond, program by program and project by project, to the domestic development plan; and (2) the plan's need for the specific kinds of technical assistance and at the proper levels be determined before-hand. Without this technical complementarity any offer of advice, technicians' time, or demonstration equipment would be largely wasted and the uncoordinated projects would impart little or no economic benefit to the country.

IRANIAN DEVELOPMENT PLANS

The tortuous process of Iran's ad hoc development planning immediately after World War II, and the unplanned juxtaposition of the Point IV program in 1950, can partly explain some of the difficulties that U.S. technical assistance encountered in Iran.

The story of the Iranian government's nationwide program of industrialization and economic development goes back to the early 1920's. Since then, a vast number of development projects were launched and several economic plans were formulated. [4] Although these plans were not, in a true sense, based on any system of calculated priorities or cost-benefit studies, the country succeeded in developing a network of modern industries, roads, communications and superstructures that seemed remarkable in their outward appearance. To some Western observers, however, these structural successes were achieved at the expense of badly needed institutional and managerial development. To these observers, the expenditure of huge sums of money on eye-catching public structures, exclusive reliance on domestic financing, and inadequate traning of managerial skills combined to produce only a small and temporary rise in productivity. [5] The Allied military occupation of Iran in 1941-1945 and its disrupting effects on the national economy (e.g., a six-times increase in the cost of living, rapid migration of workers to major cities for employment in the Allies' diverse activities, and the over-utilization of local industrial and transportation facilities) further aggravated the country's planning problems. [6]

Dissatisfied still with its past attempts at industrialization, and increasingly pressured to improve the living conditions of the masses, the Iranian government proposed in 1946 to launch a better balanced and a more comprehensive plan for new economic development. The Morrison-Knudson International, a San Francisco counsulting firm was invited to examine the economic potentialities of Iran and submit recommendations for the country's accelerated development. The company's report submitted in July of 1947 [7] was studied and revised by Iranian officials. On the basis of their recommendations, the government applied to the World Bank for a development loan. Following the advice of the Bank and the U. S. State Department, the Iranian government late in 1948 contracted for a group of American engineering firms,

Overseas Consultants, Inc., (OCI), to make a single integral survey of the country's conditions and submit a seven-year development plan. The survey was completed in August, 1949, and a five-volume report was issued. [8] In February, 1949, the Iranian Majles gave its authorization for the execution of the new plan by passing the Seven-Year Development Act. OCI agreed to stay in Iran to supervise the plan and offer continuing advice. The plan was to be financed by royalties from oil, internal credits from Bank Melli Iran, sale of government property, public borrowing at home, and loans from abroad. It was optimistically predicted that a proper execution of the plan would raise the national income by 100 per cent within the seven year period while providing employment for some 92,000 additional urban workers. [9]

In spite of its lengthy preparation and repeated revisions, the First Seven-Year Plan left unanswered a number of questions regarding its basic philosophy, major objectives, and methods of implementation. Of this an OCI team member writes:

> There was clearly present a very hazy basic philosophy of technical assistance, and widely divergent opinions as to an appropriate policy to be followed in detailed projects. Thus, the Iranian Commission was badly divided as to whether the Plan should be directed towards a basic industrialization of the country with major engineering projects, or towards a modest upgrading of the efficiency of existing techniques in agriculture and local industry. Little or no thought had been given to questions of the impact of nearly six-hundred and fifty million dollars of new investments on Iranian economy, nor to the impact of sweeping technological changes upon the mores and social structure of the country. [10]

To many Western observers again, the Plan's goal seemed very ambitious; [11] to some it appeared more in the realm of wishful thinking than of reality. [12] The planners themselves were not sure whether all the recommended projects could even be started within seven years. [13] There was already some speculation to the effect that the "landed and mercantile classes" together with the "conservative clerics" who were likely to perceive in the plan a threat to their privileges and social status might actually sabotage the entire effort. [14]

Shortly after the plan was put into operation, however, a number of important external and internal difficulties arose and held its progress down.   The nationalization of the oil industry put an end to the income from oil royalties which were the sole means of financing the plan in the first two years of operation.   The Iranian government failed to obtain a loan from the World Bank. This loan had been heavily relied upon to provide the plan's foreign exchange requirements.   No significant sale of public property was made, and no money came from private investors. A modest issue of government bonds was mainly subscribed to by the government's own financial agencies, and was later used to offset the increasing budgetary deficits.   The only domestic credit which the organization received came from the state-owned Bank Melli.

The lack of funds alone was perhaps not the only handicap. Evidently, the plan's internal administrative machinery was also plagued by frictions.   For one thing, the all-important relationship between the Overseas Consultants, Inc. and the Iranian management was not clearly defined at the outset. The American experts were originally retained to "supervise" the operation of the plan.   The supervision later was interpreted as mere advice and guidance whenever the Iranian officials needed them.   The Consultants apparently could not agree to that, particularly because they claimed that their advice was often disregarded. Another reason for the internal friction was the OCI's belief that the organization did not succeed in functioning as a non-political, business-like enterprise, as was intended. [15]

In December, 1950, the Overseas Consultants withdrew its services from the organization. In announcing the cancellation of the contract effective January 1, 1951, the Iranian Managing Director of the Plan revealed the "growing differences for months" between the foreign experts and the Iranian officials directing the program.   Western observers again charged that most of the funds originally earmarked for agriculture and irrigation in the first year of operation went instead to more spectacular and less qualified projects such as railways and new state enterprises. [16]

After OCI's departure the Plan Organization continued to operate under the direction of an all-Persian Supreme Planning Board. But, handicapped from within and from without, its progress was slow and its operations fell short of expectations.

DEMISE OF THE PLAN AND EMERGENCE OF POINT IV

It was in the midst of these financial and managerial difficulties that U.S. technical assistance to Iran was given the responsibility of rescuing the Plan from a complete collapse. As could be expected under the circumstances, the correspondence of the Point IV assistance to the Plan became, not one of technical complementarity, but mostly financial substitution: Thirty-eight of the projects approved by the Mission as of June 30, 1954, were originally the engineering and construction projects of the First Plan which were interrupted by, or postponed due to, the loss of oil revenues. [17]

Yet even in its financial relation and correspondence to the Plan, it is not clear on what basis some of the Plan projects were singled out to be included in the Point IV program while other Point IV projects were formulated outside the Plan. Nor is the functional relationship among the Plan and non-Plan projects easy to understand.

The inclusion of Plan projects in the Point IV program, so it seems, was an obvious attempt to prevent the Iranian industrial expansion program from collapsing after the oil nationalization. [18] The assistance to Fars and Rey Cement plants, the Tchitsazi Mill, Shiraz Power, and the three sugar factories was justified by Mission officials as aid to projects that were financially sound, among key industries in Iran's over-all industrial program, providing excellent opportunities for training and demonstration of improved business and industrial methods, and well adapted for later sale to private enterprise. They were, moreover, considered strategically located geographically in relation to population and agricultural production centers.

Subsequent events, and a later critical investigation [19] by the U.S. Congress, seem to indicate, however, that these projects were chosen not totally according to the foregoing

criteria but apparently by political intuition. In the words
of a former A.I.D. administrator:

> . . . funds were approved for projects, which
> in many cases, were already firm contracts of
> the Government of Iran. It had to be assumed
> that the Iranian Government, when initiating these
> projects had made economic and technical deter-
> minations as to the soundness and feasibility of
> these projects. The "crash" operation for politi-
> cal expediency was the sole basis for approval of
> these projects and a careful analysis of the pro-
> gram for the past 2 years reveals that little
> additional funds have been channeled into indus-
> trial-type projects. [20]

The reasons for the exclusion of other Plan projects in
the Point IV program are more difficult to find. In the
absence of any clear policy declarations on the part of the
Mission, it would not be easy to examine the basis on which
the exclusions were made. Many of the Mission officials who
were interviewed on this matter showed little interest in, or
sufficient concern with, it.   To them, the question seemed
either too academic to worry about, or too complex in each
case to lend itself to any kind of generalization.

A few Mission officials, however, who volunteered to
venture their personal opinions, could agree on three general
and not altogether precise criteria.   According to these
officials, the chief considerations for not undertaking or not
supporting other projects were the facts that these projects
did not help attain the United States objectives; were not wanted
by the Iranian government; and/or the government of Iran
did not wish to contribute to their financing. As will be seen
in later sections, however, there is evidence that even the
last two criteria were not always assiduously observed.

Granting the wisdom and propriety of the criteria adopted
by the Mission for the inclusion or exclusion of the Plan projects, and for the formulation of its own, the correspondence
of the Point IV projects to the domestic plan still remained
to be answered.   And even if the ad hoc nature of Point IV
operation between 1951 and 1953 could be blamed on the chaotic
political conditions of the period, the persistent and lingering

deficiencies in subsequent years ought to be explained. Why did the Mission, for example, not actively participate in the design and formulation of the Second Seven-Year Plan in 1955 when political normalcy had returned to the country? And, even more difficult to understand, why did the Mission have no effective role in the preparation of the Third Five-Year Plan?

This last plan, put in operation in September, 1962, was formulated with the aid of an independent team of "experts," (the Harvard Advisory Group) financed by the Ford Foundation, and directed by a Harvard University official. Although the Mission claims that it was always "informed and consulted" by the Group, the fact is that the outline of the Third Plan was developed in substantial independence from the Mission's thinking and planning.

This is indeed hard to understand. One great advantage of a resident technical mission is the experience it gains as domestic development evolves and the ability it acquires to advise on the formulation of subsequent plans. It is surprising, therefore, that the Mission resources were not mobilized for this one purpose, if the program were to be technical. It is equally hard to explain why the Iranian government had to invite the Harvard Group, and other technical missions, [21] at a time when the Point IV program in Iran was in full force.

POINT IV RELATIONS TO OTHER TECHNICAL AIDS

The Harvard Group was not the only technical team in the country concurrent with the Mission. During most of the Mission's life, Iran received technical assistance from a dozen or more foreign agencies and organizations.

In addition to the Mission's own contract teams financed by Point IV funds, such other agencies as the USIA, the United Nations Technical Assistance Board, and the UN agencies (UNESCO, FAO, WHO, UNICEF, SUNFED and ILO) were also engaged in assisting Iranian government agencies. Table III shows the number of foreign assistants in various fields of activity working in Iran as of May, 1965.

Bilateral assistance was offered at one time or another also by the governments of Austria, Belgium, France, Great

TABLE III

Foreign Technical Assistants Working in Iran as of May, 1965

Main Fields \ Foreign Sources	Austria	France	Germany	Israel	Japan	United Kingdom	U. N.	U.S. AID	U.S. Near-East Found.	U.S. Peace Corps	Total
Agriculture		25	4	7	2	5	36	28		21	128
Communications						2	2	6			10
Education	10	18	34		8	11	33	19	4	104	241
Health		9					11	2	1		23
Industries & Mines		3					22	2			27
Miscellaneous			1		1	4	17	26		32	81
Total	10	55	39	7	11	22	121	83	5	157	510

Source: Plan Organization of the Government of Iran.

Britain, Israel, Italy, Japan, Sweden, Soviet Union, and West Germany. So was a good deal of assistance by philanthropic organizations. The Ford Foundation, in addition to sponsoring the Harvard Advisory Group, supported Franklin Publications in its task of publishing reference books, assisted the National Teachers College for training librarians, helped the Shiraz Agricultural College and the Nemazee Vocational School, had an active program for integrated rural development, and provided individual scholarships for study abroad. The Near East Foundation, after the expiration of its contract with ICA, was offering technical aid to the Khuzistan Development Authority, the University of Ahwaz and a few other minor agencies. The Rockefeller Foundation was assisting the Shiraz Medical School. CARE was supplying food, tools and equipment to Iranian rural areas. The American Friends of the Middle East helped Iran with a library of professional periodicals, and guided Iranian students in their choice of schools in the United States. The Oil Consortium had a contract with Lafayette College to man a Technical Institute of Petroleum Studies in Abadan. There were also other individual technicians working directly with the Iranian agencies.

Without close correspondence and coordinated planning among this multitude of agencies offering technical aid to Iran, Mission activities could not be expected to produce maximum benefits. Duplication of efforts would be unavoidable, and bureaucratic frictions were bound to arise. Yet such a correspondence and coordination were not effectively present. Writes a public administration consultant about his own field:

> After arrival in Iran, I found that there was no single coordinated approach or plan for the several consultants who were to be dealing with the various ministries. Consequently each consultant was on his own to determine the best plan of attack to solve the problems discovered within his particular ministry. [22]

Not infrequently the activities of different agencies ran somewhat counter to each other. An executive officer of the Near East Foundation working on a contract team for the Mission, puts the problem this way:

> At times, Near East Foundation officials as well as Government of Iran officials and USOM/I

officials have pursued the opposite course of action, thereby spending a great deal of time and
effort trying to do things the hard way. Efforts
at times have been dissipated on many lines and
paths of trial and error to reach the ultimate
goals. [23]

The necessity for such a coordinated approach to the
problem of technical assistance at the planning and policy-
making levels is reaffirmed by one of the Mission's public
administration consultants:

It is. . . my feeling that basic progress will
be delayed until assisting agencies of friendly
nations cooperate in a mutual program as well
as in giving more substantial aid and direction.
Patchwork assistance does not seem to me to be
enough. [24]

And this lack of external coordination seems to have existed
not only between the U.S. and other foreign technical teams
but also frequently between Point IV's projects and the government of Iran's regular activities. [25] It was indeed not unusual
for a government agency to try to obtain aid elsewhere
once its request had been turned down by the Mission. More
often than not, the aid that had been refused by one organization
(or one country) was gladly granted by another organization or
nation.

It also often happened that the various Iranian ministries
and agencies simultaneously used the services of several
foreign agencies without centralized clearing to avoid duplication. In one of its quarterly reports, a Mission contract team
hired to offer technical assistance to the newly-developed
Industrial Development Center of the Ministry of Industry
and Mines states as follows:

At the present time, the Industrial Development Center has no connection whatever with any
of the activities conducted by the Ministry (of
Industry). Another major factor affecting industrial development. . . is the recent organization
of the Industrial and Mining Development Bank
(which) like the Ministry of Industry. . . will

perform many services originally planned for the Industrial Development Center. [26]

The lack of coordination among foreign technical activities in Iran, however, did not necessarily mean a lack of cooperation among the aid teams. Official consultation generally existed between the aid agencies, and particularly between the U.S. and U.N. mission, almost at all times. Personal and official relationships between their staffs (and the Iranians) were also generally cordial. In a number of projects (notably malaria control, public statistics, irrigation and land reclamation, and basic education) joint participation, too, was fairly regularly achieved.

The same "uncoordinated" cooperation seems to have existed among the staff of local agencies. Writes a community development advisor:

Cooperation between CD and rural workers from other government agencies at the village level has been fairly satisfactory (outstanding in a few instances) though no real coordination exists. [27]

One reason for this lack of necessary coordination, apart from lack of basic program planning by the Mission, should be found in the piecemeal nature of the Iranian development plans and the familiar administrative rivalry among government agencies. Every government agency in Iran naturally tried to get a share of outside funds and wanted to have a program of its own. For a variety of reasons, every organization, too, tried to get on the Point IV bandwagon. Requests for "assistance" were numerous. With no project priorities worked out beforehand, and with the quest for "cooperation," the Mission generally obliged. In some cases, this lack of necessary coordination between the Mission operations and those of national or international organizations helped some local agencies with shrewder or more aggressive leadership to receive more than their proportionate share of outside assistance. [28]

* * * * *

The task of coordination between Point IV and other bilateral and multilateral aids, in the opinion of some Mission technicians interviewed, was that of the Iranian government and not of the Mission because it was really the Iranians' responsibility to coordinate their "intake" of foreign assistance.   Granting the validity of this argument, however, still little explanation can be found for the lack of active Point IV participation in the formulations of Iranian development plans (and the resulting lack of sufficient correspondence between Mission activities and some of Iran's major development projects, including planning itself).   And in spite of courageous efforts made lately by both the Mission and the GOI toward a greater degree of over-all coordination among Iranian agencies and foreign "missions," the success has at best been limited.

References

1.   Cf. Gustav F. Papanek, Framing A Development Program (New York: International Conciliation, March, 1960).

2.   Cf. Michael A. Heilperin, "Private Means of Implementing Point Four," Annals of the American Academy of Political and Social Science(March, 1950), p. 64; H. E. Spicer (ed.)Human Problems in Technological Change (New York: Russel Sage Foundation, 1952); H. de Graff, "Some Problems involved in Transferring Technology to Underdeveloped Areas," Journal of Farm Economics (November, 1951); P. G. and D. S. Franck, Implementation of Technical Assistance (New York: International Conciliation, February, 1951); D. R. Gadgil, "Some Requirements for Technical Progress in Asia," Pacific Affairs (June, 1951); J. K. Galbraith, "Making Point IV Work," Commentary (September, 1950); R. C. Martin, "Technical Assistance: The Problem of Implementation," Public Administration Review (Autumn, 1952); and W. Vogt, "Pitfalls of Point IV," American Perspective (Spring, 1950).

3.   Charles Malik, "The Problems of Underdeveloped Countries," in World Neighbors Working Together for Peace and Plenty (Washington, 1952); and K. H. Weil, "Pitfalls of Point IV; American Methods Can Harm, Rather Than Help Underdeveloped Areas," United Nations World (September, 1949).

4.   For a short history of government planning in Iran see Economic Development in Selected Countries: Plans, Programs, and Agencies (New York: UN Doc. 1948, II, B.I, 1950), pp. 183-184; and Ali Moarefi, "The Iranian Seven Year Plan and Its Monetary Effects," Ph. D. Dissertation, Georgetown University, 1950. See also D. N. Wilber, Contemporary Iran (New York: Praeger, 1963 , pp. 173-180.

5. See particularly Elgin Groseclose, Introduction to Iran (New York, Oxford University Press, 1947); W. S. Haas, Iran (New York: Columbia University Press, 1946); A. C. Millspaugh, Americans in Persia (Washington: Brookings Institution, 1946).

6. See I. C. Lundberg, "World Revolution: American Plan," Harper's Magazine (December, 1948); and C. P. Grant, "Iran: Test of Relations between Great and Small Nations," Foreign Policy Reports (April 15, 1945).

7. Report on Program for the Development of Iran (San Francisco: Morrison-Knudson International Co., Inc, July, 1947).

8. Report on Seven Year Development Plan for the Plan Organization of the Imperial Government of Iran (New York, 1949).

9. Mosharaf Naficy, Report on the Seven Year Plan (Tehran: Majles Press, 1947), pp. 33-34. (In Persian).

10. R. K. Hall, "Seven Year Plan in Iran," in Yearbook of Education, 1954, p. 283.

11. "Can Persia Plan?" Economist (London: May 6, 1950), pp. 982-83.

12. George Kirk, The Middle East, 1945-1950 (London: Oxford University Press, 1954), p. 98.

13. John D. Lotz, "The Iranian Seven Year Development Plan," Middle East Journal (January, 1950), p. 287.

14. T. Cuyler Young, "The Race between Russia and Reform in Iran," Foreign Affairs (January, 1950), p. 287.

15. See Max W. Thornberg, New York Times, January 9, 1951, p. 16. See also his People and Policy in the Middle East (New York: Norton, 1964).

16. "Setback in Iran," Fortune (March, 1951), p. 170.

17. The Mission's admittedly "uneconomical" and unprofitable projects (e. g. , 4, 14, 21, 25, 37, 56, 68, 85, and 86) were those already started or planned under the Iranian First Seven Year Plan.

18. U. S. Aid Operations in Iran, Hearings, p. 1220.

19. U. S. Aid Operations in Iran, First Report, pp. 32-39.

20. Letter of J. B. Hollister to J. Campbell in U. S. Aid Operations in Iran, Hearings, p.1105. (Italics not in the original.)

21. Early in September, 1954, the new Managing Director of
the Iranian Plan Organization announced that the World
Bank would be invited to send to Iran a mission of experts
in industry, agriculture, communications and other fields
to help prepare a comprehensive plan. Later, in January,
1955, he told newsmen of a contract signed with an American private group to send a technical mission to Iran to
survey Iran's industrial needs. See New York Times, September 12, 1954, p. 21; and Ettela'at (Tehran, Air Mail
Edition), January 12, 1955, pp. 2-3.

22. J. J. Flynn, CTR, June 21, 1958, p. 2.

23. W. A. Fuller, CTR, April 18, 1957. See a similar complaint about the "relationship difficulties" between the US
Federal Aviation Agency Group and the UN Aviation Advisory Group in R. P. Klemme, CTR, August 14, 1961, p. 4.

24. Sterling St. John, CTR, April 21, 1958, p. 2.

25. The problem of internal coordination (e.g., synchronization of mechanical, material and manpower needs of the
projects and functional relationships among project activities) is considered an organizational rather than planning problem and is discussed in Ch. 11.

26. George Fry & Assoc., Second Quarterly Report, January,
1960, pp. 3-5.

27. R. C. Gosda, CTR, February 9, 1963, p. 3.

28. In the course of routine news gathering one day in 1955, an
Iranian newspaper reporter learned from an official of a
particular Ministry that one of the programs of that Ministry was going to be aided by two United Nations agencies.
When the text of the reporter's innocuous copy appeared
in the paper the next day, high Ministry officials were reportedly furious about the "leak" because they thought once
the news of the U. N. aid reached the Mission, Point IV
aid to that Ministry might be cut and their share of American funds might be reduced. See Ettela'at (Tehran: Air
Mail Edition), January 11, 1955, p. 3.

PART III

THE WELCOME MAT

CHAPTER 7

COOPERATION
BY THE
RECIPIENT

*To the extent that the responsibility for the effectiveness
of foreign technical assistance rests on the cooperation of the
aid-receiving country, it is imperative that the country (1)
understand the role of technical assistance in the process of
economic growth with all its possibilities and limitations,
(2) feel a real need for such assistance and (3) wholeheartedly
welcome this type of aid.*

Economic growth can be induced by deliberate alterations
in four basic socio-economic variables: (1) technical coef-
ficients of production, (2) relative factor ratios, (3) factoral
efficiency, and (4) economically relevant propensities and institutions. 1 A change in production functions is necessary in
order to make better use of facilities not yet materialized
due to the lack of scientific knowledge, supply inelasticities,
or inadequate entrepreneurial incentives. Relative factor
ratios must be improved in the direction of a fuller utilization
of existing resources, again not yet achieved due to the same
or similar reasons. Quality of factors must be enhanced in
order to increase marginal productivity of existing resources
once they are fully employed. Relevant propensities and institutions ought to be modified in the direction of facilitating a
better and fuller use of actual resources.

GRASPING THE NATURE OF ASSISTANCE

Foreign technical assistance in the form of diagnosis,
advice and/or performance can be expected to contribute to
economic growth by affecting all four of these basic development variables. First, technical aid can raise domestic output by better utilization of employed and employable resources
within the framework of existing institutions. That is to say,
technical assistance can help maximize marginal returns to

productive factors within the same scale of operation. 2 Such improved utilization of employed resources can be achieved economically by improving methods of production through available or easily adaptable techniques. Reduction of machine wastage in industrial production; a change in the methods of plowing or harvesting agricultural products; simple hygenic measures (like keeping flies away from foodstuff); curriculum revision in public education; and better filing or record keeping in business and public administration are a few examples. An increase in total output through improved use of given resources can also be accomplished by simple changes in non-economic elements, say by better enforcement of existing laws or by the enactment of improved legislation, or by instituting new business practices.

Second, foreign technical assistance can help foster economic growth by serving as a catalyst in bringing about a fuller utilization of existing but unemployed or underemployed resources. 3 Fuller utilization of available resources can be aided by technical assistance in a number of different ways. By better enforcement of good civil service regulations in recruiting, promotion and pension, public servants and government workers may be expected to work harder or longer hours. Or, with an increase in the peasants' share of the crop, they may be expected to produce proportionately more by their willingness to tend the farms more attentively. Oftentimes, it is simply the foreign technicians' way of thinking or behavior, their dynamism or their self-confidence that may introduce a new spirit into a dormant sector and trigger development. Longer working hours, greater interest in one's job, productive use of domestic hoards, or repatriation of foreign-held balances may all be stimulated by foreign technical assistance.

Sometimes, too, technical aid may involve provision of what is called a "key" resource 4 that may serve as a nucleus around which underdeveloped resources may congregate. A research-minded foreign technician may attract a group of competent potential researchers into an organized experiment. A "big name" foreign professor may gather a large number of scholars into a local university. Sometimes, these "catalytic" or "key" resources are not available to the developing country; in other cases, ignorance, inefficiency or false pride may prevent the host country from taking advantage of them. In all cases, technical assistance may play an important role. An increase in efficiency induced by a key resource may also result from the "external economies" (regional conferences, joint development plans, international facilities) that are not available to a single country, but possible through group action and group organizations.

Third, foreign technical assistance can aid domestic economic progress through the discovery and/or improvement of material or human resources in the developing country, or by way of attracting an inflow of additional resources from abroad. 5   In this category fall the creation of new skills through better training, education and health; demonstration in the proper maintenance of capital; advice for the conservation and increase of national resources (particularly domestic savings); and the attraction for foreign capital.   In all these cases, the developing country is presumed to be unable or unprepared to provide the additional resources on its own.

Finally, foreign technical aid can accelerate domestic economic development by introducing changes in the existing cultural and institutional structure in such a way as to allow the adoption of new productive techniques along with a better and fuller utilization of actual or latent resources. 6 Proper changes in the people's habits of thought, their fundamental beliefs and their incentive, outlook, aspirations and attitude are examples of transformation from a non-technical to a technical culture.   Changes in governmental philosophy and organization; in legislation affecting contracts, investment and income distribution; in the conceptions of business and public integrity; in the climate for enjoying the fruits of one's work, innovation, initiative, and enterprise are examples of improvements in the institutional field. 7

Despite these marvels that aid from abroad can render to a developing country, foreign technical assistance is not the final answer to the numerous problems involved in economic development.   As mentioned before, the frame of reference within which bilateral programs of technical aid usually operate is not broad enough to meet all the needs of a developing country.   Programs of foreign technical aid, by their very nature, may be too small in magnitude, or too narrow in scope to accomplish the near miracles which the underdeveloped areas need. 8

ACCEPTING TECHNICAL AID IN ITS OWN RIGHT

An underdeveloped country that requests foreign technical aid should know that, even in the opinion of a decidedly sympathetic group:

> Technical aid is no panacea . . . Even if pursued with utmost energy, it could not alone in a few years refashion the material basis of great and ancient societies. Feudalism, landlordism, political corruption, tradition, superstition and other barriers cannot easily be overcome. [9]

In order to be able to use foreign assistance profitably, the host country must "feel" with deep and true interest the need for this type of aid. And, if it does not know its exact needs, it should be willing to submit itself to a genuine fact-finding examination. A precise indication of such "felt need" or submission to such a critical examination is not easy. [10]   And, the yardsticks are many and varied. Under the Point IV program the host country's willingness to pay a "fair share" of the cooperative effort seems to be considered as an evidence of the recipient's enthusiasm, appreciation and support for such assistance. In a sense, this is a good measure. Unless the recipient is willing to put forth at least a minimum effort of its own for its economic development, the program can hardly be called one of self-help or mutual assistance. But because of its numerous conceptual and statistical shortcomings, the "fair-share" criterion cannot always be the unmistakable criterion.

One conceptual weakness is that "fairness" is an ambiguous term. Almost any amount of money put up by the host country can be considered "fair." [11]   Furthermore, since most of the recipients obtain technical assistance along with other types of aid, part of the outside aid received for economic assistance or defense support can always be set aside by a simple bookkeeping device as the host country's contribution to the technical assistance program. [12]

Nor does the non-payment of the fair share always mean a lack of interest in a given project. A country may actually not know its need for technical assistance; or, it may not be in a financial position to share its cost at a given time; or, it may actually contribute little to a particular technical assistance project, but use its available resources in such a way as to support other projects elsewhere.

Statistically, too, the "fair-share" criterion presents complex accounting problems. When contributions in kind are accepted as the country's share it becomes almost impossible to put a dollar value on them. As a Mission accountant has indicated, in a forestry project, for example, that is designed to make an inventory of certain wooded areas, the host country's contribution can be considered on one extreme as providing practically nothing, and on the other, as providing an entire forest. And in any case, there will always be the problem of estimating the actual value of local facilities such as land, buildings and equipment. 13

For these and possibly other reasons, the contribution of a "fair share," in the opinion of the U.S. Senate Committee on Foreign Relations is not necessarily an indication of "felt needs" or right attitude. Instead, this attitude is considered as reflected in preparation of a development plan, interest in an efficient use of outside assistance, or the willingness to undertake basic reforms. 14

This study relates the degree of enthusiasm in the host country for foreign technical aid to three elements: (a) the country's willingness to seek foreign advice for the diagnosis of its basic ills even if such advice is not accompanied by additional material aid; (b) the country's determination to gear its policies, programs, and projects to supporting foreign advice and recommendations; and (c) a minimum support of the joint projects commensurate with the country's ability to share costs. Each one of these will be briefly discussed in the forthcoming sections.

ENTHUSIASM FOR POINT IV IN IRAN

The application of the foregoing tests to the case of the program in Iran indicates that: the nature of Point IV was not sufficiently understood and appreciated by the host country; failing to appreciate the philosophy and the direction of the Point IV program, host officials were not compelled to coordinate their thinkings and actions with that philosophy or in that direction; the minimum share of the program's cost was altogether not very enthusiastically shouldered.

Demand for Money Versus Supply of Advice

A review of the available Iranian documents, as well as the newspaper accounts of Point IV's establishment and expansion in Iran, seems to indicate that the possibilities and limitations of the Point IV program were not sufficiently clear to Iranian officials in general, and to the public in particular.

To the U.S. Congress, the basic concept of Point IV in the Act for International Development was a low-cost, high-return program for the interchange of technical knowledge and skills. There was no provision of governmental grants of capital. The United States, officially and in private negotiations, was steadfastly drumming up the idea that the major effort in such a program of "self-help" must be "local" in character; and that, in spite of their low standards of living, much of the capital required in the cooperative program should be provided by the host countries themselves. Much that had to come from abroad also had to come from private agencies and/or international financial institutions.

A later report by the Senate Foreign Relations Committee is emphatic in this respect:

> Because of some misunderstanding that has arisen about the nature of this program, it should be made clear at the outset that it is neither an ECA for the world nor in any sense a capital investment program. Because of the limited nature of the program it will not require the expenditure of large sums of money. Its chief cost will be for the salaries and expenses of technicians and other personnel, and not, for example, to purchase machinery, food and raw materials. 15

This emphasis on the technical nature of the program was repeatedly brought out from the very beginning in Congressional hearings on Mutual Security authorizations and appropriations.

The Iranians, however, did not draw, or wish to draw, any hard and fast line between technical and other types of aid. It can, in fact, be shown that at the time of the establishment of the Point IV program in Iran, there was really no widespread awareness in the host country of the true nature of the program, and that the initial enthusiasm for Point IV was based on erroneous assumptions.

In the absence of official comments on the part of the Iranian government at the time, it is hard to know what Iran was explicitly seeking from the Memorandum of Understanding and its subsequent documents. Unofficial but reliable evidence, however, seems to point out that Iran accepted Point IV not as a simple "program of rural improvement" to be implemented through "advice and demonstration," 16 but in the hope of other things to come and for a variety of motives.

The people who were influential in attracting Point IV aid to Iran, and those who "cooperated" with the Mission in subsequent years, fell into divergent groups with vastly different ideas and ideals. First, there was obviously a group of informed and enthusiastic officials who welcomed the program as a useful endeavor in, and by, itself. Among these true friends of Point IV there were, of course, some who did not know exactly what the program was going to do for Iran but, by virtue of their belief in American technical supremacy, were willing to accept American guidance on blind faith. There were also some bright and capable leaders who wanted foreign advisors to help them resist non-progressive local elements, support their reformative causes, or minimize unnecessary bickering among themselves.

To a group of impatient leaders who were not very happy with previous American missions and American know-how, however, the program looked desirable mostly for its potential financial contributions. Technical assistance to them was actually a sort of unnecessary but inseparable accoutrement to financial aid -- a kind of unneeded tail fins on an otherwise desirable vehicle.

In the third category there were shrewd politicians who wanted to use U.S. technicians' recommendation or approval as a wedge to push forward their own pet projects, give respectability to their own demand for further financial aid or help them resist internal political pressure. And, finally, there were the cynics who had little faith in, or hope for the effectiveness of the program, but considered "cooperation" with an "American" program economically harmless, and politically as good as siding with the angels.

The events antecedent to, and culminating in the offer of U.S. technical assistance to Iran in October, 1950, seem to give additional credence to the contention that the country's top leaders felt a much greater need for foreign investment funds than for the American technical assistance. The need most keenly felt was indeed for U.S. (and foreign) funds to meet the foreign exchange requirements of the stalled Seven-Year Plan.

The previous attitude of the United States seemed to support these expectations. Already under the Tehran Declaration of December 1, 1943, President Roosevelt had agreed to "continue to make available to the government of Iran such economic assistance as may be possible." [17]   It is reported that shortly after the Tehran Declaration,

> President Roosevelt, following his brief visit to the country, was beginning to think "of using Iran as an example of what we could do with an unselfish American policy" of making Iran a test case of United States post-war economic and technical assistance to "all less favoured associate nations." [18]

Despite these pledges and plans, no substantial economic aid resulted from President Roosevelt's visit to Tehran until the end of the war.

Increasing American interests in the Middle East immediately after the war kindled new hopes for the implementation of the Roosevelt plan. A large segment of the Iranian public, in and out of the Iranian government, expected Iran to receive substantial American financial and military assistance under the Truman Doctrine.   But these expectations, too, proved to be illusory up until 1950. The total American financial assistance to Iran between 1946 and 1950 amounted to a loan of $25 million, almost entirely allocated to the purchase of American war surplus. The feeling in Tehran was that the United States was about to fulfill its previous pledge.

The urgency of needed investment funds was reflected in the very same Joint Statement issued in Washington on December 30, 1949, where H.I.M. the Shah accepted President Truman's offer of Point IV:

> The President appreciated the importance of the /Seven-Year/ program to the economic

development of Iran, and applications by the
Iranian Government to the International Bank for
Reconstruction and Development for economically
justifiable loans to be used in the furtherance of
the program will therefore receive the support of
the United States.   Subject to favorable Congressional action on the Point IV program, the
United States also stands ready to facilitate
Iranian economic development through the provision under Point IV and otherwise of technical
advisory assistance if requested by Iran. [19]

The Shah's own account of this encounter shows not only
his sincere conviction about urgent need for investment funds
but also his disappointment as to the kind of aid Iran was to
receive from the United States:

In late 1949 I went to America to plead for
increased economic and military aid for my
country.   I received a friendly reception, but
returned home completely empty-handed.   Instead of granting adequate funds, the American
Government allocated a token amount of Point IV
money, and the Export-Import Bank of Washington
tentatively offered us a loan of $25 million--a
small fraction of the minimum necessary to re-
habilitate our occupation-devastated economy. [20]

Further indications of insufficient appreciation of technical
assistance should be found in the report of a Congressional
Subcommittee that looked deep into the Mission's operations:

The subcommittee was told by representatives of the United States Operations Mission that
one of the most difficult tasks they had in this
period was educating the Iranian Government
Officials to the essential meaning of technical
assistance.   During this period the record would
seem to indicate that it was not United States
know-how but United States dollars in which Iran
was chiefly interested. [21]

A Mission Provincial Director reports that the government of
Iran was for some time not really enthusiastic about signing

the basic agreement of technical assistance with the United
States. And when in January, 1952, the "agreement" was
finally signed, the Mission's task of "explaining" its aims and
objectives to Iranians only just began. [22]

What was generally true in many other underdeveloped
areas seems to have been equally true in Iran. While Point IV
was braced to offer plenty of advice but not much money, the
Iranians felt they needed a considerable amount of the latter
and a minimum of the former. "It was not long before I
realized," writes a Mission advisor in the Tehran Office,
"that financial assistance was welcomed without question, but
the need for technical assistance was something which had
still to be demonstrated and sold." [23]

Numerous reports by other Mission assistants confirm
this observation. Two provincial advisors write:

> The Iranian people did recognize that they
> were pitifully lacking in school buildings and
> facilities. They did not so readily admit that
> their teaching methods were inadequate. [24]

> Many of these people . . . were satisfied with
> the schools as they were and did not feel a need
> for any training and suggestions from Point IV.
> All they wanted from Point IV was money, auto-
> mobiles and buildings. [25]

A community development specialist from Southeastern Iran
concludes:

> When we arrived in Kerman, we found many
> requests from villages for assistance . . . It
> seemed to us that the general conception of the
> CD program held by government officials, land-
> lords and village councils was that it was a
> source of easy money from Point IV. [26]

An administrative officer in the Southwest repeats this by
saying:

> I sensed the eager expectations of many that
> Point IV would develop into another operation of

> the size and scope of the American Army Persian
> Gulf Command . . . and a blossoming prosperity
> for the Ahwaz area. 27

A letter by a former Mission official to his Congressman reiterates the same fact:

> . . . these people, most of them, have no idea
> what the difference is between Point IV and the
> emergency grant, so when Point IV officials pass
> out large sums of money for emergency employ-
> ment to build projects such as streets, bath-
> houses, brick kilns, they assume that one of our
> major jobs is to give money away. 28

In view of the Seven–Year Plan's urgent need for foreign exchange at the time it is not hard to see why Iranian officials could not appreciate the limited nature of the program. This lack of "felt need" for technical assistance from the United States was occasionally admitted, perhaps inadvertently, by some Iranian officials although such formal admissions were rare. The following letters from two high government officials are candidly expressive. The first letter from a Cabinet Minister to a Division Chief says:

> Prior to the establishment of the USOM of-
> fice in Iran, the technical and agricultural de-
> velopment projects of the Ministry of Agri-
> culture, although from the technical point of view
> mostly without defects, owing to the lack of
> funds fell short . . . of their execution. 29

The second letter from a College Dean to a Division Chief states:

> Before the help of Point IV came to the col-
> lege, our budget was too small to permit us to
> purchase necessary laboratory equipment to do
> good student laboratory work. Through the help
> of Point IV, some of the laboratories are now
> well equipped . . . Point IV has assisted in build-
> ing some buildings that are very useful to the
> College work. 30

The lack of enthusiasm on the part of the Iranian people for a small program of technical advice is not hard to explain once the story of such endeavors in the country's recent history is properly reviewed. When American technical assistance under the Point IV program was offered to Iran in 1950, United States missions were not new to the country. 31 Since 1829, American religious missionaries had administered hospitals and schools in Iran, and had engaged in relief and rehabilitation activities in various Iranian cities. On a number of occasions Iran had appealed to the United States to obtain technical and financial advisers. In 1911, W. Morgan Schuster went to Tehran as Treasurer General. Ten years later A. C. Millspaugh was engaged as Administrator-General of Finances, heading a financial mission which served the country until 1927. In 1943, Millspaugh was re-employed and was given wide administrative and executive powers, heading a group of some 50 American technicians 32 on a new, but ill-fated, task force. In addition to the Millspaugh mission, the Iranian government during the war availed itself of a number of other American technical advisers for its ministries of War, Health, Agriculture, Food and the Gendarmerie. 33 In the 1940-1950 period alone, Iran availed itself of the expert advice and technical recommendations of a half dozen foreign missions, not to speak of foreign technicians working for the Iranian government and private agencies.

There were reportedly eighteen different foreign missions sent to Iran between a German-Austrian Mission in 1878 and the American Point IV program. Yet, according to a mission official, none had met with any great degree of extraordinary success. 34 Thus, while enough projects, plans and advice were already available to Iranian government offices, the means of implementing them were not. The need was apparently no longer for advice, but for putting available plans into practice. A former Point IV official acknowledges this fact:

> The files of the various Ministries were full of the learned reports by foreign experts who gave advice to the government on every phase of its activities, but usually nothing was done to put the recommendations into operation. Frequently this resulted from the fact that no funds were available to implement the suggestions that had been offered. Money had been found to make a

survey and to pay for the report, but nothing was available for actual operations. [35]

The seeming futility of the mere expert advice, and particularly the sad memories left by the humiliating failure of the second Millspaugh mission, had made most people in and out of the Iranian government extremely wary of inviting still another advisory mission to Iran. Almost everyone connected with Iranian development planning wanted "quick action and immediate results," and almost everyone seemed to think money was the key to the answer.

QUEST FOR THE VISIBLE AND THE SPECTACULAR

There also seems to have been a general lack of local appreciation in evidence not only of the Point IV philosophy, but also of its direction. Even those Iranians who could be "sold" on the philosophy of Point IV as a program of <u>technical</u> assistance and self-aid, did not always agree on the roads the mission proposed to follow. To Henry Garland Bennett, a pioneer of Point IV, the main idea was to send a minimum number of experts with modest tools and limited amounts of supplies to teach and show how local resources could be more effectively employed. In line with this basic policy of training leaders to promote peace, freedom and democracy, the Mission was expected by Congress to lean heavily toward projects that could strengthen the country's infrastructures, especially in the fields of fundamental education, basic hygiene, and rural community development.

Projects of this type, however, slow moving and unspectacular as they were, did not appeal to the impatient local leaders. Accustomed to a period of rapid industrialization during 1920-1940 when structures (large buildings, automatic factories, mountain-piercing roads) were considered true symbols of economic progress, government officials in particular, and the public in general, were somewhat cold toward the projects that emphasized ideas, attitudes and institutions. [36] What the host country wanted most, it seems, was foreign assistance for its modernization, westernization and industrialization, all considered synonymous and all considered symbolically progressive. [37]

It was, therefore, a matter of no coincidence that the one criticism of the Mission activities that invariably came up in the author's interviews with older-generation Iranians, was this very sore point. "Why," they would always sadly ask, "did Point IV not put all its resources into one big, visible project which could be seen and remembered for long as a monument to Irano-American friendship and cooperation?"

A former minister of Post, Telegraph and Telephone, not unfamiliar with American ideals and ideas, believed that Point IV could have done Iran the greatest service by establishing a modern communications system, so that the various ethnic and lingual groups in Iran could be truly united by bonds of a common language and a single communications network. An ex-assistant secretary of Health was in favor of building a few modern, fully equipped, big general hospitals in Iran's major cities. An Irrigation Bongah official who considered the shortage of water Iran's number one problem could think of nothing more important for Point IV to have done than to provide modern irrigation systems for Iran's thirsty but productive land. Several executives of the Ministry of Education were firmly convinced that if Point IV had concentrated its effort on schools and continued its initial program of building and equipping various places of learning, its success in Iran would have been assured. The same point was made even more emphatically by a Ministry of Roads official who wanted quick improvement in the sad state of Iranian roads.

The Mission's officials and technicians, on the other hand, were almost unanimous in deploring the Iranians' "edifice complex." In the field of ports and navigation, a frustrated Mission technician wrote in his 1960 report that "as long ago as 1947, studies of the transportation needs of Iran were under way by foreign experts. Physical, operational and administrative improvements were recommended, /but/ only the physical development appealed to the government of Iran." [38] The following excerpt from an Industry Division Chief's report is probably typical of the way the Mission viewed its basic role, and the desired direction of development, in Iran:

> Much effort and time will be required to change the thinking, habits and customs of the Iranians and the government. In many areas it is impossible to by-pass the horse and buggy stage. A deep understanding of the Iranian philosophy,

traditions and economy as well as cognizance of
the lack of mechanical training, is necessary for
efficient planning. For example, where a people
have no understanding or appreciation of the need
for preventive maintenance, it is ill-advised to
establish an extremely modern or push-button
complicated plant.   The Iranians desire the
ultimate plants and do not seem to realize the
need of slower progress and greater training in
operating and keeping in repair less complicated
machinery. [39]

It was evidently against views like this that the Shah
expressed his dismay, and portrayed the true pride, optimism
and ambition with which his country expected to receive
assistance from Point IV:

Some American and European economists and
engineers have peculiar ideas on how you should
go about Westernizing an economically less-
developed country. They claim that such countries
are unprepared for modern techniques, and that
therefore you should reach back into history and
encourage them to use those employed at, say the
time of the American Civil War. For example,
some point out, in Persia you still commonly see
villagers working with crude ironshod wooden
ploughs. It is argued that the thing to give them
is the type common in the mid-nineteenth century.
Don't waste time thinking about tractors or modern
implements, because the villagers wouldn't know
how to operate them, still less to maintain them.
In the same way, such economists and engineers
assert, the less-developed countries should avoid
the temptation to meddle in such complex modern
fields as antibiotics, electronics, or aviation.
The economically backward countries should learn
to walk before they run. At least as concerns
my own country, I profoundly disagree. [40]

In view of the basic policy difference regarding the type
and character of development projects, it is difficult, at least
in some important cases, to know whether the projects finally

undertaken were really acceptable to Iran, or whether they were accepted by the Iranian authorities on account of the prestige of the United States. According to the Mission, the selection and promotion of projects were always in the hands of the Iran-American Joint Commission for Social and Economic Development. The Commission was to consider only programs and projects requested by the ministries and agencies of the government of Iran. 41

Scattered reports and comments by both the Mission technicians and the Iranian officials, however, seem to indicate that this official procedure was not perhaps always meticulously followed. Many of the so-called "joint projects" were reportedly "joint" only in name. The promotion, initiation, direction and even execution were basically American. And despite the Mission's "cooperatives" and "joint funds", Point IV seemed to remain an isolated foreign island in a vast native sea. A former ICA director concedes that in most of the Iran program up to 1954, the institution being built up was American, rather than indigenous, even though many local nationals were hired and trained. 42 A Point IV Provincial Director refers to the same situation a year later:

> Owing to the absence of a well-trained and organized civil service, such as one finds in many "Point IV" countries, we were obliged at first to carry nearly the entire load of project work after receiving approval of the Ministries concerned. The projects were called joint undertakings, but most of the planning, the financing and the execution was left to us and the few local Iranians we could recruit to help us. 43

To a resident head of a large philanthropic organization who had close contacts both with the Mission staff and the Iranian agencies, the "approval" of the ministries concerned, for most of the projects was a courtesy that was almost never denied. He said in a confidential interview:

> Most of the Point IV projects are "sold" to the Iranian officials by the Mission's Division Chiefs, technicians and executives. They are not necessarily projects needed in Iran. The ministries and agencies "request" whatever project

is suggested to them because of the jeeps, the
equipment and the per diem involved, or out of
simple courtesy. In Washington, however, these
"requests" are reflected as an avid desire by the
Iranian government for Point IV help. The result is that U.S. technicians coming on their first
foreign assignment become furiously frustrated to
see lack of enthusiasm, half-hearted support and
inadequate receptivity for technical aid on the
part of the local agencies.

A forestry advisor seems to confirm the gist of that confidential interview:

During these earlier stages /of range manage-
ment/ there was little interest on the part of the
Ministry of Agriculture, partly because the work
was regarded as ineffective and partly due to the
fact that the projects were looked on as purely
American. 44

A report by a Community Development Chief reporting
in the year 1960 (i.e., four years after all the projects were
supposed to have been integrated into Iran's own development
plan) admits that the Community Development program was
essentially a U.S. activity rather than a government of Iran
activity, technically and financially supported by the USOM. 45
In the provinces, all the operating responsibility for Point IV
operations often rested entirely in the hands of the Point IV
Director. 46

Many Iranian officials interviewed by the author also
readily agreed that the projects were often more American
than Iranian. An assistant secretary in a ministry that amply
benefited from Point IV aid, admitted that he had strict instructions from the minister "to go along" with whatever project Point IV technicians suggested. The reason for this
(and similar) acquiescence with Point IV suggestions is supplied by an American-educated head of a semi-private agency
who said his Point IV advisor was doing nothing for him, but
he still was reluctant to let him go because he thought such
an action might be construed as a sign of "non-cooperation
with the United States." An old, never-left-the-country,
official of another ministry "cooperating" with Point IV had

an even more tolerant attitude. He believed that it was highly improper and inhospitable of Iranians to question the Mission's suggestions, or deny the Mission's requests. "After all," he said, "it is _their_ money and this is the way _they_ want to spend it. Who are _we_ to say, and why should _we_ say, no to them?"

Share of Costs

The absence of a basic understanding of the program's possibilities and limitations, and the lack of a distinct feeling of need for it, is confirmed by the lack of enthusiasm for paying even a minimum share of the program's costs.

Judged by the "minimum-support" yardstick, the degree of the Iranians' enthusiasm for the program seems to have been neither extraordinary nor even truly significant. The total Iranian contribution to the Point IV program during the 1950-1965 period does not seem to be more than about $60 million. This includes contributions in cash and in kind. Contributions "in kind" include use of materials and equipment, and estimated value of land, water, building and transportation facilities provided by the Iranian government. Since the value of most of these items is at best hard to determine, and in the Iranian case determined with extremely rough guesses, the figure of $60 million should be considered only as an indicative magnitude of local support. Most of this sum pertains to the period 1960-1965 when the Iranian government had to bear the major share of the program's cost. The total Iranian contribution is thus less than half of the U.S. technical aid.

The Iranian contribution between 1950 and 1954 (in both "kind" and "cash") amounted to $16.6 million. Of this total, only $1.1 million was paid in cash and $15.1 million was the estimated value of land, equipment and services provided by the Iranian government. As discussed before, the House Subcommittee on Government Operations has taken great pains to demonstrate the small magnitude of the actual cash contribution by the Iranian government in this period. The Subcommittee has also managed to get one of the Mission Directors to admit that at least part of the Iranian cash contribution had been made out of the funds generated from the sale of U.S. dollars. [47]

Yet due to the fact that during 1951-1954 the Iranian government was in a dire financial situation, the Iranians' interest in the program or lack thereof cannot be proved or disproved by these figures.   Nor can the total support of the program's activities after 1961 be considered as a proof of unmitigated enthusiasm.

A more significant indication of the lukewarm cooperation and relatively small support should perhaps be found in repeated complaints in the Mission technicians' end-of-tour reports, on numerous occasions and in almost all fields of Point IV activity, about inadequate financial support and cost-sharing by the Iranian government.   A community development advisor reports that "Community Development has been considerably hindered because Iranian officialdom (and the public in general) has by no means been convinced that the government of Iran actively desires success for this program." 48   An electronics specialist recommends that the host country be pressured to "understand its obligations as to cooperation and monetary needs" both to the foreign team and its own employees. 49   An equipment advisor complains that the lack of budget support by the GOI has "left valuable equipment supplied by the U.S. Government lying idle." 50 A public housing advisor finds his project was twice "abolished" as one of the Iranian Government's "economy moves." 51   An agricultural extension advisor states that the late approval of his project's budget resulted in the supervisor's visit to extension agents often taken up with the discussion of budget rather than discussion of technical problems concerning agriculture. 52   Other advisors also complain that their projects have been hampered by low salaries and delayed salary payment, limited supplies, inadequate transportation, and a general lack of budgetary funds. 53

PEOPLE'S ATTITUDE AND REACTIONS

Mission officials have generally and repeatedly praised the Iranian people and their leaders for their full cooperation with, and unfailing support of, the Point IV program. A bevy of letters and statements from government officials, village leaders and the rank and file has been presented in a Mission Director's story of Point IV in Iran, acknowledging their gratitude for the program. 54

That many of these letters, documents and commentaries
reflect genuine expressions of thanks for the aid received
is beyond doubt.   On more than one occasion in his auto-
biography, H.I.M. the Shah has expressed his appreciation
of American technical, economic and military aid, and wished
that there were more of them all. 55 Similar expressions
of official thanks by the Iranian leaders for the U.S. assistance
can also be found in government records, friendly newspaper
columns and private talks.

In the unofficial quarters, however, where diplomatic
courtesies and the politics of alignment do not matter much,
the subject has not been always roses.   The lukewarm
and somewhat suspicious acceptance of the Point IV concept
in both the public and the private sectors, the cautious
and somewhat restrained association of local officials with Point
IV assistants, and the lackadaisical follow-up of Point IV projects by the beneficiaries cast substantial doubt as to the
widespread popularity of the program.

The overwhelming majority of the Iranian interviewees
were privately critical of the program for one reason or
another.   Although some of these criticisms were innocently
personal and had little factual justification, they were reflections of beliefs in the limitations of Point IV. Legions of
statements and reports by the Mission's own technicians, too,
give the uneasy impression that voices of dissent were just
as frequent, if not as loud, as those of praise. 56

To the doubtful and the cynics among the Point IV critics,
the official letters of thanks produced by the Mission were
often a matter of routine courtesy for the favors received.
The appreciation by certain minor officials was also considered motivated by the writers' expectations of additional
favors.   And the least reliable of all, paradoxically, were held
to be the signed letters from the rank and file. As one
ultra-cynic put it, "in poor and illiterate societies where, in
exchange for small favors, miles of signature-filled white
cloth reels can be produced overnight for or against almost
any measure, and for or against any policy or person, the
significance of outward expressions from the illiterate masses
can not always be taken very seriously." A Mission Provincial Director seems to allude to this questionable loyalty of
the urban masses in his area.   After the overthrow of the

Mossadegh government in August, 1953, the Babolsar Provincial Director wrote:

> The PHCO people who always . . . complained
> of abuse and indecent words against them in
> Babol . . . /saw/ a crowd gathered around them
> who cheered and shouted "Long live Point IV!"
> It is just what you might expect from a poor,
> jobless, hungry, illiterate and aimless mob,
> which could bend to any wind from any direction. 57

Of particular significance among the vast array of dissenting local public opinions is the following excerpt from an article by an influenctial former Majles deputy and a well-known conservative attorney:

> Point IV aid, although noticeable in magnitude, had no noticeable impact on any aspect of
> the people's life; a good portion of it was spent
> on salaries, administrative expenses, rent, and the
> purchase of automobiles; the rest was spent on
> small and trivial activities which had no effect
> on either the rural folks or the urban population; and the Iranian people have felt none of its
> results.
> Point IV funds in Iran were wasted because
> its administrators, i.e., American officials, had
> no proper program for spending the money at
> their disposal.
> Foreign aid, unless based on a proper concept and a proper program, is not only useless
> but also harmful as was the case with Point IV
> where general increases in rents, wages and government deficits are some of the examples. 58

An editorial in one of the two largest (and semi-official) dailies in Tehran, written on the occasion of a visit by the then Vice-President Lyndon B. Johnson, is less poignant about Point IV but expresses important reservations about American aid. The editorial entitled "Johnson and the People of Iran" says in part:

> Adverse propaganda has portrayed U.S. objectives in Iran as securing a strategic bulwark

against communism, and capturing Iranian markets from trade rivals.

Point IV and other aids have not been able
to turn the immense tide of this propaganda and
to show the real motives of the United States
government and the American people.

The American modus operandi, too, is unfortunately such that it gives credence to this
foreign propaganda and distorts the public
opinion. 59

Another magazine editorial, on the same occasion, entitled
"Mr. Vice-President: An Iranian Friend of America Talks
to You," written by the publisher of an influential Tehran
weekly, again casts polite but firm aspersions on the program.
The following excerpts are a free translation from his flam-
boyant and flowery prose:

Why has the Irano-American cooperation
failed to bring forth expected results? In our
opinion, the main reason is the Americans' insufficient and occasionally erroneous knowledge
about the Iranians' unique and complicated mentality.

In attempting to cure the patient, American
healers in the arts of politics, economics and
warfare have, like Iran's own small-town practitioners, paid little attention to the fundamental
and natural process of remedy: the patient's own
consent and cooperation. And, instead of putting
the process of diagnosis, cure and care in the
hands of experienced, sympathetic, or at least
trustworthy doctors and nurses assistance was
offered through the least experienced and the least
knowledgeable technicians. Thus neither the political stick nor the economic carrot could result
in anything but harm.

The road that we have followed on your advice,
or those of your advisors, leads nowhere.

We hope you will find the right way in this
trip of yours. 60

WHY NOT POINT IV?

The underlying reasons for such views, and the Mission's difficulty in winning the necessary local cooperation are not hard to find.   The problem of winning the confidence of a dissatisfied and suspicious people whose history is replete with foreign assistance offered with ulterior motives was not easy. 61   With the notable exception of many idealistic people who labored to identify Point IV with America's traditional philanthropy and its 20th century version of disinterested political do-goodness, few people in Iran considered the Mission as an example of a non-political, altruistic, organization designed to help Iran economically and technically.   The memories of Iran's occupation by the American armed forces and America's close cooperation with the much-hated British in the Second World War, coupled with the emerging ideological conflicts between the United States and the Soviet Union were too much for many shrewd and suspicious Iranians to forget or forgive.   U.S. official pronouncements, Congressional hearings and debates, and discussions of the program in the American press regarding the political nature of the program also added support to their convictions. 62

Another reason for the people's uncertain enthusiasm was the Mission's inexperience in this part of the world. Point IV's almost total reliance on American-type public relations and its unfamiliarity with the kind of publicity fit for Iran were undoubtedly big handicaps. In the crucial months of its initial operation, the Mission engaged in a publicity campaign to put Point IV's name in the news as often and as extensively as possible. In terms of the column inches of Point IV news in Tehran's friendly newspapers and shouts of <u>Zendeh-bad Asle Chahar</u> (long live Point IV) by villagers, these efforts were successful.   For months on end, not a week passed without some Point IV "activity" or "achievement" being written up in the friendly papers. But the effect of this type of publicity on the Iranian public was not always favorable. For one thing, the Mission apparently misjudged the Iranians' fascinating custom of suspecting, if not outright disbelieving, what they read, or hear officially. For the vast majority of the Iranian masses, and a large segment of the urban population, there was only one accepted rule of communication: Seek the story behind the stories. 63 Thus, the more claim was officially made for Point IV achievements, the less convinced became the man-in-the-street about the program's benefits for him.

The exaggerated statements frequently made by U.S. officials about Iran's development potentialities, American generosity, and Point IV's omniscience added fuel to the fire. The undue elevation of hope and expectation lulled the easy-going Iranians into the hazardous belief that their salvation was close at hand, and the Mission was the medium of its deliverance. Soon after the Mission opened its doors in Tehran and in the provinces, requests for aid poured in from everywhere. People wanted everything: Plymouth Red chicks by villagers in the Taleghan valley; blackboards and chairs for schools in Brujerd, DDT for villages in the Caspian region, road-building equipment by the Ministry of Roads, a modern student dormitory for the Tehran University, etc. ad infinitum.

The Mission's obvious inability to satisfy even token expectations soon backfired. High hopes that were raised but largely unsatisfied, gave way to frustration, complaints, criticism and eventually outspoken derision of the program. The Mission, it seems, miscalculated the psychologically unfavorable effects of its grandiose promises to the deprived and envious people at a time when the government was badly handicapped and could not offer them relief of its own.

The third handicap against the program's quest for popularity was the untimeliness of the undertaking. Events in Iran following the establishment of the Mission were not particularly propitious for Point IV's acceptance by a very articulate group of Iranian ultra-nationalists. Point IV aid was extended in 1950 amid public dissatisfaction with American foreign policy toward Iran, and most apparently with the hope of remedying somewhat the situation. [64] This was in a sense a timely political maneuver to offset the Soviet charges of Anglo-American "imperialism," but in the battle to gain popularity in Iran during the years 1951-1952, Point IV activities were overshadowed by the American government's stand in the Anglo-Iranian dispute. In the face of American overt support of British interests, the Mission had a hard time convincing people that America, honestly and sincerely, intended to help them.

Fourthly, the Mission's position was weakened by repeated insistence on the non-political nature of its motives. The notes and memoranda on Point IV exchanged between the two governments gave the uneasy impression that the program was in toto an altruistic move on the part of the United States.

They said nothing about American interests in it. As it seems now, this was an unsound and unfortunate omission. The United States had legitimate interests in the Point IV program which should have been frankly admitted by the Mission as they were publicly admitted in America and elsewhere. Since the humanitarian overtone of these documents could obviously not convince the suspicious Iranians that the program was mainly for the good of their country, a frank admission of the legitimate interests of the United States could have done the program no harm while its unnecessary omission engendered a good deal of criticism and a bit of embarrassment.

An interesting example of the unbridled cynicism with which some Iranian leaders, and many of their followers, regarded the Point IV program can be found in a conversation that Director Warne is reported to have had with Prime Minister Mossadegh:

> One day in 1952 Dr. Mossadegh insisted to me that Iran needed $30,000,000 at once. "It would be much cheaper," he said, "to give $30,000,000 now, than for you Americans to have to fight your way back to Tehran." I replied that his statement indicated that he thought this program was politically motivated. I told him I thought he understood that the Technical Cooperation Program was designed to help underdeveloped areas to help themselves. "Oh but, Mr. Warne," he said, "if it weren't for our neighbours at the north you would not be here." [65]

The misconceptions and misunderstandings that the Iranians held about Point IV objectives, operations and activities were augmented by a barrage of harsh and cruel propaganda from the Iranian Tudeh Party, left-wing organizations and leftist newspapers. Characteristically, the leftist groups attacked Point IV as another "imperialistic plot" to exploit Iran and to incite the country against the Soviet Union. Although quick to grasp the Mission's blunders or tactlessness, and ready to magnify them the best they could, leftist criticisms were not directed so much against the Mission as they were against "American imperialism." They opposed anything American, including Point IV. Individual leftist accusations were often too ridiculous to be heeded by anyone except the

party faithful.   But their calculated undertones were often
effective in confirming the people's suspicion about American
motives.   The adverse propaganda was also intended to in-
tensify the nationalists' disappointment with the American
stand on the oil issue.

To overcome the rampant doubts, confusions and suspicions, the Mission needed an equally well-calculated program
of realistic and effective counter-propaganda.   Instead, it
embarked on an incredibly un-American line: denying the
obvious, and defending the inexcusable. On several occasions,
hard pressed by cunning newspapermen to explain America's
motives in aiding Iran, Director Warne offered arguments
and oratories that seem, in retrospect, strongly alien to his
journalistic background and his sharp political acumen. The
following narrative that he delivered with ostensible pride at
a medical conference in 1952 is the outstanding example.
In answer to the question about Point IV's real motive in
Iran, put to him by an obvious heckler, he said with straight
face:

> The United States of America feels that is has
> been blessed by God and that its people have in-
> herited their culture, energy, ingenuity and their
> ability to live peacefully side by side from those
> who emigrated to America from all parts of the
> earth.   America, therefore, in token of her gra-
> titude, is giving some of herself to help others
> to help themselves, believing that when other
> peoples can witness that they, too, are going ahead
> to a better future, greater hopes will come to the
> common man, and peace will be buttressed within
> every village throughout the world. America is
> striving, therefore, to help the people of Iran to
> help themselves. . . 66

Finally and perhaps the most unfortunate reason for the
people's scant enthusiasm, was the fact that most Iranian
officials, technicians, and counterparts had insufficient confidence in many of the Mission technicians. Part of the blame for
this attitude lay in the latter's personal or professional
shortcomings.   But part of the difficulty was a result of
the psychological attitude, educational background, and personal outlook of the Iranian counterparts.   Both of these
problems will be discussed in later chapters.

An evaluation of the attitude of a significant segment of the Iranian population toward Point IV by a Point IV assistant is most interesting, if not altogether flawless. An industrial management specialist's end-of-tour report says in part:

> The older Iranian (50 to 60 years of age) is of the opinion that the efforts of this Mission are only a flash in the pan, that this country has been occupied, conquered, and liberated for so many thousands of years that immediately on completion of the Mission, or before, the country will revert to its original status. The younger man in his twenties or thirties is of the opinion that he would like to do something for his country, but he is frustrated by the inefficiency, improper training, and high interest rates (36% p.a.). [67]

To overcome such misgivings about the country's future developments and to dissipate such an erroneous image of the technical assistance program, many of these oldsters had to be lured with such favors as trips to the United States, funds for pet projects, employment for relatives, and the like. Despite the apparent hazards in such undertakings, the Mission did a good job in many important cases. But once the misinformed became enlightened and the doubtful became persuaded about American know-how, their ignorance gave way to envy, if not fear, of everything American. As inadequacies became apparent, a sense of envy superceded the initial lack of information. And then, in some cases the preservation of self-interest became the source of indifference, if not hostility and resistance, toward the program.

As could be expected, the true believers in the program to the last were mostly those Iranians who, by virture of their advanced education and training, were the real "connoisseurs" of American technical know-how and felt the need for American assistance. They did not always succeed in getting what they wished for Iran, but they knew what to look for. In this group, led by the Shah himself, there were a large number of European-educated converts, but the majority consisted of former students of American education and culture.

In almost all of the informal talks and interviews held with older-generation Iranian officials, a correlation was found between the degree of professional competence in one's own field and appreciation of the United States' ability to help Iran. The less the degree of education, training and skill of the "counterparts," the greater was their certainty of their own capabilities and disregard for American know-how. Some of the older men among the superficial and the boastful were awed by American mechanical equipment; others were fascinated by American glamour; but few were convinced that America could give them more than political support or financial assistance.

References

1. The four variables listed here correspond in some respect to those suggested by Professor Edwin P. Reubens, but their coverage and directions of their alteration may not necessarily coincide with his. See E. P. Reubens, "Underdeveloped Countries: Theory and Practice of Technical Assistance," American Economic Review (May, 1953), pp. 126-130.

2. In economic jargon, this would be the same as increasing the area under the production possibilities curve by reshaping the production function.

3. This, in economic terminology, is tantamount to an increase in the area under the production possibilities curve with no necessary change in its basic shape, i. e., no change in the production function.

4. For further discussions of the catalytic role of technical and financial aid see Charles Wolf, Jr., op. cit., p. 361.

5. This would be tantamount to an increase in the area under the production possibilities curve by increasing the supply of domestic resources with or without a change in the production function.

6. This would be the same as changing both the shape of the production function and the area under the curve. Charles Wolf calls such structural reorganizations an example of technological change that may permit an escape from diminishing marginal returns associated with a given production function. See op. cit., p. 67.

7. See <u>Economic Strength for the Free World</u>, <u>supra cit</u>., p. 9.

8. For further discussions of the role of technical assistance see C. R. Wharton, "The Nature of Technical Assistance for Economic Development," <u>Economic Development and Cultural Change</u> (January, 1958); H. S. Reuss, "Foreign Aid: Misspent, Mislabeled, and Misunderstood," <u>Reporter</u> (February 6, 1958); and Charles Malik, "Some Reflections on Technical and Economic Assistance," <u>Bulletin of Atomic Scientists</u> (March, 1954).

9. <u>Christian Faith and International Responsibility</u> (New York: National Council of Churches of Christ in the United States of America, 1953), p. 1.

10. Cf. K. H. Niebyl, "Criteria for the Formulation of an Adequate Approach in Aiding the Development of Underdeveloped Areas," <u>Canadian Journal of Economics and Political Science</u> (August, 1952).

11. In the Irano-American Exchange of Notes, for example, the GOI agreed to pay its fair share in the form of "facilities, funds and services" as it determined that it could make available. The following exchange of words between Representative Porter Hardy of the House Government Operations Committee and USOM/I Director Clark Gregory is of interest:

> Mr. Hardy. So that was a complete open-end, non-specific obligation on the part of the host government.
> Mr. Gregory. That is right sir.

See <u>U. S. Aid Operations in Iran</u>, <u>Hearings</u>, p. 427.

12. The following excerpts, taken from the same <u>Hearings</u>, are also much to the point:

> Mr. Hardy. So with our economic aid we paid them the money to pay us a part of their part under technical assistance?
> Mr. Warne. If you want to put it that way, yes.
> Mr. Hardy. Maybe when we were setting up the technical assistance program, if it is a worthwhile program, we should not have required them to make any contribution.
> Mr. Warne. As a matter of fact, it might have come out to the same point; that is right.

See <u>ibid.</u>, pp. 981-982.

13. See "History of Financial Management," in RUSTEAI.

14. Technical Assistance and Related Programs, supra cit.,
    pp. 20-21. See also G. F. Papanek, op. cit., pp. 343-344.

15. "Development of Technical Assistance Programs" in Tech-
    nical Assistance, supra cit., p. 62.

16. In one of his rare undiplomatic utterances, Director Warne
    is reported to have said: "I spent nearly four years in Iran
    where we had to scratch to find anyone who could receive
    technical assistance." See U.S. Aid Operations in Iran,
    Hearings, p. 979.

17. United Nations Security Council, Official Records, 1st
    Year, 1st Series, Supplement No. 1, pp. 49-50.

18. Jacob C. Hurewitz, op. cit., p. 24. See also What is
    Point IV? U.S. Department of State, Economic Coopera-
    tion Series #30 (Washington, 1952), p. 1.

19. Department of State Bulletin (January 9, 1950), p. 54.

20. H. I. M. Mohammed Reza Sha Pahlavi, op. cit., pp. 88, 89

21. U.S. Aid Operations in Iran, First Report, p. 14. (Italics
    not in the original.)

22. H. F. Byrne, CTR, May 19, 1955, p. 4.

23. B. B. Eddy, CTR, November 10, 1956, p. 3.

24. R. E. Hensley, CTR, September 21, 1954, p. 4.

25. R. L. Amsberry, CTR, April 4, 1955, p. 2.

26. O. Nessett, CTR, June 16, 1956, p. 3.

27. J. L. Rei, CTR, May 25, 1955, p. 3.

28. Mutual Security Act of 1954, Hearings before the Commit-
    tee on Foreign Affairs, House of Representatives (Wash-
    ington, 1954), p. 490.

29. Letter from the Iranian Minister of Agriculture to the Chief
    of the Agriculture Division, USOM/I, dated February 26,
    1957. (Italics not in the original.)

30. Letter from the Dean of the Karaj Agriculture College, M. H. Mahdavi, to R. H. Warrens, Assistant Chief, Agriculture Division, USOM/I /‾1958/. (Italics not in the original.)

31. For the history of American technical missions to Iran and elsewhere, see Merle Curte, Prelude to Point Four (Madison: University of Wisconsin Press, 1954).

32. A. C. Millspaugh, op. cit., pp. 281-282.

33. For further details regarding the background of American assistance to Iran, see C. P. Grant, op. cit., pp. 33-34; and G. V. Allen, "American Advisers in Persia," Department of State Bulletin (July 23, 1944), pp. 88-89.

34. E. J. Norton, CTR, May 14, 1956, p. 5.

35. Franklin S. Harris, "The Beginning of Point IV Work in Iran," Middle East Journal (Spring, 1953), p. 223.

36. See William E. Warne, Mission for Peace (New York: The Bobbs-Merrill Co., 1956), pp. 69, 73, 74.

37. It is also interesting to note that even when appreciation was expressed for the Mission's work, reclamation and industrial projects were reportedly singled out as the type of projects which deserved particular thanks. See W. E. Warne, loc. cit., p. 132.

38. Sterling St. John, CTR, April 21, 1960, p. 4.

39. R. D. Stickney, CTR, May 9, 1956, p. 5. See also Harald Frederiksen, CTR, June 23, 1956, p. 11.

40. H. I. M. Mohammed Reza Shah Pahlavi, op. cit., p. 135.

41. For the official procedures followed in project formulation, see USOM/I, Annual Report, June, 1955 (Tehran), p. 4.

42. J. B. Bingham, Shirt-Sleeve Diplomacy, p. 130.

43. H. F. Byrne, CTR, May 19, 1955, p. 5.

44. E. H. Bomberger, CTR, January 26, 1961, p. 6.

45. C. J. Nelson, CTR, July 30, 1960, p. 3.

46. See "Provincial Administration," in RUSTEAI.

47. Supra, Notes 11 and 12.

48. Brewster Wilson, CTR, May 8, 1956, p. 6.

49. R. P. Klemme, CTR, August 14, 1961, p. 4.

50. J. W. Swann, CTR, September 1, 1962, p. 6.

51. H. M. Steffy, CTR, September 4, 1963, p. 4.

52. R. H. Fike, CTR, August 13, 1963, p. 9.

53. See, for example, the Completion of Tour Report of G. W.
     McDonald, August 7, 1958; W. F. Lundin, February 5,
     1959; C. E. Kohler, September 13, 1960; M. V. Webb,
     September 27, 1960; R. C. Gosda, February 9, 1963;
     C. F. Moberly, June 18, 1963, and W. M. Sands, June 1,
     1963.

54. See W. E. Warne, Mission for Peace, pp. 123, 133, 161.

55. See Mission for My Country, pp. 130, 293, 295, 330, 303.

56. See, for example, the Completion of Tour Report of H. A.
     Mathiesen, February 1, 1956; Brewster Wilson, May 8,
     1956; H. C. Rodgers, August 14, 1956; C. E. Pegg, Sep-
     tember 17, 1957; E. F. Overend, July 26, 1960; and J. L.
     Armon, December 18, 1961.

57. Babolsar Provincial Director, Monthly Report for August
     1955, p. 3.

58. Arsalan Khalatbari, "Aid Without Strings," Tehran Econ-
     omist (December 10, 1960), p. 10. (Free translation from
     Persian.) See also his statements on the floor of the Majles
     attacking the program by drawing a parallel between Point
     IV and the much-despised Anglo-Iranian Agreement of 1919,
     addressing the United States as follows:
        You have imposed upon us four to five hundred ad-
        visors at our expense. You have raised the costs
        of living in our country. Whatever you gave us
        in aid we paid your advisors in salaries. What-
        ever we imported with your aid dollars hurt our
        own exports.

See Mozakerat-e-Majles (Records), Legislative Day 407 (May 17, 1960), pp. 2-3. (Free translation from Persian.)

59. Ettela'at (Tehran), August 23, 1962, p. 2. (Free translation.)

60. A. A. Amirani, Khandaniha (Tehran), August 25, 1962, pp. 3-4. (Free translation.)

61. Elgin Groseclose, op. cit., p. 6; and Donald N. Wilber, Iran: Past and Present (Princeton: Princeton University Press, 1950), p. 12.

62. For the official American viewpoint regarding the importance of Point IV as a bulwark against communism, see "Text of President Truman's Speech on Foreign Affairs," New York Times, February 23, 1950, p. 3; Our Foreign Policy, U. S. Department of State, General Foreign Policy Series #56 (Washington, 1952), pp. 55-56; Some Notes on Point IV, excerpts from articles and addresses by Dr. H. G. Bennett (Washington: TCA, n. d.), p. 1; U. S. Aid Operations in Iran, Hearings, p. 794; and Point Four, U. S. Department of State, Economic Cooperation Series #24 (Washington, 1950), pp. 2, 97.

63. This custom is rooted in a cultural Iranian trait known as taghieh according to which an intelligent man is expected to keep to himself: his road, his riches, and his religion. This self-imposed discretion, traditionally crucial for self-protection and survival in the face of hostile circumstances, has gradually generated a sort of skeptical reaction toward things that are open and straightforward.

64. See George Kirk, op. cit., pp. 99-103; and Henry F. Grady, "What Went Wrong in Iran," Saturday Evening Post (January 5, 1952), p. 30 ff.

65. W. E. Warne, Mission for Peace, p. 26.

66. Ibid., p. 306.

67. E. J. Norton, CTR, May 14, 1956, p. 5.

CHAPTER
8
CAPACITY FOR RECEIVING AID

Foreign technical assistance will be mostly ineffective unless the dominant features of the existing socio-economic order (i.e., values, attitudes and institutions) in the recipient country are hospitable or susceptible to technological change.

From the standpoint of the economic interests of an aid-receiving country, the effectiveness of any foreign technical scheme, be it bilateral or multilateral, is a function of the country's over-all capacity for absorbing the aid offered and received [1]. The country's total absorptive capacity is, in turn, a function of the level of its technological and scientific development.

Different stages of development in terms of the quality of cooperating resources, organizations, and experience put different ceilings on the recipient country's ability to absorb foreign technical knowledge, processes, or institutional disciplines. The ability to absorb outside help, however, does not insure total absorption. For the ceilings to be reached at any stage of development, prevailing political, social, psychological and economic factors must be receptive to foreign assistance. In the absence of these propitious elements, while the country may be theoretically capable of reaching a certain development plateau, it may in fact never reach or even approach that level.

Nor is it to be assumed that a country that can fully absorb some kind of technical aid at some point in its development history can profitably use other kinds of aid at the same time, or the same kind of assistance at all times. Almost all countries at almost all stages of their development can use a certain amount and kind of foreign technical assistance. The difference is in the extent of such a need and the nature of its composition.

148

STAGES OF TECHNOLOGICAL DEVELOPMENT

In terms of their absorptive capacity (and need for foreign technical assistance), the countries that are bent on deliberate economic development can be placed, following the method used by Professor Walter Rostow, into a continuum marked by three distinct stages: traditional, transitional, or innovational. These categories are not necessarily mutually exclusive. It is theoretically possible for a country to be in a traditional stage in one line, and transitional, or perhaps even innovational in others. A traditional country is a country in technical infancy. Its techniques of production are simple, time-tested and almost stationary. Rapid economic (and particularly industrial) development in such a country depends almost completely on borrowed technology. That is, the country has to depend on outside help for the diagnosis of its basic problems, the assessment of its technical needs, and the establishment of a rational order of priority among these needs. [2] Progress from this stage would mean a move toward the transitional stage.

A transitional country is one which, although not yet technologically mature and resourcefully self-sufficient, is nevertheless capable of diagnosing most of its problems, and competent to devise most of the solutions. Only some basic problems, or their effective solutions, may not be adequately recognized. The need here is for certain general direction and some specific supplemental assistance. With proper direction and specific, well-tailored, assistance the country can be expected to move toward technological maturity and the innovational stage. [3]

In the innovational stage, the country reaches a level of technological maturity where it is not only capable of adopting and imitating foreign techniques, or developing compromise methods of operation, but is also in a position to produce new and original techniques in certain production lines. The country is able to push further the frontier of scientific know-how, and to become, so to speak, specialized in problem-solving. While the country can produce almost anything it chooses to produce, it cannot produce everything equally well. The choice of a given production technique in an innovational country, however, is not a matter of politico-ethical priority [4], but one of comparative technological advantage. The country has relatively greater "know-how" in some production lines than in others; it finds it economically rational to specialize in searching for and finding new solutions instead of dissipating its innovational resources too thinly over too large an area.

The type of foreign technical assistance needed in each of the foregoing stages is distinctly different from the rest. In the traditional stage of development, an underdeveloped country needs three types of skills: skills of diagnosis, skills of policy making (or therapy), and skills of operation. In its attempt to achieve a higher rate of growth, the country needs to know before anything else how much of these skills it actually needs, in what key areas the needed skills are to be filled by a transfer of technicians from abroad, and in what capacity they could serve to be most effective.

Intelligent answers to these questions can be given only by an evaluation of domestic resources that are available in the service of national objectives, defining the broad outlines of the problems involved in achieving these objectives, and by devising rational approaches to solving these problems. Since the country at this stage of growth is not totally cognizant of its basic problems (or their nature and magnitude) it is ipso facto incapable of finding all the rational solutions. Since it does not know what it needs, it certainly cannot know where to find it. If left to itself, the country is more likely to diagnose the wrong kind of problems, or to seek the wrong type of solutions.

The main task for the foreign assistant in this case is to find the kind of assistance and technicians the country needs, where to get them, at what level to use them, and in what capacity to employ their services. These "wise men" should stay in the country as long as is necessary to fulfill their task. Their "tenure" is a function of the magnitude of the problems they are expected to diagnose and the ability of the host country to learn to implement their recommendations.

In the transitional stage, a good deal of sophistication in problem-recognition is attained by the recipient country. The possibility of attributing basic ailments to wrong causes is probably at its minimum. And the need for specific skills, the levels of technical assistance, and the capacity in which foreign experts and technicians have to serve can be partly

determined by the country itself. The task of foreign technical assistants at this stage is to help the country find solutions
to known problems, and to replace existing solutions with
more effective remedies.   Here the needed assistants are
not mere executors of any particular (e.g., Western) techniques, but capable of finding compromise techniques. They
would be able not merely to train others for employment in
advanced countries, but be capable of training people for
productive work in the native environment.

Foreign technical assistance among countries that have
reached the innovational stage is truly cooperative and multilateral.   Each country has certain comparative advantages in
some technical fields, and comparative disadvantages in others.
Technical assistance among cooperating countries is thus a
two-way street, a matter of true give-and-take.[5]   In the
innovational stage, each society, although highly advanced in
one line of endeavour, can directly and immediately benefit
from comparatively greater advances made in other countries and in other lines of endeavour.

As an underdeveloped country passes from one stage
of technical growth to another, the nature, scope, or composition of foreign technical assistance, the type of technical
assistants, the level of application, and the methods of implementation would also gradually change.   The scope of
assistance changes from the most general to the most specific.
At first, foreign technical aid may have to be concentrated
on efforts to build new institutions, change non-progressive
attitudes, or upgrade the process of policy making, Or,
it may simply try to develop effective demand for technical
assistance itself by making local authorities understand
and appreciate the magnitude of their problems and their
inadequacies in solving them.

But as problems become properly analyzed and a certain
degree of connoissance in problem-solving is achieved by
the host country, foreign technical assistance would move
toward narrower and more specific techniques of production
and operation.   These techniques themselves change from
relatively primitive and crude to relatively advanced and
sophisticated.

Technical assistants in these stages of the host country's
development fall in different categories in a spectrum of

ingenuity and skill.   At one end of the spectrum are top-
level "experts-at-large" (brilliant problem-finders and brainy
trouble-shooters) who can devise practical and effective solutions to problems of a broad and fundamental nature in an
age-old setting. At the other end, there are specialized technicians who can provide standard solutions to routine problems that emerge, in a familiar pattern, in an industrializing
society.

The level of application begins at the top of the governmental (or commercial) structure, and seeps down to small
political or business units. Depending on the area and scope
of assistance, and allowing for important exceptions, the
methods of implementation, too, would start with direct
performance, move into training and demonstration, and end
in occasional consultation and advice.

In short, when a country is least technically advanced,
it needs a few, most highly experienced, experts or general-
ists who can help it obtain the relatively uncomplicated,
compromise techniques essential to its development. At
this stage the country neither needs, nor can use, specialized
technicians who know their job well but little beyond that.
When the country becomes technically mature, however, it
would need specialists in specific areas and at a very high
level of sophistication. Strange as it may seem, foreign
"top notch" experts are needed not when a country is developed, but when it is in its early stages of technical growth.

IRAN'S DEVELOPMENT STAGE

At the time the U. S. technical assistance program was
offered to Iran the country's socio-economic conditions roughly
resembled those of a nation entering into the transitional
stage. [6]   That is to say, the country had, in addition to a
long history of cultural and scientific achievements, a good
many years of experience with Westernization, industrialization and deliberate economic development. Of this the Shah
says:

> I sometimes think it curious that we are not
> better known to the West, for we have from an
> early date exported our culture, much as America
> today provides technical assistance overseas
> through her Point Four programme.

And:

> When applied to a land as far advanced as
> Iran, the standard jargon about underdeveloped
> countries--which of course we Persians also
> employ about ourselves--may give false impres-
> sions as to just where we stand in the scale of
> progress. [7]

At the signing of the Point IV agreement, Iran was in the
midst of carrying out its First Seven-Year Development
Plan, with some degree of experience behind it. The country's
technical needs were for specific types, and in certain
specific areas, mostly in planning, resource mobilization and
administrative techniques.

For the absorption of most of the technical aid she
received under Point IV, it now seems that Iran was either
inadequately prepared or more than adequately provided
for.   And in lacking some of the essential pre-requisites
for the optimum absorption of U.S. technology, she shared the
fate of many other developing countries.   As in the latter,
an intricate chain of political, socio-cultural, and techno-
economic factors played their part in forming the major obstacles to her effective use of Point IV aid.

Part of the problem was historical in its origin. Part
of it was due to the inappropriate circumstances under which
the aid was offered.   The rest had to do with the incommuni-
cability of the techniques in the local setting.

The Legacy of Underdevelopment [8]

Politically, the legacy of an autocratic system of government up until the turn of the century, the absence of a truly
national and ethnic unity up until the advent of Reza Shah after
World War I, and the memories of foreign "imperialism"
manifested themselves not only in the instability of the political institutions but in an ever-widening gap between the
felt needs of the governed and the satisfaction offered by the
government. [9]   The deep-rooted suspicion of foreign schemes
and motives became particularly acute when the latter was
supposedly supporting the government against the interest of
the governed.   The inadequate support of the union was partly

due to the fact that after long periods of foreign domination and frequent abuses of fundamental human rights by the "feudal" classes, most people in Iran, rich and poor alike, had developed the basically anti-social attitude that the government, and government-type organizations, could not be expected to do much good for anybody anyway.

Culturally, the individualism and fatalism of the people, particularly the rural folk, were to blame. In the wake of long periods of foreign oppression, exploitation and intervention, these people had become self-protective and apolitical. Indifferent to national welfare problems and aloof toward the government, they had developed an effective, self-centered modus operandi based on passive resistance and active localization. This mode of behavior involved an overt enthusiasm for (if not subservience to) the outsiders' rule, and a web-like, behind-the-scenes maneuver to engulf and assimilate the foreign element.

Among the urban population -- industrial workers, artisans, entrepreneurs, bureaucrats and the intelligentsia -- where the essence of Iran's modernization, progressiveness and dynamism were to be found -- a good deal of sagacity, courage, and technical ability was inordinately dulled by skepticism, emotionalism and disoriented nationalism. [10] Business conservatism, the well-known preference for white-collar jobs, and a desire for quick profits (in real estate, commodity speculations or foreign trade) added their weight. [11]

Socially, the crippling of the country's economic growth and ability to receive foreign technical assistance could be attributed to a system of land ownership which (until recently) discouraged adoption of better methods of agricultural production; a bureaucratic hierarchy in which economic success was seldom the basis of social status or prestige; and a highly abstract and impractical system of education which generally produced an elite of fairly competent theoreticians with no corresponding complement of technicians and operatives. [12]

Techno-economically, the impediments to an effective absorption of technical aid were the shortage of basic surveys and statistics, infancy of scientific and technological research, and, above all, the inadequacies of the Iranian administrative machinery through which the bulk of Point IV aid was to be implemented. The government administration was plagued by inordinate centralization, lack of organizational continuity, and reliance on confusing procedures. The civil service structure was afflicted with personalized methods of recruitment and promotion, instability of tenure and low salaries.   The cadre of civil servants suffered from over-staffing, insufficient skill, and inadequate tenure. [13] Inappropriate centralization denied necessary authority and freedom of action in the field, and drove away the creative and imaginative talent. [14] The lack of organizational continuity, basically due to a lack of organizational philosophy (but intensified also by frequent changes in the composition of government leaders) was inimical to an orderly operation of development projects. [15]

Domestic Receptivity to Point IV

It was against the background of such mentality, traditions and institutions that Point IV assistance was offered and carried out in Iran. Thus, neither the sequential settings nor the concurrent happenings seemed optimally hospitable to its reception.

It may be argued that the foregoing obstacles to rapid economic growth and the prevailing conditions in Iran are part and parcel of the political economy of underdevelopment and the very characteristics of backwardness which foreign technical assistance is supposed to change. And, thus, they should not be considered contra-indications of receptivity. A former Mission Director seems to convey this notion when he says:

> . . . in the completely stable political situation that would furnish an ideal setting for Point 4, it is unlikely that any technical assistance would be needed. The Point 4 program is almost necessarily conducted in a country where it is needed most and most difficult to perform. Iran was such a country. [16]

This argument would, of course, have validity only if foreign technical assistance were a universally identifiable category, i.e., one thing to all countries and at all times.

But the preceding discussions of this chapter showed that foreign technical aid takes on different characteristics and different composition for different societies at different stages of development. What may be the raison d'etre of a particular aid program in one country may not be the rationale of aid to another nation. In fact, the very point of this Chapter is that a given socio-economic situation that would warrant, and could profitably use, a given program of a certain magnitude and composition may actually prove irresponsive, if not inimical, to a scheme of different magnitude and/or composition.

In the case of Iran, the intention here is not to argue that during the 1950's the country was irresponsive to any kind of foreign technical assistance. The argument is that the magnitude and composition of the technical aid offered under Point IV were not ideally suited to the existing socio-economic order. Here are some of the reasons:

Development Without Banner

First, the elan vital necessary to have gotten the people (i.e., the rank and file) on the road to rapid economic development and behind Point IV was not sufficiently strong. In the initial phase of Point IV operations (1950-1953), the Mossadegh movement as a combination of ultra nationalism and anglophobia offered a facade of a national purpose necessary for the development urge to blossom; but the movement did not last. Weakened by its inherent contradictions and incapable of resisting external pressure, it ended in vain, leaving as its legacy a sense of utter disillusionment and futility.

The development effort that followed the downfall of Mossadegh was directed toward bringing order out of the chaos. But the national will to develop, although strong in government circles and among the ruling group, had few roots among the masses to whom anything beyond their immediate horizon was strange and suspect. The Iranian development plans seemed to have no existing philosophy or fiery purpose for the bulk of the city folks, and no understandable lure for the rural population. The majority of the people who would be affected by these plans either did not understand them or did not get sufficiently excited about them to give them their full support. Some even considered non-cooperation with public agencies -- tax evasion, draft dodging, or political opposition -- as socially or religiously justified. [17]

Until the early 1960's when the Shah raised the banner of a new "white" revolution from the top, none of the historical forces responsible for rapid economic development and increased national power such as religious or ethnic solidarity, desire for racial grandeur, external ideological or military threats, or even general xenophobia was strong or widespread in Iran. The only discernible common purpose was a desire for a quick change toward a higher standard of living, sometimes perhaps for the change's sake, and apparently often without willingness to undergo the necessary painstaking adjustments to the new disciplines and values. A Mission educationist's appraisal of the situation is the following:

> The existing philosophies found in Iran are at a "crossroads." Everyone visualizes change but there seems to be an unwillingness to pay the price which is required to bring about lasting and effective changes which could promote positive development. "Hurry!" seems to be the by-word, and materialism the medium. [18]

Minarets Without Holes

The second reason underlying the inadequate receptivity toward Point IV assistance seems to have been the absence of sufficient time to get local agencies braced for using foreign advice and know-how. Part of this problem was the lack of a central organization on the Iranian side to estimate the needs and control the means of satisfying these needs. In the early, crisis-ridden, days of Point IV operations the urgency of broader national problems apparently left the government ill-prepared to set up such an organization. Even when normal times came back, and the situation was improved considerably, the weight of the old procedures could not be totally lifted. Until early in 1961 when a foreign assistance coordinating bureau was set up in the Plan Organization, requests for aid were made by individual ministries or agencies directly, and generally without prior clearing with each other. And within the requesting ministry or agency, the minister or the agency chief usually served as the coordinator. Program direction and project support were thus mostly personal, and seldom carried out on a continued, institutional basis.

In the absence of a proper Iranian organization to request and handle the Point IV aid in most of the period, the Iranian government often received American technicians without prior determination of their professional qualifications, and without knowing beforehand where, with what, and with whom they had to work. [19]   In one case, according to a Mission official document, "it was soon apparent after arrival of the labor standards specialist that the Ministry of Labor was not prepared financially, organizationally or morally to accept assistance on a broad front in the field of labor standards." [20] In another case, that of agriculture, the Mission reports that at the time the aid was offered, the Iranian agricultural institutes had very few programs into which it would move and help them.   The American technicians did not understand the Iranians' approach, and they did not understand the American approach and procedures. [21]

In the field of city planning, a Mission adviser's lament was that he was "to do city planning without any governmental unit capable of sustaining a program which by nature has to be projected into a considerable future. [22] The same problems apparently existed in the area of business education. "The business education situation in Iran when I arrived," writes a Mission technician, "was very simple -- there were no textbooks, teachers, equipment, schools or appreciation of the place of education for business in the school pattern of Iran." [23]   Sometimes the prior preparation was similarly so scanty, or the conditions for utilizing foreign technical aid so inopportune, that the situation was not remedied during the entire tour of the project technician. [24]   Due to the lack of prior, coordinated preparation, the execution of a single project was often reportedly the responsibility of several different agencies.   The financial support came from the Plan Organization; technical advice came from the Mission, or the United Nations, or both; operating responsibility was in the hands of a third agency, and supervision entrusted to still another one. [25]   Each agency naturally wanted to have the final say on the project direction, and the result was sometimes unnecessary friction and interminable bickering among agencies.   In the case of Project 82, for example, eight different organizations and departments were reportedly involved with none having ultimate responsibility. [26]

The absence of institutionally-based division of labor among public agencies could not have been so frustrating if it could be substituted by a continuity of personal collaboration among individual ministers and organization chiefs. Even if ideal personal relations (and team-work spirit) were impossible to establish, a modus operandi based on a live-and-let-live philosophy could surely have been found in the interest of all. But such a method of "getting along to go along" required considerable political stability and long tenures of personnel. And the average tenure of high offices in Iran was generally so short as to prevent any real administrative relations on a personal basis to be formed. During 1950-1965, the Mission and its divisions had to "cooperate" with ten prime ministers and at least nine ministers of agriculture, ten ministers of commerce, nine ministers of education, eleven ministers of finance, eight ministers of health, six ministers of industry, ten ministers of interior, ten ministers of labor, seven ministers of post and telegraph, nine ministers of roads, seven managing directors of the Plan Organization, and a host of Bongah administrators. [27]

The unfavorable effects of this instability on maintaining a consistent approach in the aid process have been the constant peeve of the Mission assistants. [28] Writes a Mission Division Chief:

> Since I have been aboard, I have had three different Ministers (of Agriculture and Co-Directors of the Agricultural Division). Each new Minister reshuffles, dismisses and retires key people in the Department and Bongahs, and replaces them with those of his choice. Even those who are capable usually do not stay in office long enough to carry out a program which they have planned before someone else comes in and starts planning another program that tends to disregard the original. [29]

An education advisor's lament as recently as 1965 tells the same story:

> With the frequent changes of Ministers of Education (seven in six and a half years) come changes in personnel all the way down the line. This is a definite drawback for long-range planning as each new administrator has to be filled in on what has happened. [30]

The turnover, thus, was not limited to top officials. A team sent by the Governmental Affairs Institute to improve the Plan Organization's management reportedly had to train four personnel managers in three years, as the latter were constantly shifted around. A turnover rate of 50% was reported in one Ostan Community Development program. A motion picture advisor in Tehran complained about a personnel turnover of 70% in trainees and qualified technicians in film production. An evaluation of the cost of this turnover is made by one of the Mission technicians in the field of agriculture:

> It requires Rls. 10,000 to give basic training to a recruit for one year. To establish this newly-trained agent on the job requires Rls. 123,175 for the first year, and to continue his employment beyond the first year costs Rls. 85,000 annually. This is an expensive investment unless these men continue in service. Yet during the past five years fully one third of the personnel trained for agents have left the extension services. [31]

These rates were perhaps not typical of the situation in every field. But even their rare occurrence must be indicative of the underlying difficulty: grabbing the minaret, without having deep enough holes to put them in.

Too Many Teachers and Too Few to Teach

A third difficulty with the Iranian reception of technical assistance was the problem of providing appropriate "counterparts" to cooperate with foreign technicians, learn from them, and replace them in due time.

The crucial importance of competent, dedicated and enthusiastic counterparts can hardly be exaggerated. If foreign technical assistance is to take root in the host country and be eventually terminated, technical knowledge of foreign technicians must be imparted to the natives as soon as possible. Here the professional quality and personal qualifications of counterparts make all the difference. A Mission technician has recognized this point when he says:

> The progress to be expected of any technical assistance project is directly related to the attitude of the least convinced local counterpart. . .

the unconvinced local counterpart can often use
his influence to negate everything the American
advisor proposes. [32]

Finding proper counterparts, however, was one of the
most vexing problems for the Iranian government. Sometimes,
the inability to have counterparts ready before foreign advisors
arrived, was, as mentioned before, due to inadequate planning, lack of information about the number of available
advisors and the dates of their arrival. But often, even with
advance knowledge and sufficient interest, it was not easy
to find enough qualified local technicians to work with foreign
advisors.   In a large number of cases actual counterparts
(or individuals ready to be trained as such) were simply not
available for several months or even for almost the technician's
entire tour of duty. [33]   A Ministry of Agriculture official confided that when a forestry survey team of six technicians came
to make an inventory of Iranian forests, the Forestry Bongah
had absolutely nobody who could follow what they were up to,
and when they left after two years, nobody was trained well
enough to replace them. [34]

The difficulties in recruiting competent counterparts were
many.   At the beginning of the program when leftist attacks
were rampant, some capable people were reportedly not too
keen on being identified with Point IV. [35]   Then there was the
problem of finding local technicians for the projects and concepts that were new to Iran (e.g., public health, agricultural
extension, business and public administration).   And where
this was not the case, the potential counterparts were found
among those who were almost all educated in Europe and
knew only French or German -- Iran's former "second"
languages.   These technicians, even when eager to learn and
cooperative, were often in need of interpreters to communicate
with Mission technicians.

Sometimes also good people were available in the private
sector, but could not be lured in, because of the Iranian administrative regulations and low pay.   Writes a Mission
technician:

Recruitment of qualified technical personnel
to date has been slow and tedious. Not for lack
of capable applicants, but rather because salaries

offered by the government of Iran are so low as
to be unattractive to prospective employees. For
example, after advertising in the local newspapers, between fifty and sixty applicants were
interviewed, many of whom were well trained and
technically qualified individuals. Not one vacancy
was filled as the result of these interviews.
This was because better employment was available elsewhere in various private oil and chemi-
cal companies. [36]

Occasionally, also, the "old timers" that served as official counterparts had a kind of 19th-century European under-
estimation of American culture, intellectual capacity and
political leadership. Some of them were so proudly convinced
of their own "cultural superiority" as to doubt America's
ability to help them with anything except money; they were
thus unwilling to serve as counterparts. Of this, a sympathetic
Mission advisor writes:

The Iranian people are extremely conscious
and proud of their heritage. A people with such
ancient social and religious customs is not as
receptive to cultural changes as one that has a
social heritage of a different kind. [37]

Many of these deficiencies - almost totally unavoidable,
and not altogether surprising - were apparently so much
beyond the Mission technicians' expectations that their usually
gentle and resigned attitude toward local counterparts turned
sour on occasion. Thus writes an unhappy Mission engineer:

Sufficient care was not taken to determine the
competence of the applicants . . . The ability to
speak English fluently many times outweighed
other more vital requirements. Men without
training or experience in construction were employed as engineers. In one case, a tennis player
with a good command of English was placed in
charge of a construction program in one of the
provinces. [38]

A city planning advisor complains that his "counterpart" was employed daily as a street cleaner at 50 cents a day. [39] Another Mission technician writes:

> Iranian specialist personnel is not selected for qualities which would make them better trainees or better Community Organization workers. Many of these trainees had to return to National Headquarters as totally unsuitable for the work. Some of them were later sent to another province where more time was wasted on them. This process still goes on. The turnover from this region (Ostan II) has been fortunately only about 50%. [40]

An extension advisor reports that 40 "agents" and "specialists" selected to be trained in extension methods and principles were ministry employees between 25 and 65 years of age who had no field experience whatsoever, and had never worked in a village. [41]

Absentee Teachers and Learners

Ranking close to the problem of unavailability, inadequacy and incompetence of counterparts was the fourth factor: the lack of an effective program for discovering and utilizing foreign-educated Iranian talent (including the Mission's own trainees and participants) as counterparts and/or follow-up men. Since the late 1920's, hundreds of Iranian students had gone abroad, mostly to Western Europe, for advanced studies and training. Most of these reportedly 14,000 students, [42] and particularly those who were sponsored by the government had gradually returned home. But many of them were not utilizing their foreign training in the right fields or to the fullest extent. Engineers and technical trainees had become business managers, factory administrators, or plain bureaucrats. Physicians and accountants had gone into politics. Many had found their bilingual skills more lucrative than their professional training. The lack of proper care in the selection of their original fields of study, coupled with the abstract and purely academic nature of their training (and the glamour of politics in the countries in which they studied) were all responsible for the inadequate utilization of their talents.

The absence of a proper placement program was equally
to blame.   This fact was belatedly acknowledged by one of the
Mission's keen observers who, in his short tour of duty,
recognized that Iran had rich sources of human talent, but the
Iranian society often did not contribute to the release of
that talent. [43]   The same was true in the case of reportedly
some 15,000 Iranian students studying abroad.   To utilize
their knowledge, skills and capabilities, the government
needed an up-to-date central file and a far-reaching recruitment program.   To bring these students back and place them
in their fields of study, the Ministry of Court and the Ministry
of Labor both established special placement bureaus, and
many well-trained students were lured back and properly
placed.   But still the vast reservoir of these talents remained
virtually untapped.

The major grievance of a would-be returnee centered
about the difficulty of finding suitable positions in Iran -- a
complaint that was not totally unfounded.   Part of the reason
was the fact that the majority of the students had almost no
guidance from the government in choosing their fields of
study abroad.   Consequently their specializations were sometimes too broad or too narrow for the country's needs.
Oftentimes, however, the difficulty lay in the absence of an
up-to-date and efficient placement system.   The returnees
who were interviewed were invariably grieved about having
several immediate job offers abroad, but could not find any
at home without pull or connections.

A similar complaint was about the unproductive uses made
of the returnees' skills and talents in the positions they did
manage to get.   Sometimes the organization in which they
worked was not quite ready to absorb their ideas.   Often, they
had little technical help from their subordinates, and had to do
everything themselves.   Occasionally, they were hampered
in their work by incompetent or venal bosses.   And due to
these and similar organizational deficiencies, their recommendations for the most part fell on deaf ears.

Most important of all, however, was the complaint that
they were discriminated against in their home country because
of their nationality.   Many of the returnees considered their
education and experience equal, if not superior, to those of
the foreign assistants as they had the same or higher degrees
from the same or better universities in Europe or the United

States.   And they could hardly consent to receive salaries as low as one fourth to one third of those of foreign technicians.   Not only did the government itself have a relatively low ceiling on the salaries the Iranians could receive in government positions, but foreign contractors also were committed in their contracts with the government to observe similar ceilings in the case of their Iranian employees. It was thus not too infrequently that a bright returnee was discretely urged by his foreign employer to leave Iran and apply for work in the firm's headquarters in the United States at a several times higher salary.

The situation, as far as the utilization of technical skills was concerned, was perhaps slightly better (but not vastly different) for the Mission's own trainees and participants sent abroad.   Even when the participants were chosen with sufficient care, and when their foreign training was successful, effective use was apparently not always made of their foreign experience.   The Mission itself undertook an evaluative study to determine the impact of the participants' foreign training on their subsequent positions in Iran. Of the 284 participants (69% of the total) who returned to Iran and were interviewed by the Mission in 1956 only 25% believed that their foreign training of three to twelve months abroad was "fully utilized." Against this, 28% claimed their training was used "little or not at all," and 40% thought theirs was only partly utilized. [44]

Not too infrequently a Point IV participant was removed from the job for which he was being trained in the United States or elsewhere.   And despite the Mission's frequent protests, such shifts did not appreciably slacken. The participants who stayed abroad more than three months, often found their former government positions given to someone else. Sometimes the trainees were old enough to be retired upon return to Iran; occasionally they were retired while being trained abroad.

On more than one occasion the Mission technicians themselves deplored the government's heavy reliance on foreign experts at the expense of many well trained Iranians whom it had failed to use. [45] A glaring, and not a fortunate indication of the failure to utilize local talent, is to be found in the increasing migration of Iranian technicians and professional men to the United States and other parts of the industrialized world.

The total number of technical and professional men emigrating each year from Iran to the rest of the world is not known as the government does not officially authorize such movements, except under special circumstances, and there is no published list of these. The number of Iranian immigrants to the United States, however, is available from U. S. sources and can serve as a partial indication of the situation. According to the figures supplied to the author by the U.S. Immigration and Naturalization Service, between June, 1950, and June, 1964, some 1800 operatives, craftsmen, foremen, managers, technical and professional men and women born in Iran immigrated to the United States in search of better and more productive opportunities. Of these, more than 75% were individuals of high academic and practical qualifications who were admitted to the United States for permanent residence.

Against this number of emigrants, the total number of U.S. assistants sent to Iran during the same period was around 550. As can be seen, the total number of Iranian specialists leaving Iran for the U.S. was more than three times the number of U.S. technicians, advisors and administrators sent to Iran. [46] The figures are of course not always comparable, but a closer look at the categories regarding types of technicians exchanged, shows that the majority of the Iranian emigrants were in the same fields, if not exactly of the same kind, as the American technicians going to Iran.

Even if the U.S. and Iranian technicians were in no comparable or competing groups, the occurrence of such an exodus from the country could not be treated lightly. Except for a few individuals with unusually advanced and complicated training not yet practical in Iran, the vast majority of the emigrants could, under propitious circumstances, be profitably employed to the country's great advantage. Thus, to the extent that the Iranian emigrants were of the same type and in the same category as the Point IV technicians, U.S. technical aid to Iran was not an additional assistance, but a make-up for the Iranian loss of technicians and technical manpower.

And, in the majority of cases in the exchange of Iranian technicians for Americans, Iran was a net loser, as the incoming American technicians were by far costlier, much less familiar with the working environment, sometimes unmistakably inferior to the emigrants, and almost always in need of

additional help.   Where the exchanged technicians belonged
to different categories, the gain to Iran in receiving American
aid was obviously offset by the loss of its own talent, and
the net gain was not always positive. U.S. aid was of course a
compensating factor in the right direction, but totally inadequate in this respect.

* * * * *

In the absence of sufficient attention to the legacy of
underdevelopment in Iran and the impediments to an optimum
absorption of Point IV aid discussed above, the Mission
apparently misjudged Iran's particular stage of technological
development (and the type of aid needed by the country).
Thus the kind of aid offered, the level at which it was applied,
and its composition left a good many urgent local needs
neglected, while duplicating at the same time a good deal
of local talent and effort.

References

1. For a more recent discussion of this subject see John H.
    Adler, Absorptive Capacity: The Concept and Its Deter-
    minants (Washington: The Brookings Institution, 1965).

2. In this case the country resembles an individual who is
    eager to learn but unable to choose a proper program of
    study for himself. He does not know what body of know-
    ledge in his sphere of interest is available, where to be-
    gin, and how to go about using what is available to his ad-
    vantage. He needs almost complete tutelage in curriculum,
    class schedule, learning methods, etc.

3. Here the country presents the case of an intelligent adult
    who knows his interests, aptitude, and capabilities but
    needs training and guidance. Within certain broad guide-
    lines, he can be trusted to choose his program of self-
    improvement, and to proceed to learn on his own, with
    only occasional advice here and there.

4. See W. W. Rostow, The Stages of Economic Growth (Cam-
    bridge: The University Press, 1960), p. 10.   The stages
    discussed here bear no correspondence to Professor Ros-
    tow's and except for resemblance in categorization are not
    related to his.

5. There is undoubtedly a good deal of practical experience
    and theoretical knowledge that foreign technical assistants
    acquire while aiding countries in the traditional or trans-
    itional stage. But these gains, apart from being ancillary

to their task of giving assistance, are largely useful in other underdeveloped countries and perhaps not much in their own economies.

6. This does not mean, however, that in certain specific arts and crafts the country had not reached the innovational stage, or that in some others perhaps, she had not left the traditional stage.

7. Mission for My Country, pp. 16, 302.

8. For a fuller discussion of these impediments, see Jahangir Amuzegar, "The Role of Technical Assistance in the Development of Underdeveloped Countries with Special Reference to Iran," Ph.D. Dissertation, University of California, Los Angeles, 1955, Ch. V.

9. Cf. Alfred Bonné, State and Economics in the Middle East (London: Paul and Co. , 1948), p. 4; William Haas, op. cit., p. 94 ff.

10. Cf. R. D. Gastil, "Middle Class Impediments to Iranian Modernization," Public Opinion Quarterly (February, 1958); A. J. Fisher, "Persia between Feudalism and Terror," Contemporary Review (August, 1952).

11. Cf. Heshmat Ala'i, "How Not to Develop a Backward Country," Fortune (August, 1948); E. Sykes, "Some Economic Problems of Persia," Royal Central Asian Journal (July-October, 1950); M. R. Solomon, "The Structure of the Market in Underdeveloped Economies," Quarterly Journal of Economics (August, 1948). For a decidedly critical view of the situation, see R. T. Fitzhugh, "Swapping Cultures," and "Foreign Aid in Iran," Wall Street Journal, March 24, 1960, and May 29, 1960.

12. Cf. T. E. Gregory, "The Problems of the Underdeveloped World," Lloyds Bank Review (October, 1948); for a broader aspect of the same problem, see R. R. Wohl, "Technical Assistance: Retrospect and Review," Bulletin of Atomic Scientists (March, 1954), and P. M. Hauser, "Cultural and Personal Obstacles to Development," Human Organization (Summer, 1959).

13. For a fuller discussion of Iran's administrative problems relating to economic development, see E. A. Bayne, The Managing Director (New York: American Universities Field Staff, June 30, 1960); Jahangir Amuzegar, "Administrative Barriers to Iran's Economic Development," Middle East Economic Papers, 1960.

14. See the Completion of Tour Report of A. P. Donovan, August 27, 1960, pp. 3-5, and Harold Winer, June 12, 1955, p. 19.

15. A decidedly critical observation by a Mission advisor of the Iranian administration can be seen in P. E. Taylor, CTR, July 31, 1954, p. 3.

16. W. E. Warne, Mission for Peace, p. 134.

17. For an account of the private investors' reluctance to deal with government agencies, see George Fry & Assoc., 2nd Quarterly Report, January, 1960, p. 5.

18. See W. B. Wlech, CTR, September 8, 1956, p. 2. See also the Completion of Tour Report of P. W. Weiser, December 13, 1958; T. R. Thompson, June 18, 1959, p. 41; and Sterling St. John, April 21, 1960, p. 12. For a discussion of the problems of financing industrial development in Iran, see R. E. Benedick, Industrial Finance in Iran (Boston: Harvard University Press, 1964).

19. See, for example, S. A. Miller, CTR, September 15, 1960, p. 3.

20. See "Labor, " in RUSTEAI.

21. See "Agriculture, " in RUSTEAI.

22. I. J. Alten, CTR, January 10, 1959, p. 3.

23. B. I. Blackstone, CTR, September 5, 1959, p. 2.

24. On the plight of one such project -- Port Management -- see Sterling St. John, loc. cit., p. 5.

25. See Harald Frederiksen, CTR, June 23, 1956, p. 10.

26. George Fry & Assoc., Report of January, 1957, p. 3.

27. "In the past four years," writes an education advisor, "there has been no less than eleven deans of the Vocational Teachers' Training College. " See A. S. Goss, CTR, May 13, 1963, p. 10.

28. See J. E. Schumacher, CTR, October 24, 1960, p. 3. See also M. J. Regan, CTR, April 21, 1955; and E. L. R. Bilodeau, CTR, November 4, 1958.

29. H. E. Hendricks, CTR, February 1, 1961, p. 4.

30. A. S. Goss, CTR, April 14, 1965, p. 5.

31. H. S. Johnson, CTR, November 19, 1958, p. 7.

32. C. D. Jackson, CTR, February 25, 1960, p. 7.

33. See E. H. Bomberger, CTR, January 26, 1961, p. 3, and H. J. Burgi, CTR, August 25, 1960, p. 4.

34. See also T. S. Kampmann, CTR, July 12, 1960, p. 3.

35. After some outbursts of anti-Americanism early in 1952, the Mission Director wrote the following to Washington: "It will take some time, patience, and careful work to win again the full collaboration of the Iranian officials with whom we must work. This is because at least the new figures in the government will be wary of close identification with us until it becomes clear that the association will not be a political liability in Iran." See Sixth Weekly Report of the TCI Director to ICA/W, August 2, 1952, p. 1/

36. T. L. Swenson, CTR, April 30, 1959, pp. 4-5.

37. Frank Nearing, CTR, January 22, 1959, pp. 2-3.

38. L. J. Deming, CTR, December 4, 1954, pp. 10-11.

39. I. J. Alten, CTR, January 10, 1959, p. 3.

40. V. P. Shook, CTR, May 5, 1956, p. 9.

41. R. B. McDaniel, CTR, July 17, 1958, p. 2. See also Brewster Wilson, CTR, May 8, 1956, pp. 5-6.

42. See Robert Hall, op. cit., p. 28.

43. J. A. Fitz, CTR, August 30, 1960.

44. See Follow-Up Evaluation Study of Iranian Participants (Tehran: USOM/I, 1956), p. 16.

45. See particularly Harold Winer, CTR, June 12, 1955, p. 19. and G. W. McDonald, CTR, August 7, 1958, p. 5. See also Jahangir Amuzegar, "Technical Assistance: Sense and Nonsense," Social Research (August, 1960).

46. The figure excludes Iranian graduates of American universities remaining in the United States without having an immigrant status as yet. Against this exclusion, account should be taken of a small number of immigrants who later changed their minds and returned to Iran.

PART IV

THE ORDER, THE ORGANIZATION AND THE ORGANIZATION MEN

CHAPTER

9

ABILITY TO OFFER AID

The effectiveness of foreign technical assistance will depend not so much on the aid-giver's wealth and technological superiority as it does on the cultural, technical and political preparedness to offer the type of aid needed by the recipient nation.

As the needs of recipient nations differ from time to time and in different stages of economic development, so does the ability of advanced countries to meet those needs. This ability differs from country to country, and essentially hinges upon the cultural and technical affinities between the aid-giving and the aid-receiving nations.

The need for foreign technical assistance is generally associated with economic underdevelopment. But economic underdevelopment itself is a relative concept and cannot serve as a denominator of absolute needs.

UNDERDEVELOPMENT AND THE NEED FOR AID

Unfortunately, there is neither a common standard nor a generally accepted yardstick for measuring relative degrees of economic underdevelopment or the need for help. Usages and definitions are numerous and varied. Suggested measuring rods are even greater in number.

A definition by the U. S. Congress of the term "underdeveloped area" is contained in a Senate Foreign Relations Committee reference to "area where low standards of living generally prevail."[1] An official publication of the U.S. Department of State defines the economically underdeveloped areas as the "nations whose economic life provides the lowest standards of living."[2] According to these definitions, the low level

173

of income (as reflected in such factors as health, education, food consumption, non-human energy utilization, and industrial investment) can serve as the best indicator both for the degree of economic underdevelopment and the extent of the need for outside assistance.

The eligibility for technical assistance by the United States under the Point IV program is contingent, inter alia, upon the state of "economic underdevelopment," i.e., the low average per capita income. Thus, says Point Four:

> The annual income of the people of a country is probably the most representative single indicator of their standard of living. It also provides the most logical criterion for dividing the countries of the world into general groups of well-developed, intermediate and underdeveloped countries, in order to make comparisons between them in terms of several criteria which can indicate or roughly measure their need for assistance. [3]

Potentiality for development evidently is not a crucial factor in this definition. For diplomatic reasons, apparently, it is axiomatically assumed that the people of the underdeveloped areas, while unable to produce the raw materials and finished goods necessary for their well-being, would be capable of producing them if assisted by advanced technical knowledge and capital equipment. Implicit in this assumption is the belief that the level of income in all underdeveloped areas is below what it could be if external economic and technical aid were available. In this view, the existence of a low-income country that may be incapable of further development seems to be ruled out. By the same token, the ability to help underdeveloped nations is assumed to be the same for all advanced nations and apparently depends solely on their wealth and/or technological advancement.

In the confines of this study, particular attention is given to the concept of underdevelopment. The prefix "under" before the word "development" connotes the failure of the existing situation to measure up to a common standard, norm or goal. Thus, the term "economic underdevelopment" here implies the practical possibility of reaching a higher goal.

That is to say, a nation that considers itself underdeveloped must not only be dissatisfied with its existing economic status and desirous of further economic progress; it should also be capable of attaining a higher plateau of economic development. In this sense, an underdeveloped area may be defined as an area rich in potentialities, inhabited by a nation which not only feels economically retarded, and desires accelerated economic development, but is also capable of attaining a higher level of living.

Depending on the extent of its resource potentials, its technological advancement, its popular urge for development, and its capability of attaining national objectives, each developing country falls into a particular category or stage of growth and, as discussed before, needs a particular category or type of aid.

The ability of an aid-giving country to supply the particular types of aid needed in the developing country thus depends on (a) an adequate affinity or familiarity with the recipient country's problems, and (b) an adequate supply of technical and organizational resources to deal with them. The conditions of effective assistance can therefore be ideally met when cultural and technological gaps between the aid-giver and the aid receiver are the smallest. The wider the gap between the cooperating countries' stages of technological development, and the further apart their cultural patterns, the more difficult it will be for the advanced country to assist its partner in progress. For the reasons advanced below, technical cooperation between two countries, one in the innovational stage and the other still struggling to get out of the traditional stage, would be most difficult, and only rarely effective.

NATIONAL CHARACTER AND
INTERNATIONAL ORIENTATION

Under the hypothesis of "cultural affinity," the ability of an advanced nation to aid an underdeveloped country is partly a product of its national character, and partly a matter of its international orientation. A nation that is unsure of the universal acceptability of its own institutions, or disinclined to impose its way of life on other peoples, cannot extend its technical assistance beyond limited areas. Nor can a nation that is for long committed to a policy of non-intervention in the internal affairs of other nations advocate changes which obviously jeopardize the stability of the status quo in a friendly state, particularly when these changes must occur not only in the techniques of production and exchange but in the very institutions that support these techniques.

"Liberal opinion in the western world," Niebuhr points out, "rightly stresses the necessity for technical assistance in raising the productivity of the whole non-industrial world. But it usually does not recognize that, even if every form of exploitation is avoided in this development, it is not possible to transmute an agrarian culture into a technical civilization without vast cultural and social dislocations." [4]

In the words of a national Advisory Committee studying the problem on a global scale:

> In most underdeveloped areas, changes in some psychological, social or political factors are necessary before maximum benefit can be obtained from additional capital or improved technology; in some cases, economic and technical progress is virtually impossible without far-reaching changes in customs, institutions or underlying values and attitudes. [5]

A former Point IV Director also admits that without establishing and strengthening sound and efficient institutions in the recipient country, very little that Point IV Mission could accomplish through their expert advice and guidance would be of much lasting value. [6]

The role of foreign technical aid in establishing and enforcing institutions that underlie technological change in each developing country is, to be sure, very delicate. This role cannot be played equally well by all advanced nations and in all underdeveloped areas alike. Depending upon the recipient country's needs for development, the success of foreign technical assistance would depend on the ability of the advanced nations to offer that particular type of aid required to meet those needs.

PROBLEMS IN U.S.-IRAN TECHNICAL COOPERATION

The solution to Iran's socio-economic problems at the eve of Point IV aid required (a) a comprehensive and all-embracing technical assistance program in which the influence of non-economic factors were carefully weighed and heeded, (b) an organization not too alien to the local environment but sufficiently advanced to induce local emulation, and (c) a group of perceptive and knowledgeable experts who could look beyond the immediate horizon of their specialized fields and devise specific solutions to fit local problems.

On all three of these scores, the Mission's role was severely handicapped by several factors. One of these factors was the inadequacy of program planning which was discussed before.   Another factor was the particular nature of the Mission organization and the characteristics of its technicians which will be discussed later.   The purpose of this chapter is to discuss the inherent difficulties which the United States as a nation faced in offering technical assistance to a country like Iran.

Without getting involved in the polemics of the so-called "national character," [7] it can be argued that the United States as a nation (and despite significant individual and geographical exceptions to such a generalization) was culturally, economically and politically too far apart from Iran to be able, ideally or perhaps even very effectively, to assist the latter in solving most of its technical problems.

Cultural Disaffinities

To begin with, the American advanced "industrial" discipline and culture was just beginning to appear in Iran. And prior to Iran's recent Westernization and more recent "Americanization," it was perhaps totally foreign to it. The secret of American material progress, what Niebuhr calls American "historical dynamism" [8] seems to be rooted in three fundamental traits: optimism, self-confidence, and positivism. [9] Americans generally see the bright side of life, seldom doubt their ultimate success, and possess a magnificent power of positive thinking.   With optimism comes the trust in one's future, incentives for improving one's life through cooperation, and a conviction in the existence of solutions to every problem. From self-confidence arise strength, enthusiastic work and personal satisfaction. Pragmatism and positivism engender a "scientific" spirit (e.g., "there must be black and white answers to every question"), and a desire for efficiency (e.g., "there must be short-cuts in achieving any goals"). This culture,

based on the nordic and Anglo-Saxon traits, emphasizes pre-
cision, pragmatism and utility.

A contrast between this cultural heritage and the Iranian
individual and national make-up is somewhat striking. [10] The
Iranian culture often shows strong traces of fatalism, exaggerated artistry, and good life. Analytical reasoning is often
subdued by emotions. Creative thinking often becomes an easy
prey to facile imitations. Relationships are personalized, seldom formal and very rarely institutional. As pointed out before,
conditioned by history-long preoccupation with political instability, economic insecurity, and social injustices, the Iranians have become somewhat pessimistic about their life, uncertain about social cooperation, and driven to follow a lonely,
individualistic route.

Problems are magnified out of all proportion or altogether
left to be solved by themselves. Answers, when found, are
generally imprecise, neither black nor white. Confidence in
individual or national ability to solve problems is in some cases
unduly small, and in others overly exaggerated. Constructive
actions are often hampered by too many negative observations,
too much hesitation, or a leisurely pace.

Due to the existence of such fundamental differences in
national values, attitudes and behaviour, cooperation between
Mission assistants and their counterparts was naturally difficult. Insufficient familiarity with each other's differing ways
of life often created considerable misunderstandings. American optimism, for example, was interpreted by most Iranian intellectuals as either incredulity or downright ignorance. [11]
American self-confidence was often regarded as a sign of a
superiority complex verging on condescension. American
pragmatism often appeared materialistic and expedient.

The Mission technicians, in turn, often interpreted Iranian emotionalism as a sign of psychological and social im-
maturity; their love of exaggeration as a tendency toward un-
truth or hypocrisy; their craving for a good life as apathy or
laziness.

Such characteristic conceptual differences in appraising
the value of time, teamwork, trust, objectivity and democracy
also made the necessary understanding between U.S. advisors
and their Iranian collaborators difficult, if not impossible.

The Iranian counterparts seemed to find their American advisors "too much in a hurry" with little or no sympathy for the Iranians' leisurely pace.   American advisors, on the other hand, seemed to find such harmless Iranian traits as the attempt not to lose face (or not to admit ignorance) intolerably immodest, if not plainly untruthful. [12]

The native personnel having little understanding or appreciation of teamwork, delegation of authority and assumption of responsibility, appeared aloof and uncooperative toward foreign technicians. The American trust of their fellowmen and their confidence in complete strangers often seemed to the Iranians a sign of immature experience and naivety. The importance of personal relationships, friendship and "connections" for getting things done in Iran struck the Americans as contrary to their traditions of impersonality, equality of treatment and objectivity. To the rank-conscious Iranian, on the other hand, the American egalitarian heritage (e.g., inviting the jeep driver to eat or associate with high government functionaries on their trips) seemed bizarre and uncalled for.

As a result of these misunderstandings, American assistance and counsel were not always accepted without reservations and were not always adequately appreciated or enthusiastically followed.   In the face of this lack of enthusiasm and appreciation, American advisors were easily discouraged, often felt taken advantage of, or saw no reason for fulfilling their jobs beyond the strictest call of duty. [13]

Techno-Economic Gaps

A more inhibiting factor in the Irano-American technical cooperation was the gulf between America's highly advanced and sophisticated state of the arts and Iran's relatively new experience with modern American technology.

At the risk both of great over-simplification and inadequate correspondence, some contrasting figures about the levels of technical and educational progress may be cited as illustrations of the gap between the two countries' stages of economic and technological development. In agriculture, less than 17 per cent of U.S. population were engaged in farming in 1950, producing food and fiber valued at about 7-1/2% of the national income. [14]   In Iran an estimated 70% of the population were working on the farms, yet producing not more than 30% of

Iran's domestic products. According to a Mission agricul-
turist, in terms of the number of families capable of producing for themselves and other families, Iran was at about
the year 1660 of the United States. [15]

In the field of industry the amount of capital invested per
worker in 1950 was approximately $1,000 or about 1/2% of the
figure in the United States. The installed horse-power per
actively employed worker in Iran was no more than 0.30 h.p.,
while the corresponding figure for the United States was 7 h.p.
According to a Mission electrical specialist, Denver, a typical
U. S. city with similarities to Tehran, had sixty times more
power per capita. [16]

Of even greater importance for the purpose of absorbing
foreign technology was perhaps the gap between levels of
education in the cooperating countries. In the year 1950, when
Point IV operations started, there were only 110 elementary
school teachers in Iran for every 100,000 children of school
age. The United States had close to 3000. Iran had only a
daily newspaper circulation of 5 per 1000 of population; the
United States figure was more than 350. There were merely
10 radio sets for each 1000 of population in Iran, and roughly
700 in the United States. The total number of letters handled
by the Iranian Post Office was approximately 38 million; that
of the United States, 44 billion. [17]

The average productivity of the Iranian worker was estimated to be 150 international units for the primary producers,
128 for the secondary producers, and 340 for the tertiary producers. [18] These figures were approximately one fifth of the
levels prevailing in the United States after the Second World
War.

These contrasts may still not be able to measure the true
significance of the educational and technological gaps between
the two countries and the importance of these gaps as a barrier
against the transfer of advanced technology. But the manifesta-
tions of these gaps were evident everywhere. For one thing,
due to a lack of a common conceptual ground for operation, the
United States was inadequately prepared to offer Iran the type
of discipline and institutions that were more in line with the
Iranian tradition; she also had difficulty in finding the type of
men who could put these disciplines and institutions to work.
More on this will be said in Chapter 11.

Trained in schools, organizations and factories equipped with most modern tools, and accustomed to a rich and prosperous way of life, most American technicians with some notable exceptions could not help but "think big" in everything. Their conceptions of a minimum operational scale, of standard equipment, of needed tools had few parallels in the Iranian way of thinking. They often could think of nothing but the best and the latest -- the only things with which they had worked and were familiar. Sometimes, the most modern American equipment was what Iran really needed. Often, a good number of substitutes would do. And sometimes there was need for completely new devices.

A Mission Provincial Director, announcing the inauguration of the Fars Cement Plant, expressed his unmitigated glee over the fact that the factory was "a practically push button type, the equal of which can be found in very few other countries." [19] A public safety advisor said:

> It is the ultimate aim of this advisor to begin
> a replacement program for all equipment that is
> considered obsolete by U.S. standards and to be-
> gin pilot programs that will demand their own
> expansion. [20]

Too often the technicians' recommendations were to scrap instead of repair; to mechanize instead of using manual labor; to purchase fancy equipment instead of devising local tools. In the field of agriculture, for example, where technical deficiencies were the major reason for attracting Point IV aid, a good deal of the funds went for the importation of unsuitable agricultural machinery from the United States under the guise of giving "real stimulus" to the Iranian farmer to seek better and easier ways of performing his farming operations. This fact was later acknowledged by one of the Mission's own agricultural technicians:

> A vast amount of . . . machinery has also
> been made available, including threshers, com-
> bines, plows, discs, etc. Some of the machinery
> has not yet found a place in Iranian agriculture . . .
> The situation was due partly to the selection, and
> partly to the Iranian farmers' not accepting the
> machinery; or they have not been economically
> proven favorable because of low labor costs. [21]

A "demonstration" Children's Home was built (Project No. 77) for the "design" of which $15,000 alone (i.e., the cost of an average house in Iran) was paid to a famed American architectural firm. Equipment for demonstration schools, utensils for home economics classes, and tools for machine shops, although of standard American varieties, were obviously too fancy for Iran, too expensive for Iranian agencies, and too out of place in the native setting. Writes a Mission advisor:

> Point 4 started the Home Making program and the people like it. But they are now demanding something more practical than they are getting. At present Home Making is not dealing with the basic needs of the people but rather is catering to the daughters of the well-to-do.[22]

While, according to an Iranian senator, state hospitals connected with the Tehran Medical School lacked enough bandage materials for dressing wounds, [23] the school reportedly received some fancy electronic equipment which few among the staff could use and which had to remain partly idle for want of accessories. As a Tehran University professor put it, the difficulty with Point IV was its attempt to show how much better people can live aspirationally, without their having the wherewithal to actually live that way. [24]

Socio-Political Problems

The United States' limitations in offering technical assistance was not only evident in its inadequate cultural, economic and technological affinities with Iran; they also manifested themselves in the Mission's inability to move far and fast in the socio-political arena. [25]

The American system of political economy based on private enterprise and price mechanism, was ill-fitted to the system of political economy followed in Iran. Not only was the United States ideologically opposed to state planning, but having had little to do with national planning problems, she lacked enough convinced and experienced planners for overseas assignments. U. S. technicians, brought up in the ideals of democracy and free enterprise, were in the uneasy position of not only tolerating, but actually promoting state direction and control. Even when these technicians had little interest personally in proselytizing free enterprise or democracy, they usually lacked the background and qualifications for the new task of state planning.

One of the basic objectives of the Point IV program in Iran was to assist the country in the establishment and promotion of democracy and free enterprise. [26] Yet the type of democratic practices and institutions that the United States was bent on promoting (e.g., a parliamentary system and local autonomy) were believed by many responsible people in Iran not the kind of politico-economic system that the country needed or could adopt advantageously. [27] In the opinion of many well-meaning people in Iran, a freely-elected parliament in the hands of unscrupulous politicians with vested interests could, if nothing else, obstruct the passage of desirable social legislation. And freedom of the press, speech and assembly, unchecked by a sufficiently strong sense of national or individual responsibility, could do more harm than good to the development efforts. [28]

To some American technicians this made sense. But to many it did not. In the words of a U.S. legislative committee:

> Democratic practices as we understand them require a high sense of public responsibility and the acceptance of rules and values different from those that are the heritage of the Asian nations.

> To the illiterate masses the operation of democratic machinery represents confusion. In the democratic process opposition performs a valuable service. In the Orient the idea of a loyal opposition is neither understood nor respected. It has no constructive function. [29]

Yet, to many technicians in the field, and to some influential members of Congress, there was only one road to salvation, and that was American democracy and free enterprise.

And, there was another impasse. The need for some socio-economic reforms (later carried out in Iran under the Shah's leadership and through his Six-Point Program) lay at the source of Iran's economic ills as much as deficiencies of technical know-how and the scarcity of capital did. Iranian poverty was as much a result of social, political, economic, and

moral problems as it was the outcome of lack of scientific
knowledge and absence of accumulated wealth. [30]

The Mission itself seemed to think that unless changes in
the unfavorable attitudes, motivation and institutions were
profound and far reaching, an economic development scheme,
even if started with foreign technical assistance, would have
little chance of ultimate success. Discussing the role of a
religious institution in Northeastern Iran -- the Holy Shrine --
a disappointed Provincial Director wrote:

> In effect the Shrine is the biggest absentee
> landlord in Khorasan, perhaps in Iran. In con-
> nection with the Shrine there is the clergy which
> exert a powerful, though negative, influence upon
> the people. The Shrine is an enormously rich,
> sprawling inefficiently-run institution. It would
> seem that before any satisfactory economic
> progress is made, political and social reforms
> must be instituted. [31]

Yet, the Mission as a U.S. agency was obviously unable to take
such initiative.

Part of the reluctance to openly suggest necessary reforms was a reflection of America's respect for, if not fas-
cination with, different ways of life and revulsion for imposing
her way of life on others. From the very beginning of the
Point IV program warning signals had come from all quarters
against going too fast. There were emotional pleas for pro-
tecting national ethos and preserving native color. There was
also moral admonition against the United States trying to reform developing societies in "the American image."

Part of the reason for loathing to press for social reform
was the self-imposed restraint by the U. S. government
to avoid being accused of meddling in other countries' affairs.
Although the urge to develop, and socio-political changes accompanying economic development were considered by a Senate Committee studying the problem as "crucial" in deciding
the ultimate success of technical assistance, it was found that
neither of these factors was "within the control of the United
States," and in fact, "highly improper, as well as self-defeating
for the United States to attempt to dictate." [32] Treading
boldly on the same theme, President Eisenhower said that the

United States had "no desire or intent" to change other people's "chosen political, economic or cultural patterns." Following the same line, the ICA observed that "if in the implementation of our assistance programs, we were to attempt
to dictate the form of economic policy that other countries
should follow, our efforts would be worse than useless." [33]
And still another part of the reason for the Mission's inability
to press for reforms was the inevitability of a strong Iranian
reaction to any such "interference." In the face of the Iranians' pride, nationalistic fervor, and mistrust of foreign dicta-
tion, any undue pressure by the Mission would have backfired.
Witness the Shah's evaluation of the foreign assistants' role:

> My father employed many foreign specialists,
> but always he made them understand that they
> were merely assisting the work of an on-going,
> essentially Persian administration; in no way
> should the foreigners imagine that they were in
> charge of any of our regular Government agencies
> here, either in an executive capacity or as ad-
> visers who fancied that they were directing things
> from behind the scenes. [34]

Indicative of the Mission's wise reluctance to press hard
in favor of needed social reforms is the manner in which two
of Point IV's most significant programs, land reforms and
community development, were carried out. [35]   A similar attitude was taken toward the thorny problem of excess government employees. The report of a roving Committee of the U.S.
House of Representatives that visited Iran in 1956 put it this
way:

> The /Iranian/ Government payroll is heavily
> loaded; estimates supplied to the study mission
> indicate that its numbers could be reduced by at
> least 40 percent. But against such a drastic re-
> duction must be weighed the fact, demonstrated
> repeatedly in other countries, that communism
> spreads most rapidly among unemployed white
> collar workers. [36]

A thoughtful public administration advisor in the Mission
sums up the analysis of this chapter in the following verdict:

> I believe there is now general agreement that
> as a Division, as a USOM, as a nation, we do not

know as much as we need to know to assure
maximum effectiveness of technical assistance
programs. [37]

Due to this inadequate national preparedness to offer the
technical aid needed by Iran, the Point IV assistance was not
always of the right kind and composition. Some of the same
type of assistance and advice offered, through some of the same
technicians, to countries in the innovational stage of technological development might have been more effective. And by
the same token, a similar type of assistance offered by similar
types of technicians from another advanced country of greater
cultural affinity with Iran (and less political power) might have
gone much further. More on this will be said in Chapters 10
and 11.

References

1. The Act for International Development, 1950 (Washington:
   Senate Report 1371, part 2, March 24, 1950).

2. Point Four, U. S. Department of State, Economic Cooperation Series #24, p. 15.

3. Ibid., p. 103.

4. Reinhold Niebuhr, The Irony of American History (New
   York: Charles Scribner's Sons, 1952), p. 118.

5. Economic Strength for the Free World, supra cit., p. 7.

6. J. B. Bingham, op. cit., p. 130.

7. E. g., Geoffry Gorer, The American People: A Study in
   National Character (New York: Norton, 1948).

8. Reinhold Niebuhr, op. cit., p. 118.

9. Harlan Cleveland speaks of an "objective" and "deperson-
   alized" system of human relations in the United States
   where optimism about human progress, pragmatism and
   practicality minimizes the necessity for human judgment
   and personal prejudice in decision-making. See his Overseas Americans, pp. 139-140.

10. For a "western" description of the Iranian mentality (not
    altogether a flawless study and not much appreciated in
    Iran), see H. H. Vreeland, Iran (New Haven: Human Re-
    lations Area Files, 1957), particularly Ch. XXIV.

11. R. D. Gastil shows how Iranian "cleverness" is often con- trasted by Iranians with what they consider American "simplicity." See op. cit.

12. See I. J. Alten, CTR, January 10, 1959, p. 3.

13. More on this will be said in Ch. 11.

14. By 1960, the percentage of U.S. population engaged in farming dropped to less than 9 per cent. of total popula- tion. The figure for Iran is not available.

15. W. E. Carroll, "Agriculture," in RUSTEAI, n.p.

16. J. W. Howard, CTR, July 11, 1956, p. 7.

17. Figures from the annual Statistical Abstract of the United States (Washington: U.S. Department of Commerce), and Statistical Yearbook (New York: United Nations).

18. Alfred S. Ray, "The Problem of Economic Development in Backward Areas with Special Reference to Iran," Ph. D. Dissertation, University of Michigan, 1951, App. C. 1. For the definition of the international unit, see Colin Clark, Conditions of Economic Progress (London: Macmillan, 1951), p. 19.

19. USOM/I, Monthly Operations Report to Washington, Au- gust, 1955, p. 12.

20. Z. L. Wilkins, CTR, May 13, 1964, p. 5. (Italics added.) For the technicians' advocation of American techniques and methods see below, Ch. 11, Competence and Expertise.

21. R. E. Griffin, CTR, March 28, 1957, p. 6. Even when the equipment could be profitably used in Iran, they were not always the same type and make, resulting in greater parts cost, mix-up in parts and needing separate transla- tions for parts books and separate instructions on each make of machine. See R. O. Gustafson, CTR, January 4, 1954, p. 2.

22. Obed Williamson, CTR, July 3, 1961, p. 8.

23. See the statement of Senator Jamshid A'alam on the floor of the Iranian Senate, January 11, 1963 as reported in Keyhan (Tehran, Air Mail Edition), January 11, 1963.

24. More on this will be said in Ch. 11.

25. See supra Ch. 3.

26. Section 402, Parts (a) and (c) of the Act for International Development, 1950.

27. For the type of democracy for Iran favored by His Majesty, see Mission for My Country, Ch. 8.

28. For a more recent discussion of the Iranian political structure, see Leonard Binder, Political Development in a Changing Society (Berkeley: University of California Press, 1962).

29. Report of the Special Study Mission to the Middle East, U.S. House of Representatives, 84th Cong., 2nd Sess., House Report No. 2147 (Washington, 1960), p. 207.

30. The necessity for such reforms was not limited to Iran, but equally applicable to the whole underdeveloped world. Cf. A. Q. Dabir, "Asia's Need is Moral Not Material," Islamic Review (January, 1953), pp. 17-18.

31. H. C. Landenheim, "Khorasan," in RUSTEAI, n. p.

32. Technical Assistance and Related Programs, Senate Report No. 1956, May 1956, p. 8.

33. Criticisms of the Foreign Aid Program, supra cit., p. 95.

34. H. I. M. Mohammed Reza Shah Pahlevi, op. cit., p. 302.

35. See F. J. Moore, CTR, August 9, 1960, pp. 3-4, and H. L. Naylor, CTR, May 11, 1957, p. 17.

36. Report of the Special Study Mission to the Middle East, p. 58.

37. L. O. Wolcott, CTR, April 19, 1961, p. 7. (Italics not in the original.)

CHAPTER 10

POINT IV ORGANIZATION AND MANAGEMENT

The success of a program of foreign technical assistance depends not only on the inherent efficiency of its administration but even more on the exemplary character of that administration in the native country.

The necessity of administrative efficiency and sound management in a program of foreign technical assistance hardly requires elaboration. It is the program's organization that may encourage or stifle technicians' initiative, use or misuse their time, and guide or misguide their efforts. Even the best of technicians can do little without organized direction and support.

Efficiency requirements are too familiar to need elaborate discussion here. Simply put, an efficient administration requires an appropriate process of direction, work distribution, staffing, coordination and job evaluation. Proper direction of a technical aid organization in a foreign country requires a delicate balance between guidance for the solution of domestic problems and replacement of domestic responsibility for local initiative. Efficient work distribution requires tailoring the program to fit local possibilities for best work accomplishment. Good staffing means using foreign technicians to the best of their ability in providing local personnel with necessary technical experience. Coordination requires proper timing in the use of manpower, equipment and materials through sustained administrative efforts. Job evaluation requires periodic control of activities in order to measure the degree of accomplishment and to avoid duplication of activities.

In many developing countries where significant administrative barriers to economic development exist it is more essential that the foreign mission's administration and

189

management serve as a model of organizational efficiency. Strong leadership, a minimum of delays and red tape, effective direction of technicians' time and efforts, and the use of administrative procedures adapted to local needs would not only give local agencies a model to emulate, but would also save the program embarrassing setbacks and avoidable mishaps.

POINT IV ADMINISTRATION IN IRAN

In view of the delicate and trying circumstances under which the Point IV program had to operate (e.g., distrust of the program's motives, the emergency nature of many of the projects, the uncertain process of annual appropriations, and the difficulty of recruiting suitable technical advisors in a short time), there was a far more compelling need for a sounder organization to compensate for these deficiencies.

A review of the Mission's own account of its organization and management, particularly in the early phases of the program, however, seems to indicate that the Mission's administration did not only fail to make up for existing draw-backs but sometimes accentuated them.

Philosophy and Orientation

Frequent shifts' in the structure of the Mission organiza-tion without a continuous, homogeneous leadership was one of the problems. The program's administration in Iran closely followed administrative changes in Washington. As Technical Cooperation Administration became Foreign Opera-tions Administration, the International Cooperation Adminis-tration, and, finally, the Agency for International Development, so the country organization starting as Technical Cooperation for Iran, was later changed to U.S. Operations Mission/Iran and finally to American Aid Mission/Iran. And these changes were not in the alphabetical designations only. In inter-nal management, the Mission had its own fund at first, a series of joint-funds for each activity during 1952-1953; a Master Joint Fund (MJF) in 1954; and a Special Activities Account (SAA) in 1956 and after. There were also frequent shifts in the structure of the Mission divisions. [1]

Each change in the personality of the Mission Directors, Division Chiefs and project supervisors ushered in a new and somewhat different philosophy and orientation. In order to ensure maximum flexibility in handling the Point IV program under the extremely delicate and highly volatile situation in Iran during most of the period, broad authority had to be vested in the Mission Directors (and the American Ambassadors as their superiors). But since the scope of the authority was not (and perhaps could not be) clearly defined, it fell to the Mission Director (or the American Ambassador) to decide personally on both programs and procedures.

In a period of less than ten years, the Mission had five different Directors of dissimilar taste and temperament, working under five different Ambassadors of similar diversities. As one former academician in the Mission put it, the Point IV program in Iran was closely tied to the character of the Mission Directors and Division Chiefs. One Director, with a love of farming and resource development, sent most of the technicians out to the remote provinces, and stretched the program in all directions. Another urbane Director deemphasized provincial operations and tried to build up the headquarters' strength. One wanted to operate at the village level; the other wished to work at the ministry level. One had a liking for public works and big public projects; another one favored private enterprise and small industries. One was a "go-getter" with little patience for traditional procedure; another one wanted every single operation documented down to minute details. One had an obsessive flair for showmanship and publicity; another was shy and self-effacing. [2]

Some of the Mission Divisions also apparently experienced a similar lack of continuous leadership. The Chief of the Industry Division said in 1954:

> The Division had had four acting chiefs during the previous two years, all excellent technicians but with little administrative and executive experience. The morale of both American and Iranian personnel was low, the relationship with the Plan Organization poor, and unsatisfactory action and progress had been made in most of the projects. [3]

In the opinion of another Industry Division Chief, the seventh since the activity was established, the result of "such lack of continuity in leadership" was nothing but disgruntled personnel. 4

Of the various Mission programs only health and sanitation activities were carried through a separate organization called the Public Health Cooperative, modeled after the Latin American servicios, outside of the Iranian Ministry of Health and somewhat outside of the Mission itself. The reason the health program was singled out for this form of organization, according to a high-ranking Mission official, was that the first Health Division Chief had been in Brazil prior to his assignment to Iran in 1951, and was "sold" on the advantages of this type of organization. So he wanted his division to be organized accordingly. Other than this, the official said, there was no reason for the health program's being organized as a "cooperative," or for other programs not being so organized.

Another example of the shift in philosophy and approach of the Mission Divisions following changes in the personality and character of Division Chiefs can be seen in the Community Development program where five different persons directed it between 1954 and 1960. According to one of the Division's own staff, both the Division's diagnosis of community development problems and its approach to their solution varied with the background, interests and personalities of Division Chiefs. And as a result of these vacillations, few people in Iran could find out what community development was all about.

The frequent changes in leadership seem to have been also true of the Provincial Directors. In all of the ten Ostans where the Mission had provincial offices as of November, 1951, Provincial directors frequently changed. Between November, 1951, and November, 1958, alone each of the ten provincial offices had at least four different directors or acting-directors. Some provinces had as many as nine different ones.

The influence on Mission operations of personalities and points of view was not limited to Directors, Division Chiefs and Provincial administrators. Individual technicians, too, influenced the projects' direction according to their own judgment. 5

The essential problem in the Mission's philosophy and leadership is vividly portrayed in the following report by one of the Mission Directors:

> I find the task of bringing Mission operations into a consistent pattern extremely difficult to accomplish. This is a vast, sprawling organization, and sometimes I have the feeling that I have turned the horse's head but that the body keeps going right down the road. [6]

This "headless" movement of the Mission organization is confirmed in numerous reports of the Mission staff. In the opinion of a community development technician, the greatest obstacle faced by the community development staff was the lack of clear designation of duties, authority and responsibility as well as the frequent contradictions of policy directives. [7] Another technician in the same Division reported that his Ostan chief had to manage Ostan activity for six months with nothing to guide him with regard to either finances, personnel or program. [8]   A provincial sanitary engineering advisor complained that there was no written nor stated policy from the Public Health Department in Tehran or the Section Chief. The closest thing to a policy was the general thinking and action of the Public Health Chief. [9]

Direction and Work Distribution

Frequent changes in the personalities of Directors and Division Chiefs would not have had such adverse effects on Mission activities if the Iranian Co-Directors were given broader responsibilities.   But, as stated before, the Mission was pretty much an American government agency, directly connected with the American Embassy in Tehran and, for all practical purposes, responsible mainly to Washington.   Its elaborate structure, management, procedures, working hours and salary scale were mostly foreign to Iran.   Even after the so-called "integration" in 1956, the Mission continued to operate as a separate agency, outside the Iranian bureaucracy and more or less the same way as before.   As a critic put it, the entire program was American -- a show almost entirely written, produced, directed and played by American talent, using a number of Iranian bit-players and a few score of extras.

The Mission staff, even the local personnel, were in effect employees of the U.S. government, paid out of funds that, altough "joint" or "special" in name, were outside of the Iranian Treasury and financial regulations.   Staff loyalty, in the case of the Americans, was unmistakably toward the United States, although some of them had a good deal of sympathy for Iranian causes. 10   For the Iranians, the loyalty was peculiarly mixed.   As Iranian citizens they were expected to promote their country's best interests; but as Mission employees, they had to follow U.S. policies and directives.

In the nature of the undertaking the Mission's guidance and direction of projects were perhaps not only a legitimate exercise of power on the part of the party which paid the lion's share of the program's cost but maybe also an intelligent exercise of choice on the part of the party who was supposed to know better.   Nevertheless, to the extent that the U.S. government had the ultimate say in deciding policies and directing operations, it was probably hard to convince the Iranian officials that they were helping themselves, that this was their problem, and that they had to put in their best efforts.   In fact, leaving the deciding vote in U.S. hands was perhaps a welcome opportunity for the cautious Iranian bureaucrats to evade responsibility for project direction and thus avoid criticisms of project failures and deficiencies.

Acceptance of responsibility by local authorities and their participation in project formulation and implementation were not only desirable in the very nature of joint operation but also indispensable because of the limitation of Mission resources.   In field after field, and activity after activity, the Mission technicians were complaining about the program being too thinly spread. 11   In the words of a lonely city planner, the area assigned to him was 600 miles long and 200 miles wide, comprising some 30 cities. 12   One single labor training advisor was given the task of running an ambitious nation-wide program in skill improvement, apprenticeship, and adult in-service training. 13   In community development -- a completely new field in Iran -- some 150 village councils reportedly had to be organized by one single field worker. 14   In agricultural extension -- another new field -- three specialists and eight agents were reportedly given the task of training, supervision and administration in 3600 villages scattered over 170,000 square miles. 15

Technical and managerial advice to Tehran Tchitsazi Mill (which later took 26 private American technicans and 18 European mechanics to perform) was, for a long time, left in the hands of two Mission engineers. [16]   Advice to the Agriculture Department in Khorasan, an area larger than France, was the duty of one single agriculturalist. [17]   Assistance in the educational programs of two larger Ostans (Kerman and Baluchistan) was the task of one lonely educator. [18]

Recruitment and Staffing

Staffing was probably one of the most vexing problems of the Mission throughout the years. Recruitment difficulties kept the Mission's strength constantly below par. Vacancies for foreign technicians at the headquarters and in the provinces were not always filled; those that were filled did not always meet the actual and urgent needs; and the men and women who did meet the needs did not always stay long enough on the job to show expected results.

According to one of the Mission's Provincial Directors, the recruitment of Americans for Iran from the very start ran into competition with recruitment for missions in other countries which were more attractive. [19]   Those who volunteered for work in Iran in the early years were, according to a Mission document, recruited on the basis of "canned" job-descriptions prepared in Washington.   In the early period, staff needs of the Mission were reportedly also determined in Washington, and until the technician arrived in Iran, nobody was sure just exactly what he was going to do. The Mission Director met with every new arrival, and it was usually during this meeting that the technician learned about his actual assignment. [20]

Since most of the technicians hired in the early period were evidently recruited not for a specific job in a specific area, many had to be moved around from one job to another and from one area to the next. A public administration advisor had four different assignments in a two-year tour of duty. [21] An animal husbandry technician, employed as a cooperative specialist, served as community development specialist, agricultural extension advisor, farm machinery advisor, and an agricultural economist. [22]   A soils and land classification advisor started work as community development advisor; was detailed as "operations officer" to the same Division; transferred to the Public Health Division as a "program assistant";

and wound up his tour as an advisor to the Bank Omran. [23]
An accounting advisor started work as an assistant to the Plan
Organization; later, he was detailed to the Ministry of Finance
to work in the Internal Revenue Department; then to the
Master Joint Fund Organization for improvement in the pro-
curement and property records; then to the Tehran Slaughter-
house for the design of an accounting system; then to the
Tobacco Monopoly for establishing a system of cost accounting;
and finally ended up as Acting Comptroller of the Mission's
Master Joint Fund.   And all of this in only two years. [24]

Extension of the program beyond what could be reasonably
accomplished was thus responsible for the necessity of
employing available technicians sometimes outside their fields
of specialization and beyond their professional usefulness.
This factor, in turn, intensified the turnover problem. The
following candid account of an educator is most interesting:

> I, the only American in the (Western
> Azarbaijan) Ostan, was left not only in charge of
> the Education Program, but likewise in charge of
> everything else.   It is true that I have had
> considerable administrative experience, but I
> was totally unacquainted with the administration
> of a branch Point IV regional office. [25]

Another secondary school educationist had an equally interesting
account of his own. He says rather imperiously in his final
report:

> I came to Iran with the understanding that I
> was to be a Secondary Education Technician, but
> in the process my scope of activities had broad-
> ened to include such areas as vocational education,
> home making education, normal school, cur-
> riculum revision, fundamental education, school
> administration, elementary in-service training,
> budget and fiscal problems, and several other
> interesting areas. [26]

Yet in his recommendation to the Mission, he includes a
suggestion, "that perhaps the technician could be of more
value if he could focus his attention on a somewhat restricted

area.'' Another vocational educationist reported that although he was to be the vocational agricultural education advisor, he served in the capacity of an advisor in ''all phases of education'' because he was the only American advisor in Shiraz. [27]

In some cases, non-specialized or unfamiliar Mission technicians were put in charge of ''joint projects'' where the native contingent included some adequately-trained Iranians with more advanced degrees and occasionally greater experience. [28]   The resulting effect on the Mission's professional prestige as well as on the Iranian technicians' morale was recognized by the Mission technicians themselves. A trade and investment specialist who was given an administrative job advised the Mission that:

> Temporary assignment of a technician to projects with which he is not fully acquainted, or for which he is not trained not only causes hardship to technicians but creates an opportunity for unfair criticism by outsiders. [29]

A public safety specialist warned against expanding his project without additional technicians, counterparts and commodity funds. [30]   A technical services specialist cautioned against extending his project beyond what could be done and done well. [31]

Indicative of the seriousness of similar situations in the early years is the fact that not until 1957 could the Mission establish a firm policy of requiring that a person recruited for a specialized field work in his field after he arrives at the post. [32]   The situation improved toward the end of the decade, however, and starting in the 1960's most of the problems came under reasonable control.

Internal Coordination

Due to a lack of effective planning and direction, discussed before, the Mission had an insurmountable problem of internal coordination of its material and human resources. As mentioned in Chapters 5 and 6, in the first few years of operation, the lack of synchronization of supplies, equipment, and technicians was particularly acute.   Closely connected with this

lack of synchronization of human and mechanical factors
seems to have been the inadequate backstopping of the projects
from the headquarters in Tehran. A chief sanitary engineering advisor complained that his advisory staff was larger than
the entire public health divisions of 25 missions throughout
the world, yet the project had been carried on for three
years without secretarial help. [33]   A provincial nursing
advisor blamed the lack of transportation facilities not so
much on shortage as on poor planning and misuse. [34]   An
agronomist, voicing the sentiments of a large number of
the technicians interviewed, protested against advisors being
required to perform too many clerical jobs and other duties
of a non-technical nature. [35]

More serious than the inadequacies of typists or transportation vehicles seems to have been insufficient technical
support given to the various projects, particularly in the
provinces. A large number of projects were without an advisor
for several months and this lapse of time between the departure of one technician and the arrival of his successor
usually resulted in setting the project back much longer than
the actual time elapsed, and slowing up the rate at which the
new technician could show accomplishments. [36]   The Kerman
community development block, for example, was once without
a qualified chief for five months. [37]   The agricultural extension in the same Ostan was at one stretch without an advisor
for eight months. [38]   Teacher training was stopped for almost
twelve months in Eastern Azarbaijan because there was no
advisor available. [39]   Trade and Industry Divisions in the
same Ostan had been without an advisor for about a year. A
range management specialist who was departing from Iran
complained that although he had resigned six months prior
to his departure, his replacement was not in sight. [40]   And
even until 5 months after his departure the Mission could
not find a successor for him. [41]

In the absence of clear program objectives, continuous
policy direction and trained counterparts, the departure of
a technician naturally resulted in discontinuing the project.
Even when the project was not completely abandoned, it
would be difficult for the new technician to pick up the pieces
or to determine just where the former technician was heading.
Most often, by the time the new technician arrived, local
enthusiasm and support for the project had diminished if not
vanished.   There was always the problem of leaving a good

deal of equipment and supply idle while the technician was not available.   And once the technician finished his tour of duty and left, his Iranian counterparts were left in the air, remaining idle and receiving no direction.   Sometimes the counterparts had to be let go after the technicians left. A sanitary engineering advisor reported that at the time of his arrival his section had fifteen loose-end projects left uncompleted by the previous Section Chief. [42]

Juxtaposed to a number of important cases where the Mission had expanded its operations faster than they could be adequately manned or supplied, there are indications that, in other instances, it did not know exactly how to keep its staff occupied.   In the heyday of Community Development activity in the country, for example, a Provincial Director wrote:

Since there has not been enough work for the specialists lately, five of the eight specialists have been transferred to their respective ministries with their jeeps retained in our motor pool. [43]

Another Provincial Director reported:

Total personnel for the provinces has been reduced during the past two months from 143 to 114 without any serious curtailment of operations. [44]

And, according to a Mission technician:

From May to October, 1955, I was virtually without a definite assignment and for that reason I requested a transfer to Washington or to another mission, but my October request was not forwarded to Washington until March, 1956. [45]

In another case, a community development advisor's report reads:

Some of the more qualified field technicians who were not being used to full value and were

immobile in the field due to lack of transportation, were brought in the Ostan office to fill
administrative positions yet unfilled in the staff
quota. [46]

Part of the problem of ineffective use was due to the
necessity of getting acquainted with project and programs
the technicians knew very little about. An agricultural
credit advisor, for example, admits that his entire period
of duty in a four-month assignment was spent on "reviewing
the background of the project and becoming acquainted with
the program." [47] A "support" technician's one-year tour
of duty was spent one fourth on "orientation," about one
half on "temporary assignments" in four Ostans, and the rest
on "surveying the agricultural situation" prior to placement
as a permanent advisor. His own appraisal of his one year
duty was that the orientation was inappropriate, apprenticeship unnecessary, and his accomplishments in his acting
advisor's role difficult to measure because the time was too
short for him to gain the confidence of the Iranians and to
understand the local situation completely. [48]

In a significant number of cases, the haste in recruiting
people for the rapidly expanding Mission organization aggravated the turnover problem. The number of Mission technicians who "did not work out" and had to be sent home is not
revealed by the Mission. But it was privately conceded that
the percentage was not negligible. A report by a high State
Department official puts the figure of those who did not "make
the grade" as high as 25 percent. [49]

An adjunct to the problem of excessive turnover was the
problem of short tenure. The Mission's regular tour of duty
was only two years. Although a number of technicians stayed
for their second, third, and occasionally fourth tours, the
majority of the technicians had no more than a two-year
sojourn -- a period unduly short under the circumstances. The
two-year stay would probably have been adequate had the
technicians been thoroughly familiar with their assignments.
But given the nature and type of the Mission operation and the
conditions under which they had to work, two years seem to
have been inadequate. The first few months following the
technicians' arrival were admittedly taken up by such chores
as finding suitable quarters, getting "oriented" in the language

and country courses, studying the background of the project to which they were assigned, and altogether "feeling their way around."   The last month or two at the end of the tour were also mostly spent on "getting ready to go" (e.g., making travel arrangements, selling household furniture, saying good-bye to friends, etc.).   The active work period was thus even less than two years. In too many cases, the technician had to leave just about the time his usefulness had begun. Of this says a Mission advisor at the end of his second tour of duty in Isfahan:

> At the end of the first tour in my self-evaluation, it was uncertain who learned the most, the Iranians or myself. Now with confidence I leave Isfahan feeling that I have been able to contribute to their educational progress. [50]

In the absence of adequate coordinate planning, policy direction and continuity of leadership, the success of each project fell upon individual technicians' own initiative and talent.   Where the project advisor was competent, dedicated and alert, progress was assured.   Otherwise it went by the wayside.   A dissatisfied Mission technician confided in his interview that during his tenure in Iran the Mission consisted of 200 technicians each one on his own, and, all of them constituting 200 "one-man" lands. Too many projects, he said, were virtually discontinued because technicians had no uniform concept, no common time horizon, and no group interest.

The Mission held regular staff meetings, attended by all Division Chiefs, for the avowed purpose of making policy decisions and coordinating division activities.   Yet, many of the Mission officials who were interviewed seemed little informed about the activities of other divisions and were mostly concerned with their own divisions.   Some were not even fully aware of the relationship between their endeavors and those of other technicians.   The concern for this lack of mutual orientation, and the frustration involved in it, are plainly visible in the following frank statement by one of the Mission's public administration advisors:

> I find a universal belief that, though hundreds of millions of dollars have been spent in the program of this mission, virtually nothing has

been accomplished except furthering the wealth
and interests of the so-called "thousand families
of Iran." Publicity on our program is so poor
that even /Mission7 technicians do not have
information to correct this attitude. I, for
instance, know virtually nothing of what has
been accomplished in other /Mission7 programs. [51]

Job Evaluation

The story of the Mission's financial management and its
difficulties is well publicized elsewhere and need not be
repeated here. [52]   The contention of these documents (i.e.,
the allegations that the Mission had no adequate or accurate
financial reports, a very ineffective budgetary control of its
activities and made virtually no real end-use checks of its
expenditures), however, can be seized upon to explain the
reason for another administrative deficiency: difficulty of
project evaluation.   In the absence of effective budgetary
control, evaluation of projects and programs was very difficult.   And in the absence of job evaluation, duplication
was bound to occur.

Fundamental Education, Community Development and Agricultural Extension were all doing essentially the same thing:
teaching villagers some elementary principles of clean and
comfortable living.   In the opinion of a Mission technician,
much of the work of the engineering staff in Community Development could "under proper cooperative stimulation," be
delegated to the divisions of Public Health, Roads or Education,
thus preventing the encouragement of laxness created by the
existing duplication. [53]   An agricultural extension advisor
echoed the same feeling in his own work: specialists or agents
in the Community Development, he said, were doing exactly
what an extension agent was doing, namely, carrying out
educational programs for rural people. This, to him, seemed
to be "the most cumbersome, overlapping program in the
country." [54]   A rural credit specialist also felt that Community Development was in competition with other divisions
of Point IV, "each going its own direction, each working hard
in its own field, each anxious for special attention for its
accomplishments." [55]   A community development advisor
confided that individual jealousies, friction and personality

conflicts within these divisions influenced their respective programs out of all proportion and made the whole operation anything but continuous.

Duplication of activities and rivalries among technicians seems also to have existed occasionally between the Mission's so-called "direct hires" (i.e., own staff) and the staff of its "contract teams." In the field of public administration, for example, the Mission had a relatively large division of its own as well as two contract teams: A Governmental Affairs Institute team, helping the Plan Organization renovate its administration, and a University of Southern California team, running the Institute of Administrative Affairs at the University of Tehran. In the field of industrial management, too, the Mission had, in addition to its own large division, a contract with George Fry & Associates to reorganize existing public factories, and another agreement with Stanford Research Institute to man and run new government plants under the Second Seven Year Plan. There were other contract teams in several other fields of Mission activities: A Near East Foundation team in community development; a Utah State Agricultural team in the Karaj Agricultural College.

The struggle for recognition among individual technicians of different teams in the same field frequently seemed open and sometimes fierce. And since individuals' loyalties were often primarily to their own institutions, professional jealousies and friction between these teams and the Mission divisions could not, apparently, always be prevented. It was probably in reference to these problems that a specialist, assigned to evaluate the Mission's Community Development program (and the Near East Foundation's role in it) said:

> It is difficult to secure full integration, and Mission teamwork in community development, when the community development advisory services are contracted out to a private agency, no matter how cooperative, well-intentioned and dedicated that agency might be. [56]

The same complaint was echoed by another Mission advisor who found his "greatest single matter of concern and embarrassment" in the "presence, and parallel or contradictory action" of other "well-meaning but uninformed short-tour

American personnel." What was needed in the program was, in his words, "a well-integrated, non-duplicating clearing-house procedure to get the best use out of each individual." [57]

* * *

A special survey made by a U.S. Senate team sums up the discussion of this chapter. According to this survey (1) the program in Iran was spread too thinly over too many projects; (2) a disproportionate number of total Mission personnel were concentrated in the Tehran area; (3) the complex administration and operational systems presented by the Mission were too advanced for the country; and (4) there was much administrative work done by the Mission which could have been performed equally well in Washington. [58]

To what extent these difficulties, inconsistencies and duplications could have been avoided, is hard to know. [59] Many of them were undoubtedly unavoidable. But the curious fact, as a Mission public administration advisor confided, is that, while the Mission was constantly asking the Iranian agencies to put their houses in order along the lines recommended by its administration specialists, it never asked the specialists to put its own organization on an administratively scientific basis. [60]

References

1. See U. S. Aid Operations in Iran, First Report, pp. 15-16.

2. American ambassadors, too, differed in personality and character. One was the prototype of an old-time mission-ary do-gooder; another was a good example of a cunning trouble-shooter; and still another had the manner of a high-handed 19th-century Victorian envoy.

3. R. D. Stickney, CTR, May 6, 1956, p. 2.

4. W. F. Benning, "Industry," in RUSTEAI, n. p.

5. Of the engineering team of the Industry Division, according to one of its Chiefs, "one was a power expert steeped in government-administered activities, the other a proponent of private enterprise," each trying to follow his own intui-tion. See ibid.

6. Letter of Clark S. Gregory to the Regional Director, NEA, Foreign Operations Administration, dated June 9, 1955.

7. H. L. Galt, CTR, November 30, 1957, p. 8.

8. Cf. E. D. Harmon, CTR, January 7, 1960.

9. P. W. Weiser, CTR, December 13, 1958, p. 4.

10. A report of the Near East Foundation team working in Iran under a Mission contract makes the team's loyalty unmistakably clear:

> As we are working for the Iranian government, we must loyally support the Iranians' decisions. The only exception to this is in a case where we believe those decisions are contrary to U. S. Government policy.

See "Near East Foundation Contract," in RUSTEAI, n. p. (Italics not in the original.)

11. R. E. Hensley, CTR, September 21, 1954, p. 8.

12. I. J. Alten, CTR, January 10, 1959, p. 2.

13. Hans Gaidies, CTR, November 4, 1958, p. 2.

14. E. D. Harmon, loc. cit., p. 3.

15. L. B. Williams, CTR, May 19, 1959, p. 3.

16. W. F. Benning, CTR, February 25, 1958, p. 3.

17. W. W. Leake, CTR, April 17, 1956, p. 4.

18. D. K. Brumbaugh, CTR, February 16, 1961, p. 3.

19. H. F. Byrne, CTR, May 19, 1955, p. 3.

20. "History of Personnel Operations," in RUSTEAI.

21. F. M. Richter, CTR, December 30, 1958, p. 2.

22. C. L. Martin, CTR, January 3, 1959, p. 2.

23. This technician's appraisal of his own achievement was a simple admission that his work in Iran happened to be so stimulating that:

> I now want to broaden my background by further academic studies in preparation for future assignments abroad.

See J. T. Hegland, <u>CTR</u>, February 27, 1960, p. 7. (Italics added.)

24. His own evaluation of the results of these assignments was that: the dictionary of business terms that he helped prepare was not published; his recommendations for improvement in auditing practices were not followed; his task was given to George Fry before he was through with his "plan for a comprehensive Controller Division in the Plan Organization"; his work on internal revenue was postponed because it was deemed "politically expedient" by his Division Chief; and his work in the Slaughter House encountered an impasse. See A. A. Gauthier, <u>CTR</u>, October 19, 1956, pp. 1-7.

25. A. K. Garretson, <u>CTR</u>, August 22, 1955, p. 12.

26. J. R. Brown, <u>CTR</u>, August 1, 1955, pp. 8, 11. (Italics not in the original.)

27. See E. F. Vandrell, <u>CTR</u>, October 20, 1960, p. 2.

28. A simple electrician, for example, was reportedly made the head of a labor training branch in which a young Iranian with an advanced degree in labor economics was to be a "trainee."

29. S. da Silva, <u>CTR</u>, August 25, 1956, p. 6.

30. F. A. Jessup, <u>CTR</u>, February 10, 1960, p. 5.

31. G. B. Gregg, <u>CTR</u>, February 9, 1957, p. 2.

32. See "History of Personnel Operations," in <u>RUSTEAL</u>

33. A. D. Swisher, <u>CTR</u>, September 20, 1960, p. 11.

34. A. Des Marais, <u>CTR</u>, April 29, 1957, p. 11. See also George Fry & Assoc., 2nd <u>Quarterly Report</u>, January 1960, p. 3.

35. J. G. Morrill, <u>CTR</u>, September 8, 1956, p. 14.

36. See E. M. Harmon, <u>CTR</u>, May 14, 1959, p. 9, and J. A. Fitz, <u>CTR</u>, August 30, 1960, p. 6.

37. See E. D. Harmon, <u>CTR</u>, January 7, 1960, p. 3.

38. See L. B. Williams, <u>CTR</u>, May 19, 1959, p. 2.

39. See N. A. Pitts, CTR, August 19, 1959, p. 1.

40. L. R. Short, CTR, June 18, 1955, p. 13.

41. See J. O. Stewart, CTR, October 10, 1957, p. 2.

42. As far as he himself was concerned, "every one of his plans was started, but few of them were carried through." See P. W. Weiser, CTR, December 13, 1958, pp. 4-5.

43. See Babolsar Director's "Report" in USOM/I, Monthly Operations Report to Washington, March, 1956, p. 3.

44. See Kermanshah Director's "Report" in USOM/I, Monthly Program Summary for September 1956, (Airgram to FOA/ Washington), p. 4.

45. A. A. Gauthier, CTR, October 19, 1956, p. 7.

46. H. L. Galt, CTR, November 30, 1957, p. 8.

47. D. W. Andreson, CTR, January 23, 1961, p. 11.

48. C. W. King, CTR, April 5, 1960, pp. 1-4.

49. Harlan Cleveland, op. cit., p. 169.

50. J. A. Colman, CTR, July 24, 1961, p. 7.

51. R. P. Loomis, CTR, October 14, 1958, pp. 9-10.

52. In addition to the works previously cited in this study, see the Report of the Staff Survey Team, Subcommittee for Review of the Mutual Security Program, U. S. House of Representatives, Committee on Foreign Affairs, 86th Cong., 2nd Sess. (Washington, 1960), pp. 17-24.

53. H. L. Galt, loc. cit., p. 8.

54. A. N. Renshaw, CTR, October 26, 1955, p. 23.

55. H. C. Rodgers, CTR, August 14, 1956, p. 14.

56. Paul Phillips, CTR, August 8, 1957, p. 4.

57. E. D. McCullough, CTR, June 28, 1961, pp. 6-7.

58. Norman Armour, op. cit., pp. 1219-1220.

59. With regard to the Mission's conspicuously abundant transport facilities, for example, a Mission specialist suggests:

> I believe it was a mistake to assign automobiles to development specialists. They could have done the necessary traveling by using donkeys, bicycles or camels. See O. Nessett, <u>CTR</u>, June 16, 1956, p. 4.

60. For a discussion of similar administrative and organizational problems in other countries, see Loren Tesdell, "The Administration of Technical Assistance in Iraq and Jordon," Ph. D. Dissertation, Stanford University, 1950.

CHAPTER 11

KIND AND
QUALITY OF
ASSISTANTS

The effectiveness of a program of foreign technical assistance is a function not only of the educational background, professional experience, and personal qualifications of its experts, specialists and technicians but also of their additional qualifications for overseas assignment.

Foreign technical assistance, i.e., the imparting of advanced technical skills and know-how is a process of cross-cultural transmission, adoption and adaptation that involves human relations. It only works through people. And it is the qualifications of the people who give and receive technical aid that determine in the last analysis the success of the program. It is foreign technical assistants who, as individual human beings, can discover the host country's problems, devise the necessary program to fill its needs, gain the confidence of the people they work with, give them necessary support and encouragement, and transmit to them their know-how. On the receiving end, too, it is the native technicians -- the counterparts -- as individual human beings who can express their felt needs, show understanding and appreciation of outside efforts, have the wisdom and courage to adopt new techniques, and cooperate with foreign assistants to develop new institutions and attitudes.

At the core of this human problem of technological transfer lies the necessity for aid-givers and receivers alike to understand and appreciate each other's interests, competence and dedication. The ideal effectiveness of foreign technical assistance would be directly related to the mutual understanding between foreign assistants and their counterparts.

ELEMENTS OF EFFECTIVE PERFORMANCE

To insure a maximum of understanding and a minimum of friction between the cooperating parties, technical assistants should possess the particular elements of successful perform- ance generally required for overseas assignments. [1] These elements are discussed here in six distinct but interrelated categories. First, it is technical skill and competence in one's discipline; second, dedication and enthusiasm for one's mission; third, an ability to communicate with people in other countries; fourth, empathy and adaptability to other cultures; fifth, a capacity for leadership and organization in an unfamiliar environment; and sixth, a talent for maneuverability in the face of new impediments. In short, foreign assistants should be endowed with qualities of character, understanding and adapt- ability far beyond what is considered indispensable in their own country. [2]

In order to gain the respect and confidence of the host people, essential to an effective transmission of techniques and/or institutions, technical assistants ought to possess thorough competence in their fields, and be considerably more advanced in their thinking and practice than the average native counterparts. This is particularly imperative in countries with a long cultural heritage and a proud history of scientific or technical achievements of their own.

In order to be able to motivate people in the host country, technical assistants need to have greater enthusiasm for their jobs and profound dedication to their missions. Measuring up just to the call of duty and fulfilling one's assignment responsi- bly but without personal interest will not be enough. The need is for a "missionary" zeal and an eager interest in one's task that can serve as a model in the host country.

In order to convey basic ideas, skills and institutions to the host people across language and cultural barriers, technical assistants need to find a way into the people's minds and hearts in order to be able to communicate with them. Language is only one barrier to overcome, and contrary to what is generally believed, perhaps not the most important one. A reasonable awareness of local problems and a workable knowledge of the country's customs, work habits, and organiza- tions are far more crucial. A knowledgeable, tactful and friend- ly technician who does not know the local language but can easily establish close working relations with local personnel can leave a much longer-lasting impact than a distant, self-centered snob who can outwit the natives in their idioms. Technical assistants, as effective teachers, should have patience because new ideas, skills and techniques take time to be thoroughly absorbed and routinized and cannot always be hurried.

In the absence of an ingrained cultural affinity with local personnel, technical assistants should be capable of putting themselves in the natives' shoes and looking at the problems from the natives' viewpoint.   They should be able to mingle with their counterparts, travel if necessary, and refrain from enjoying privileges too dissimilar to those available to the natives.   They should be tolerant, if not respectful, of harmless native mores.   They should show a cooperating, instead of patronizing, attitude, never condescendent toward the natives.   They should be willing to share responsibility with local counterparts, and if they cannot be completely self-effacing, at least they should let the counterparts take major credit for work accomplishments. Without such cultural empathy and adaptability, no amount of professional competence can quite do the job.

Leadership and organizational ability is needed to get maximum results from the assistance effort.   Teaching a particular discipline well, and demonstrating a particular process accurately are only part of the aid task. The crucial problem is the ability to mobilize local resources -- will, wit, wisdom and all -- in the service of the desired goal. Often enough, all a technical assistant should do is serve as a focal point around which scattered local talent can congregate -- a catalyst that can set dormant forces in motion.

Last, but no less important, technical assistants should possess a special talent for political maneuvering under unfavorable circumstances and in inopportune times.   Good diplomacy in getting one's advice accepted and applied by the recipient is often as important as the advice itself. Technical assistance, in the last analysis, is a process of change, hopefully for the better. And change usually breeds resistance. By crushing the resistance the goal may not always be reached. Frequently, it would be far more advisable to by-pass the stumbling blocks rather than push one's way through them.

Policy-level advisors, by the nature of their assignment, naturally become involved in the internal affairs of the local government.   Their effectiveness, therefore, depends on the people's confidence in their political integrity and professional objectivity.   It is in this rough and tumble that a talent for diplomatic path-finding becomes indispensable.   And, the greater the cultural, economic and political disaffinities between the cooperating parties (discussed in Ch. 9) the more important loom these qualities.

POINT IV ASSISTANTS IN IRAN:
NATURE AND PERFORMANCE

The Iranian socio-economic problems to which mention was made in the preceding chapters, and which needed foreign technical assistance, were of three hierarchical orders. At the surface were the tangible, mechanical problems of operation, e.g., better plowing in agriculture, water purification in health, audio-visual instruction in education, and the like. Underlying these were the less tangible problems of administration and institutional support, e.g., organizational stability, efficiency in recruitment, and proper relationship between authority and responsibility.   And the least tangible of all were the problems of individuals' incentives and attitudes, e.g., the desire for self-development, respect for the law, and co-operation with the government.

For an effective aid to the solution of these problems, Iran needed two types of foreign technical assistants: (1) a few broad-gauged program planners and coordinators to work as general experts at the highest level of government planning and administration; and (2) a larger number of specialist and technicians who could be assigned to various specific projects for a limited time as devisors or advisors. The Point IV program in Iran seems to have sought after both of these categories with some measure of success.   But its success was neither spectacular nor widely appreciated by the host officials.

In the numerous interviews held with the Iranian government officials, the Mission's Iranian staff, local counterparts and independent observers, no other aspect of the Point IV operations came as often or as impassionately under discussion as the qualifications of Mission technicians for their assignments. The general concensus of the interviews was that among Point IV technicians: (1) old and retired officers, or young and brusk upstarts, were in the majority; (2) most of the technicians were unfamiliar with Iranian problems; (3) many were not even as good as their counterparts; and (4) those who were good in their own right generally undertook responsibilities far beyond their personal or professional ability.

As will be shown below, these opinions went somewhat wide of the mark, and were mostly rooted in the lack of mutual understanding discussed in the previous chapters.[3] Most of the Iranians, coming into contact with American assistants for the first time and frequently not being able to communicate with them directly, misunderstood, misjudged and mishandled their foreign advisors. Most of the Americans, too, in foreign assignments for the first time and unaccustomed to their new environments, misunderstood, misjudged and mishandled their counterparts.

Competence and Expertise

In the matter of competence, the reason for the Iranians' adverse opinions about American technicians was not so much the latter's technical qualifications per se as it was unfamiliarity with individual assignments. True enough, some of the assistants may not have been successful even at their home base; but the majority were reasonably versed in their professional fields. What made them less than fully successful in Iran was perhaps the fact that they were frequently too small for the big job, or too big for the small job.

For the tasks at the policy or decision-making levels, i.e., in dealing with touchy problems of socio-political institution-building, the Mission lacked what the natives considered first-rate experts. The tasks of formalized planning, administrative reform, community development and industrial management required experienced and sophisticated experts. Such experts, having established sufficient reputation for themselves, could use their skill, judgment and advice in (a) instilling necessary confidence in the local staff, (b) diagnosing the basic problems mostly by ingenuity and intuition, (c) developing the needed approach to problem-solving, and (d) upgrading the process of decision-making among local authorities.

But, here the Mission had its greatest administrative difficulty: people of this caliber were in limited supply, unwilling to leave their regular jobs in the United States for any length of time, and/or uninterested in overseas assignments at Point IV salaries and employment conditions. With the exception of a few individuals of the required caliber, the majority of the Mission staff consisted of technicians who, in their own milieu and supported by familiar physical and institutional backstopping, could do a good job. But they were almost helpless without those supports: they could not devise new methods of operation or improvise new techniques of management. As specialized technicians, they naturally lacked the broad professional grasp, the mental outlook, the inquisitiveness, and the persuasive powers of experts.

The jobs needing technical assistance at the operational levels (e.g., teaching and demonstration in the techniques of such things as pest control, audio-visual instruction, sanitary engineering, industrial management or labor safety) were also not adequately helped because they did not always lend themselves to the Mission technicians' particular skills and know-how. As mentioned in Chapters 9 and 10, U.S. technicians were either too narrowly specialized to be of optimum use in the local setting, or were only effective in association with special and familiar cooperating factors (e.g., American-made equipment, American supplies and American management). For these reasons they were in many cases no better than, and occasionally even inferior to, local technicians and specialists.

To repeat, the solution to many of the well-known and well-publicized problems of Iranian agriculture, education or health required, in addition to the general knowledge in the field, flexibility, initiative and a wide variety of training and experience. Most of the Mission technicians, however, were too specifically trained to be able (or willing) to deal with existing "elementary" problems (or elementary solutions). To many of these technicians the problems they were asked to solve had only historical relevance: they neither had experienced nor had studied them at home.

Mission technicians were required to make decisions, or to advise, on matters for which they were not adequately prepared -- a fact about which they were often very frank.

They were not experts. What made them so was the fact that they were working in a country other than their own, and with different (or inferior) methods of operation. And often, either out of conviction that the American way was the best way, or because they themselves did not know any other way, they had to rely almost completely on U.S. techniques and methods. The examples used in their teaching were frequently taken from U.S. experiences or textbooks, and totally unknown and incomprehensible to students and trainees in Iran.

One education advisor, for example, was frankly proud of the fact that his "continuous day to day operation had been to express and present American educational techniques and philosophy." [4] Another technician boastfully stated that although modern plumbing was not known in Iran as it was found in the U.S., wherever funds were available, he attempted to install plumbing in the manner in which it is done in the United States. [5]

The difficulty, however, was not limited to the importation of big, fancy and unsuitable machinery discussed here and in Ch. 9. Thinking too big made most of the problems look small and easy for the foreign technicians to solve. And the less familiar the foreign advisor was with the local terrain, the easier the road appeared to him. The following testimony by a Mission assistant is much to the point:

> I sometimes think we are better advised to hitch our wagons to a lamp post rather than to a star. I think we underestimate the problem. We set ourselves goals which are unattainable within the time we have. We fall into the error of thinking that simple technical assistance is sufficient to change patterns of behavior which have cultural roots. [6]

Sometimes, this insufficient appraisal of Iran's problems was due to an insufficient familiarity of the Mission technicians with techniques that were locally-tested and appropriate for local conditions, although totally out-of-place in America. A school construction engineer, for example, discovered that unlike the United States where central heating and air conditioning made the orientation of a building largely inconsequential, Iran

had to pay sufficient heed to proper orientation in order to
protect buildings from the heat of the sun in the hot seasons
and get full benefit of it in the winter. [7]

The general principle for most of the technicians seems
to have been the old adage of "what is good for the goose must
be good for the gander." A community development engineer
confesses this in vivid and unadorned terms:

> At the beginning of my assignment, I found
> that I had to make quite an adjustment from the
> usual type of construction work that I had been
> following, to the type common in this country.
> Such things as Shefteh foundations and brick walls,
> pole and mud roofs, mud and straw plaster, and
> brick arches constructed without supporting
> forms, were things I had never seen or heard of.
> My first reaction was that it all needed changing
> to concrete foundations, hard brick walls, metal
> roofs, wood framing, etc. I was soon informed
> that some of the local type of construction had
> been built for many, many years, that it served
> well the needs of the local people and, of most
> importance, that the cost was very low. [8]

Harlan Cleveland cites the statement of an engineer in a Mission
contract team as follows:

> One trouble with an American when he comes
> here at first and has never had experience in
> this type of construction which is mainly just
> mud, he does not know what to do. The reaction
> is "Why not build something more permanent?"
> But you soon find out that they just cannot afford
> anything else. It is remarkable what they can
> do with what they have got. [9]

The fact that the American techniques were not the
ideal type for Iran or could not be easily communicated is

evidenced by the experiences and observations of another Mission advisor:

> Most Americans are presenting technical ideas that even other Americans are unable to understand unless they have a similar background and training. This technical information is furthermore presented to a translator who lacks the necessary background and training, and who is supposed to express the message in a language that does not even include many of the words necessary to express the thought. [10]

It was perhaps due to such complications that the recommendations made by a telecommunication specialist, a nursing-education advisor and a customs regulations technician were, to their great dismay and disappointment, not adopted by the Iranian agencies. [11]   These and many other such recommendations were basic and useful in an American setting but were perhaps void of applicability in Iran because they were made mostly out of an Iranian context.

On the whole, for the small engineering problems, at the village level, U.S. technicians were too refined and too precious: they found their jobs too trivial, boring and inconsequential.   Writes a community development organizer:

> I was directed in my thinking of the application of engineering to Iranian agriculture to forget about engineering as we think of it in the States [and look] to somthing very basic and very elementary. At the risk of deprecating my capacity as a professional engineer, for this job, I will say that what seemed needed was some sort of an experienced and proven ingenue (sic) to make the most of little [or] nothing. [12]

For many of these jobs, local technicians were more adaptable and even more knowledgeable, as acknowledged by other specialists in the same field. Pondering the depth of the advice

by a colleague who told him to forget all he knows when he
goes on an overseas assignment, one of the specialists
says:

> Perhaps it was his way of cutting me down to
> a more humble approach to the job in hand, to
> shed my seven league boots and walk in the foot-
> steps of my counterpart for a bit. [13]

The belief in the absolute superiority of American institutions, techniques and tools which a Division Chief considers
"overconfidence in the American wisdom," was, in his
opinion, one of the worst stumbling blocks in the implementation of the program. Says he:

> We Americans too frequently believe that our
> way of life can quickly be imposed on foreign
> people when we ourselves are most reluctant to
> accept new ways, be it even a different brand of
> coffee or cigarettes. [14]

Although often disturbed and occasionally jolted by the Iranian
experience, the belief in American omniscience was for some
technicians never really shaken.

As a Provincial Director summed it up, his and his
colleagues' difficulties were mostly due to the novelty of
the experience:

> We Americans out here are amateurs, rank
> amateurs. No one has ever done this sort of
> thing before in this way or on this scale of
> magnitude. [15]

Indications of the advisors' deficiencies in professional
qualifications may be found in the quality of their completion-
of-tour reports, and their own evaluation of their usefulness
in their assigned tasks. The extent of perception, clarity of
organization and profoundity of recommendations in these
reports can serve as a measure of their authors' diagnostic
ability, analytical capacity and expertise in finding appropriate
solutions. The annals of their accomplishments can attest
to the degree of their success.

Of the 450 reports available in the Mission files that were reviewed by the author, the majority varied in both size and content. In form, there were reports of only one or two mimeographed pages; and there were some over fifty, with the majority between five and fifteen pages. In content, they ranged from a travelog-like, letter-to-an-aunt variety, to something worthy of publication in a professional journal. The majority, however, dealt with a description of the existing situations. Well over half of these reports were no more than an abstract collection of generalities, trite euphemisms, or familiar stories. Many seemed more concerned with justifying the raison d'etre of the reporter rather than his findings and recommendations. Some were simply self-glorifying reports, critical both of the projects' previous accomplishments and the chance of its future success without the reporter. With the notable exception of a few, they seemed to show an amazing lack of concern with the significance of the reporter's contribution in the totality of the assistance effort.

The most striking feature of most of these reports was their conspicuous simplicity in diagnosing the problems involved or deeper understanding of the solutions required. An auditing specialist's report to the Ministry of Finance, for example, contained two recommendations for urgent action, one requiring that immediate steps should be taken to secure full administrative discipline in the Ministry, and the other asking for a current copy of laws, regulations and procedures to be furnished to every employee concerned. [16] A sanitary engineer's account of his "contributions" to the Iranian economy lists the following: (1) convincing the engineering staff that a water supply is a public health responsibility; (2) making an effort to have regular staff meetings which resulted in one such meeting being held in his two year tour of duty; (3) giving his counterpart more confidence in himself; (4) preparing or having several "papers translated"; and (5) making many good friends and contributing to better under-standing between his country and theirs. [17]

A public health physician's conclusion was that Iran "can make no really lasting progress until she has a literate population and is able to train her own personnel to meet her own needs in her own institutions and with her own facilities." [18] An agricultural technician found it difficult to set "definite milestones" on the progress made but was sure

that the people of Iran were receiving "lasting benefits" from
his services and a majority of them appreciated the work of
Point IV personnel. [19]

A home economics extension advisor found the Iranian
village problems to be: "poor nutrition, low home-food production, poor sanitary conditions, low incomes, poor health, insufficient clothing, inadequate housing." The objectives of the
project entrusted to this advisor were in her words "better
farm and home living, a balanced diet, conservation of natural
resources and raising the standard of living through better
nutrition, sanitation, income, clothing and housing." The
difficulties the advisor foresaw in achieving these objectives
were "illiteracy, taboos against women living or traveling
alone, religious beliefs, lack of good translators, lack of
cooperation among ministries." The advisor's recommendation was to remove these difficulties in order to reach the
goals. [20]

A public administration consultant concluded his report
by saying:

> After nearly two years' experience it is the
> consultant's opinion that in spite of . . . the Min-
> istry of Interior's highly political complexion,
> more acceptable performances may be expected
> in the future from the Ministry if modern systems
> of management are installed and an organization
> to provide sound information on which to base
> sound decision is established. [21]

A water resources specialist whose 36-page report started
with a 4-page history of Iran since the year 2000 B.C., and a
5-page history of water development in the last 1700 years,
had only one page of conclusions and recommendations, the
gist of which was that (1) the Irrigation Bongah was seriously
handicapped by lack of well-trained personnel; (2) existing
irrigation projects were handicapped by inadequate planning
and programming; (3) no new projects should be started; and
(4) the Division should be channeled into proper planning and
training of Iranian engineers along the lines of a Bureau of
Reclamation planning office. [22]

A trade and investment officer's one-year tour report was only 3 pages long, and its essence was that (1) considerable suspicion of foreign private capital existed in Iran, (2) the Iranian law to encourage foreign investment was not adequate, and (3) the establishment of a special private credit institution (not detailed) was needed. [23]

Of a customs advisor's report whose contribution was apparently not clear even to the Mission, the Mission Director said:

> As [the report] lacks discussion of problems and difficulties encountered in the course of the author's work, so it also fails to reflect adequately the contributions made by him in his assigned areas. [24]

The chronicles of technicians' achievements contained in some of these reports are also interesting. One technician's tour of duty was spent on the "preliminary" proposal for "several major development programs" but nothing came of them due to the shortage of planning engineers and lack of funds. [25] An agricultural economic advisor who first served in the Industry Division proposed a training program in this field for the Ministry of Agriculture employees but "after two postponements of the initial phase of the training course," his tour of duty expired and he departed for the United States. [26] An electrical power specialist reports that at the end of his first year in Iran, accomplishment on a nationwide basis stood in the position of a signed contract to supply 50,000 KW of steam power for Tehran and an incipient program for a nationwide survey of power used which was never made because ICA withdrew its support. [27] A planning and design specialist admits that during his tour of duty no major area-planning projects were undertaken. [28] A telecommunication advisor was "painfully aware" of the fact that the Ministry's improvements during his tour of duty were "pitifully small." [29] A procurement specialist who "strongly" recommended that his project be continued had nothing to say about his accomplishments except that "he enjoyed the full cooperation" of the local agencies involved. [30]

Interest and Dedication

In the opinion of an American missionary living in Iran, the Mission staff consisted mostly of "a new brand of career bureaucrats interested in vacations, home leave, comfortable cars, and big offices--the type of things that in his opinion are tolerable in Washington, but not in the host country." Too many technicians, in his view, kept staying on the job for which they had no competence, interest, or enthusiasm.

Views such as these were not widely shared by other Americans living and working in Iran, but they fell on sympathetic ears among the Iranians. The fact of the matter, however, was that many of the Mission's advisors had an unusual yearning for service, and some of them accomplished their tasks far beyond the call of duty. This was particularly true in the first formative year when the Mission staff consisted of a few individuals of strong religious convictions and almost a zeal for proselytizing their sectarian belief through good work. During the turbulent Mossadegh era, too, when the Mission acted both as the guardian angel of the American educated Iranians and the grand savior of the Iranian economy, a group of earnest and hard-hitting enthusiasts ran the Mission's headquarters and provincial offices.

At the time of the Point IV enunciation and the almost missionary enthusiasm that immediately followed, many dedicated Americans volunteered for Point IV missions. As the program's purpose, orientation and leadership became increasingly political, however, more and more of the early enthusiasts shied away, and more and more mundane groups were attracted. As Point IV missions expanded in number and size not only in Iran but all over the world, too, the drain on personnel became acute and the spiritual character of the early staff began to change. More and more earthly pleasure-seekers or escape-finders started to join.

In its full complement the Mission had many assistants with personal dedication, professional interest, intellectual curiosity, and ideological convictions; but there were also others who were motivated by the lure of greater material rewards, attraction of superior executive or advisory positions, excitement of new adventures, and the possibility of establishing a new career.

Personal Rapport

Establishing close rapport with native personnel was another problem for the Mission staff. The mistrust of the program's goals on the Iranian side, and cultural differences between the two nations dampened local confidence in the objectivity of foreign advice and foreign advisors.

American advisors were not accepted or judged independently of their allegiance to an admittedly cold-war agency of a Great Power. Whatever counsel they offered was often appraised by the skeptics in the shadow of a "there-must-be-an-ulterior-motive" suspicion. Sometimes the alleged motives were real, but often purely fancied. And the more fancied the motives, the less were the chances of success from close association with the U.S. government. Advice and order from the Mission's "contract teams" seemed much better tolerated than similar counsels or commands from the Mission's "direct hires." And, the recommendations of international teams not connected with any Big Power enjoyed even better reception.

There was also the problem of manners and morals. Some Iranian officials, particularly the European-educated among them, found their American counterparts, except for a few notable exceptions, no match for them in urbanity, blandness or sophistication. The American informality of manner (e.g., allowing technicians to wear sport shirts in the office, to chew gum or put their feet on the desk while talking to ranking government officials) was partly responsible for the Iranians' reaction. But part of the difficulty was also due to the modest, rural, or small-town backgrounds of some of the technicians, making them look insufficiently suave for the intricate formalities of the Iranian bureaucratic establishment.

The problem also was complicated by the considerable unfamiliarity of Mission advisors with the Iranian traditions, customs, and social relationships. With the exception of a few, Mission technicians were unacquainted with local conditions at the time of their arrival in Iran. Hired directly from the U.S. labor markets or transferred from other overseas assignments, most of the advisors had no previous preparation save a short orientation course in Washington for living and working under Iranian conditions. A provincial officer's account of his experience offers an interesting testimony:

> Upon our arrival, my wife and I were introduced to [the] personnel officer whose greeting to us was, "Just the people we have been waiting for

to go to Ahwaz.'' It took us a few days of research
and inquiry to find out about Ahwaz and the results
were not encouraging. [31]

To another technician, even most diligent reading of the
"post report," the few books on Iran borrowed from the Pen-
tagon's library, and quizzing of good friends who had been
there failed to uncover what he felt was a dependable picture
of Iran "de jure." [32]   A labor training advisor lamented that
at the time of his arrival he was "without pertinent knowledge"
of the actual social conditions of life and industrial work in
Iran. [33]   A public health nurse whose four-page report was
regarded by the Director as "succinct and unembellished",
acknowledged the fact that her nonfamiliarity with local
customs often required "longer planning or complete change
of programs proposed." [34]

Language was also a problem. With the exception of the
American-educated staff, the majority of government officials,
participating teams and local technicians were not fluently
conversant in English and could not communicate directly
with Mission advisors. Thus, from the start and for the most
elementary discourses most of the Iranian professional counterparts were in need of English translators and interpreters.
But English not being a commonly used language in Iran until
World War II, neither the Iranian government nor the Mission
could find enough competent translators and interpreters.
Most of those who applied and were hired as such were poor
substitutes. Often not knowing the language well enough, and
almost invariably ill-versed in the technical jargon, these
interpreters had to embellish the translations on their own, or
make short sentences out of complicated statements, as their
knowledge and the occasion permitted. The situation was
particularly grave in the case of demonstrations and teaching
of technical subjects where there were no corresponding or
close expressions in Persian, or none that the poor interpreters could find.

If only a few Iranian government officials knew English
well enough to converse with Mission advisors, fewer in the
Mission staff knew Persian to fill the gap. Except for a few
"old hands" among the Mission staff, none knew French or
German proficiently enough to communicate with European-
educated Iranians. The slight language familiarity that the

counterparts acquired by association with American advisors, and what the advisors learned in their Farsi classes, was not sufficient to let them converse in the highly technical language of modern technology.

The transmission of skills and know-how was thus handicapped from the start not only by the lack of a common language but by the difficulty of translation. This was true just as much in teaching industrial mechanics (where there was a lack of standardization for technical terminology relating to equipment and parts of a machine) [35] as in teaching public administration for which there was no literature in Persian. [36]

Adaptability

The adaptability to local circumstances of the Mission personnel was not particularly smooth or painless. Coming in most cases directly from the United States, and having little or no overseas "hardship" experience, too many Mission advisors found living and working in Iran unusually hard. Of those who chose to finish their tour of duty, despite themselves or because they found the discomforts compensated by other satisfying factors, not all could aspire to achieve "reasonably perfect" adjustment. The majority had a hard time putting themselves in the natives' shoes; nor could they succeed in appreciating local customs.

Spiritually, the adaptation to local conditions for the majority of Mission technicians was hampered by virtue of their strong convictions about American values and ideals. Brought up in a dynamic culture whose "bulldozer techniques" emphasized action, speed and concrete results, they could not adapt to a slower tempo of life or appreciate values that were vastly different from theirs. As a consequence, many were shocked into a philosophical tolerance of native values or else into their total rejection. The majority who were philosophically resigned to their assignments chose a "live and let live" policy of least involvement, operating within the framework of certain pre-conceived ideas about life and work in Iran. The more resigned an advisor was, the more he tended toward a sort of mental ossification, willing to accept cultural clichés, half-truths, and innuendos about Iran.

The importance of personal relationships in getting things done, for instance, was interpreted by some Mission staff as giving favors (e.g., positions, fellowship grants, demonstration equipment) to a small minority of influential Iranian officials or their protégés. Similarly, having accepted the cliché about the Iranian love of flattery (and their dislike of open, direct and straightforward dealings) some Mission assistants indulged in accepting compliments from shrewd Iranians to the point of gradually becoming duped by them. Or, they put themselves so much on guard against accepting what was open, direct and straightforward that they became incredulous of everything where the catch was not apparent.

The technicians who were successful in their work in Iran and left a favorable personal and professional impact on the country were those who could strike a balance between the clichés they were led to believe and their better analytical judgement. But not everybody could succeed. Many seemed to agree with one of their colleagues that an adaptability to the local situation was not only unnecessary, but perhaps also harmful. Commented a Mission specialist:

> Getting to know the Iranian in correcting difficulties is another matter of conjecture. It is felt by this individual that to become familiar is to fall into the inertia of Iranian thinking and thereby lose his American identity and become a non-entity. [37]

There were others in the Mission also whose tactless criticisms of Iran and its people, and their open disregard of Iranian sensitivities, left an indelible black mark in the annals of the Mission operations. [38]

Materially, it was even harder for the Mission technicians to adjust to the exacting discomforts of the Iranian life. In spite of Washington's admonitions, and occasional attempts by some of the technicians to live as the natives did, the difference between the level of living enjoyed by the Mission staff and that of their native counterparts was embarrassingly conspicuous. Mission salaries and living allowances were invariably more and generally two to three times higher than the native counterpart's. Mission technicians lived in some of the best available quarters in Iran, enjoyed entertainment facilities exclusively provided for them, and had extensive import privileges not available to the native personnel. Although this mode of living still perhaps left some of the uniquely American conveniences (ball games, favorite TV shows, family physician, and shopping centers) out of their reach, there were additional compensations (large quarters, servants, travel, parties) not generally available to them in the United States.

Whether or not these gains were any match for the losses they suffered is a matter of personal judgment. The fact remained, however, that to the natives the Mission technician's life looked far more lavish than was expected of them under the circumstances. As a member of one of the Mission's contract teams explained it, it was virtually impossible for him, even without ostentatious display, to live the way the Iranians did. In one of his annual vacation trips, he admitted to have spent upward of $2,000. This may not be a particularly large sum by the United States standards, but it was a year's salary for most of the people who worked with him. Two other young assistants in his team, living together in a fine residence, had a cook, a butler, a maid and a driver-- privileges available only to the highest and the most independently wealthy government officials in Iran. Sometimes the facilities available to the American clerks and secretaries were more elaborate than the Iranian professional personnel could hope for.

Where the Mission assistants were competent, dedicated and likeable, their lavish level of living was only envied by their counterparts. But where they lacked the necessary qualifications, these priviledges were resented and the effectiveness of their assistance was correspondingly minimized. The resentment was particularly noticeable in the case of those technicians who were most obviously of an inferior quality and still could not put up with the slightest inconveniences in their daily living. [39]

Many of the troubles, frustrations, and shocks of the Mission technicians or their families resulting from uncomfortable or unsafe living quarters, the dirty and unkempt surroundings, polluted water, and the absence of household appliances [40] were conditions not exclusively Iranian, and largely predictable before the technicians set out for their overseas assignments. Yet, of the Mission technicians sent to

Iran, according to Harlan Cleveland, "about 25 families a year
or about two a month, were being sent home for reasons
ranging from the wife's morale to the husband's morals, from
the health of a child to the frustration of his father in trying to
'get things done' in an unfamiliar environment." [41]

Leadership Quality

For most of the Mission porjects, such things as the
approval of the Joint-Commission, the green light from Washington, and the accompanying facilities were relatively easier
to obtain. The catch was the advisor's ability for organization
and leadership. As a Mission technician was quick to realize,
the importance of organizational ability was no less that that of
technical competence:

> I soon found out, that teaching forestry and
> techniques was just a small part of the job. The
> difficult job was teaching good work habits,
> decision making . . . and the appreciation of
> absolute accuracy and integrity. [42]

Another observing technician, a regional sanitary engineer,
came to the conclusion that sanitary engineering in Iran was
more a human relations problem than technical because as long
as conditions of attitude and environment "were not ripe for
accepting a new sanitary practices, they would surely fail to
take root." [43]

For doing their jobs well, U.S. technicians thus needed
much more than purely professional competence; they had to
have an ability (a) to convince their counterparts and trainees
of the necessity for change; (b) get them motivated enough to
want to accept change; (c) help them individually and as a group
to institute necessary adjustments; and (d) organize their efforts
through proper channels to obtain results. In this process the
technician needed not only the persuasive power and convincing
dedication of a gospel preacher, but also the smooth maneuvering of a shrewd administrator. Without these qualities, the
technician's recommendations, no matter how sound they were,
could soon be shelved and forgotten.

Most of the advice and recommendations that Iran received
from its previous foreign advisors was never put to use,

partly because the latter did not know how to get those recommendations accepted and implemented.   The Mission was
no exception. Cites a port administration advisor:

> Too often, projects and programs have with-
> ered for lack of acceptance and follow through
> on the part of local management. . . Most often
> this can be attributed to the reactions to advice
> of men not educated to the broad-gauge level,
> no matter how well they may be trained tech-
> nically. [44]

Statesmanship

The same difficulty existed when technicians lacked what.
Cleveland calls a "sense of politics," i.e., an ability to re-
concile their inner feelings and ideals with the political
requirements of their assignments.   Some of the Mission's
non-career personnel were not only weary of many Iranian
administrative procedures and social practices, but so bluntly
critical of them as to minimize their own effectiveness and
embarrass the Mission administration. The case of a Mission
vocational educationist is one in point. Explaining the reasons
for his lack of accomplishment in the fields of administration
and supervision, he complains:

> Where incompetent political favorites domi-
> nate over practical judgment, it is extremely
> difficult for an advisor to overcome the resulting
> effects. [45]

In this tactless judgment, and in thinking that foreign
technical assistance can be offered in a political vacuum
or in an antiseptic environment, this technician was not
alone.   Due to a lack of proper orientation, many other
Mission advisors, wanting to teach people to do things the
right way (i.e., the American way), were tactless in pointing
out the wrong ways. In many cases, the advisor seemed to
deal with his counterpart (whether he was a mayor or a public
company manager or a department head) in a condescending,
patronizing manner.   "I am going to make a better man out of
you," he would say, or act as though he were saying the same.

In other cases, the advisors shied away from anything
that might be construed as interfering with their counterparts'

wishes and methods of operation. They were simply content to go through the formalized motions of presenting their reports without bothering about the necessary informal, personal prodding and arm-twisting that were required to get action. Consequently, some of the reports were received with rousing cheers but were duly shelved after an empty gesture.

OVER-ALL SUITABILITY

How many of the Mission technicians were suitable for their work in Iran, and in which of these categories they scored high, it is not easy to know. The majority of the Iranian officials and technicians interviewed firmly believed that very few of them, i.e., certainly not more than 25% and perhaps about 20%, were useful to Iran. Some put the figure as low as 5%. Their reason for finding such a high percentage of the Mission advisors ineffective was that the majority of Mission technicians were not able to find solutions for Iranian problems within the Iranian context.

A similar response was obtained by analyzing the results of another study, designed to find out from a group of Iranian counterparts and associates of American technicians what particular qualifications they thought a good foreign technical assistant ought to have. Seventy-five percent of the answers emphasized communicability, knowledge of history, customs, tradition, and preferably the language of the host country. The same number of answers called attention to cultural adaptability, particularly a tolerance of native mores. Sixty-five percent of the answers stressed thorough competence (including professional flexibility for devising compromise techniques). Thirty percent indicated diplomacy in selling one's ideas. Twenty percent pointed out dedication. And ten percent mentioned organizational ability.

Although the study was not intended to probe the interviewees' evaluation of the Mission technicians, their general attitude toward foreign technical assistance and the ranking of answers with heavy emphasis on competence and awareness of local problems may indicate the technicians' relatively heavier deficiencies on these scores. [46]

* * *

The substance of the interviewees' evaluation and the conclusions of this chapter are summed up by one of the Mission's own keener analysts.   In his opinion, American advisors go to foreign countries with technical competence, savoir-faire in U.S. techniques of administration, and impatience for success, but they never reach their maximum effectiveness because of a lack of orientation in the customs, administration and values of other countries, deficiency in foreign languages, and local resistance to their ideas due to their lack of understanding or lack of salesmanship.   He continues:

> We U.S. AID technicians tend to be generally lacking in the skills necessary to (1) identify the source or cause of resistance to apparently sound ideas, and (2) be effective and persuasive salesmen of our "technical service wares." Without these skills, our technical competence and experience are rendered useless. [47]

References

1. See Harlan Cleveland, The Overseas Americans, Part III; and John Ohly, A Proposed Outline for the Study of Technical Assistance to Less Developed Countries(Washington: ICA, 1960).

2. See D. H. Blelloch, "Export of Technology and the Clash of Cultures, " in Yearbook of Education, 1954.

3. See particularly Ch. 9.

4. D. K. Brumbaugh, CTR, February 16, 1961, p. 6. (Italics added.)

5. R. V. Bernhart, CTR, July, 1954, p. 3. (Italics not in the original.) See also supra, Ch. 9, Notes 19 and 20.

6. F. E. Furguson, CTR, June 17, 1957, p. 5. For a discussion of similar underestimations of the problems involved, See R. A. Moore, CTR, July 16, 1956, pp. 2-3.

7. L. J. Deming, CTR, December 4, 1954, p. 12. Another construction engineer admits that after two years in Iran, he could not say he knew Iranian materials of construction. See W. H. Sletten, CTR, May 8, 1956, p. 7.

8. D. R. Cannon, CTR, July 17, 1956, p. 2.

9. Harlan Cleveland, loc. cit., p. 130. (Italics added.)

10. R. E. Fort, CTR, August 25, 1956, p. 7.

11. See the Completion-of-Tour Report of C. A. Baillet, April 26, 1960; M. G. Chapus, August 1, 1957; and W. Shaw, September 17, 1960.

12. W. H. Sletten, loc. cit., p. 4.

13. B. B. Eddy, CTR, November 10, 1956, p. 3. The ingenuity of local workers admittedly sometimes really amazed the Mission technicians. See I. H. Helander, CTR, January 23, 1956, p. 2; and A. E. Thurston, CTR, March 31, 1955, p. 6.

14. W. F. Benning, CTR, February 25, 1958, p. 3.

15. E. D. Conroy, CTR, June 10, 1954, p. 4.

16. See S. H. Conover, CTR, August 8, 1956, p. 6. (Italics added.)

17. C. F. Bain, CTR, September 24, 1960, pp. 7-8. Of this technicians's accomplishments cited above verbatim, the Mission Director admitted they were not "spectacular."

18. G. G. Browning, CTR, June 5, 1957, p. 5.

19. B. R. Gardner, CTR, November 13, 1956, p. 14.

20. A. E. Smith, CTR, January 30, 1960, pp. 2, 4. (Italics added.)

21. J. P. Thew, CTR, April 24, 1958, p. 5. (Italics not in the original.)

22. W. E. Wheeler, CTR, June 13, 1954, p. 36.

23. R. D. Stickney, CTR, September 19, 1957, pp. 2-3.

24. William Shaw, CTR, September 17, 1960, p. 1.

25. H. F. Tolley, CTR, May 14, 1956, p. 2.

26. D. W. Hubbard, CTR, September 13, 1956, p. 3.

27. John Howard, CTR, July 11, 1956, p. 5.

28. C. C. Hampshire, <u>CTR</u>, November 16, 1955, p. 2.

29. Norman Snyder, <u>CTR</u>, July 2, 1959, p. 9.

30. D. H. Eldridge, <u>CTR</u>, June 26, 1956, p. 6.

31. J. L. Rei, <u>CTR</u>, May 25, 1955, p. 2.

32. B. B. Eddy, <u>CTR</u>, November 10, 1956, p. 2.

33. Hans Gaidies, <u>CTR</u>, November 4, 1958, p. 2.

34. H. H. Castro, <u>CTR</u>, September 22, 1960, p. 3. Some of the Mission technicians seemed unacquainted even with standard works and publications on Iran. An education advisor, for example, who consulted the author in 1955 about the possibility of organizing an American university task force to study Iranian educational problems was totally unaware of the extensive and penetrating study of the subject published by the Overseas Consultants, Inc., as far back as 1949.

35. See R. E. Cox, <u>CTR</u>, January 16, 1956, p. 4.

36. The apparent helplessness of some Mission technicians in the face of the language barrier is indicated by the somewhat amusing statement of a Mission engineer:

> Any document in Farsi, when one is not familiar with the written language, may serve as an engineering degree; it may even be translated as such, if the occasion warrants it. This is mentioned to show the complete dependence of American technicians upon Iranian personnel.

See L. J. Deming, <u>CTR</u>, December 4, 1954, p. 10.

37. W. H. Sletten, <u>CTR</u>, May 8, 1958, p. 5. The ironic fact is that the Mission's Acting Director submitting this technician's report to Washington praised it as one that could provide "good orientation material" for field workers arriving in Iran in the future.

38. A Mission technician, for example, begins his completion-of-tour report by saying:

> To a land of poverty, starvation, confusion and inaction Mr. and Mrs. M. J. Regan arrived May 16, 1953.

See M. J. Regan, <u>CTR</u>, April 21, 1955, p. 2.

39. Some of the examples cited by the Iranians who talked to the author ranged from a nurse who was raging mad because it took three days for her house radio to be fixed, to a technician who volunteered for travels in the country where the per diem was significant but could not stand the lack of western-style toilet facilities.

40. Cf. Harlan Cleveland, op. cit. , pp. 47-49.

41. Ibid. , p. 169.

42. A. B. Williams, CTR, November 21, 1960, p. 3.

43. S. W. Brandon, CTR, April(?) 1954, p. 2. (Italics added.)

44. Sterling St. John, CTR, April 21, 1960, p. 13.

45. E. F. Vandrell, CTR, October 20, 1960, p. 10.

46. The interviews were conducted by Mr. M. Soraya on behalf of Dr. Wayne Unterriner.

47. T. J. Edwards, CTR, July 25, 1963, pp. 8-10.

PART V

THE AFTERMATH

CHAPTER 12
ASSIMILATION OF ASSISTANCE

The success of a program of foreign technical assistance in the last analysis depends upon the ultimate integration of its activities in the host country's developmental programs; and this depends on the integrability of its approach, techniques and methods in the local environment.

The ultimate assimilation of foreign techniques and institutions into the country's order of operation is indeed indispensable for the routinized performance and organic growth of aided projects. A successful program of foreign assistance in any field of endeavor, or at any level of operation, is certainly a program which leads to its own gradual termination in that field or at that level. [1] The noblest charity, it is said, is to prevent a man from accepting charity, and the best alms are those that enable a man to dispense with alms.

To meet the criterion of integrability, a program of foreign technical assistance (in any aspect of economic growth, through any process of implementation, and at any level of operation [2]) should be so suitable to local conditions as to give a promise of ultimate absorption into the country's own development efforts without further foreign stimulation, support, or subjugation. Since the aid needed in each aspect, process, and level of technical cooperation is different in every case, the total composition of foreign technical assistance should be especially tailored to suit local exigencies. This composition or composite of aid will be discussed in a later section under strategy and tactics of assistance. Strategy involves such considerations as the level and direction of aid; tactics involve specific techniques and methods of implementation.

THE ADVENT OF INTEGRATION

Both the intention of Point IV, and the desire of the Iranian government from the beginning of the program was to have Point IV activities assimilated into the Iranian development agencies in due time. But no one, in or out of the Mission, had ventured to suggest when the due time would be for such an assimilation. Consequently when the Mission, early in 1956, decided to integrate its activities into the Iranian agencies most everyone was surprised.

The Mission's official explanation of the "integration" decision was simple, and brief. It contended that the aim of Point IV operations had always been to have its personnel act in an advisory capacity and not to assume administrative responsibility. The existence of certain emergency and unusual conditions in Iran, the argument continued, made it necessary for the Mission to try to obtain "relatively quick impact" from Point IV activities. And this, in turn, required centralized operation within the Point IV organization. Later on, when the unusual conditions largely disappeared, the integration of projects and trained personnel into the related agencies of the Iranian government became necessary and had to be put into effect without further delay.

The skeptics had a different explanation. Since the "integration" decision came shortly after an investigation of the Iranian aid operations by the House Government Operations Committee (which put the Mission under heavy fire for irregularities in handling U.S. funds and property), they argued that the Mission's decision was an obvious attempt to avoid the blame for similar difficulties in the future and to absolve itself from further embarrassments for its past performance.

Whatever the real reason was, the fact of the matter is that there was no concensus on the timeliness of the integration decision. A special study of U.S. aid to Iran at the time had this to say:

> Today in Iran, "integration" is taking place; that is to say, United States aid projects are being turned over to Iranian ministries, with United States personnel playing only an advisory role. Certainly in the long run, integration should take place. But I am inclined to feel that it should not

be pressed too rapidly; that it is doubtful whether, in many instances, the Iranian personnel are really ready to take over. In some instances, we found that where integration had already occurred, the Americans were by necessity still, in effect, directing and not just advising. [3]

As it seems now, there was a good deal of merit in this skepticism. The obstacles to even a partial integration of the Mission activities into Iran's own program of socio-economic development were not at the time few or far between. The basic developmental needs that were originally pivotal in the establishment of the Point IV organization in Iran had not yet been fully met. If the Iranians were not able to carry out their economic development program without Point IV administration during the early years of the 1950's, there was no reason to believe that they were suddenly prepared to do so in the middle of 1956. Over two-thirds of the projects undertaken by the Mission had not yet been completed; some of them had just started; and a few were still in the stage of planning and preparation. There hardly seemed any technical or economic reason for an immediate transfer of these projects to the Iranian administration.

Still further, the gulf that existed between the Mission's administrative system and that of the Iranian government in wage and salary levels, personnel regulations, accounting and auditing procedures, and the whole concept of management did not allow for an easy integration without new arrangements. In view of the Iranian government's financial conditions still scarred by the cessation of oil revenues between 1951 and 1954, it was virtually impossible for the Point IV program to be financed entirely by Iran. At any rate, the take-over of the program by the Iranian government required at least a "phasing out" period which had not been sufficiently worked out.

The timing of the integration process was apparently subject to disagreement among the Mission officials themselves. A Deputy Director, voicing the minority opinion, believed that integration should have come much earlier and without allowing such a long separation of the Point IV organization from the Iranian agencies. A Division Chief, on the other hand, had the feeling that the move was utterly premature, and that the Iranian agencies were not at all prepared to take over the

program.   In his opinion, the new concepts of the program
had not yet taken root; not enough people were convinced of
the advantages of new techniques; and the atmosphere was
not sufficiently changed.

Those in the Mission who would have favored an earlier
integration believed that the reason their colleagues did not
approve of their idea was because execution is invariably
more comfortable than giving advice.   Those who would have
delayed integration, on the other hand, attributed this rationali-
zation to "sheer politics" and saw no technical or professional
necessity for such a move at the time.   Almost everybody
seemed to agree, however, that integration took place at an
inopportune time; to some it was too soon; to others, not
soon enough.

POST-INTEGRATION DELUGE

Scattered "proofs" of the untimeliness of integration in
1956 can be found in the operational difficulties reported by
the Mission staff in subsequent months.   Judging from the
experience of a sanitary engineering advisor, the feeling of
dependency of the Iranian officials upon the new American
"advisors" (and their former executive colleagues or co-
directors) was not changed by a change in name.   The advisor
apparently was still exposed to a great deal of pressure from
the Iranian directors to use his influence in short-circuiting
administrative channels to expedite requisitions, promotions,
and other agency affairs. [4]

A labor training advisor felt that there was a reluctance
to accept technical assistance now that it was not backed up
by material and moral support as in the pre-integration period.
Obviously lamenting his loss of authority, he deplored the fact
his advice was judged not only by what it would do for the
country, but scrutinized in regard to its political implications,
making technical assistance very difficult for him. [5]

A public health physician, who believed that almost all
technicians would have delayed integration until the Iranian
administrative machinery was clearly ready for it, [6] spurned
the administrators' decision in favor of integration on the ground
that the Iranian "concept of face" was against the admission that
any advice was needed, and therefore no advice could effectively
be given.

The <u>administrative</u> differences between the two systems that stood in the way of smooth integration are exemplified in a report by an industrial engineering advisor:

> The efficiency of my office was greatly impaired when I was integrated with the textile division of the Plan Organization. Due to low salaries paid to Iranian clerks and typists, it /was/ impossible to employ qualified bilingual office personnel. The short weekly work period (35 hrs.) further handicaps the technicians, and work which at its best /was/ very slow, /was/ further retarded. [7]

Typical perhaps of the <u>procedural</u> difficulties encountered in the continued implementation of projects after integration is the report of an agriculture advisor who was charged with the responsibility of assisting the transfer of agricultural equipment and commodities from the Mission to the Ministry of Agriculture:

> Ministry of Agriculture officials were never before confronted with the handling of commodities in such quantities and were not prepared to receive same. There was and remains still a lack of strong procedural methods to ensure smooth operation. When transfer of property is completed, much additional assistance and guidance will have to be extended to the Ministry of Agriculture to assure proper handling and final end-use of the property turned over. [8]

Indicative of the <u>budgetary</u> difficulties faced after integration are the reports of several Mission advisors, complaining about lack of funds for project operations, delays in the payment of employee salaries, lack of means of transportation, and altogether a prolonged period of budget starvation. [9]

Symptomatic of the Mission difficulties in the <u>follow-up</u> operations is a report of another Mission assistant. Although his observations relate to only one field and only one <u>Ostan,</u> they seem to have had wider coverage:

> Our staff still has a pump to install after two years. The cracked Khalilabad reservoir

still stands as a monument to poor design and
ineffective follow-up.   There are 18 villages in
which we have wells without pumps.   Countless
holes are in the ground without mustarah (toilet)
slabs.   Chlorination of Kermanshah's water, and
the clinic for Javanrud and Kamyaran all hang in
limbo.   Training schools for the agricultural
school are set aside after the departure of the
Mission assistant. [10]

The over-all let-down in the Mission activities after integration was particularly pronounced in some fields more than
others.   In the opinion of a chief sanitary engineering advisor,
writing in 1960, there was so much retrogression in the Iranian
sanitary engineering program that only the completion of the
new Mission-initiated activities in 1961 could place the Iranian
capabilities once again at the level existing on the eve of integration. [11]   Reaffirming the need for re-establishing pre-
integration projects was also the fact that long after Project
72 (Training and Demonstration in Rural Public Health) was
considered "completed and successful," the Mission concluded
a new series of project agreements with the Ministry of
Health (Project Nos. 207, 208, 209, 210, 211, 212, 213, 214,
215) in almost every phase of the previous projects in order
to continue previous operations through advisory services.

The reasons for most of the difficulties with a smooth and
successful integration of the Point IV program into the Iranian
development machinery can be found in the program's conceptual and operational shortcomings discussed separately in
the previous chapters.   By way of summary, they will now
be presented in a more related manner under the headings of
strategy and tactics of assistance.

Deficiencies in Strategy

As discussed in Part II of this study, the short-range and
expediential nature of the Mission's operations did not offer a
coherent cluster of developmental projects which could be later
on fitted into a larger development scheme. Inadequate correspondence of Point IV projects with the Iranian Second
Seven Year Plan, and insufficient coordination with other technical aid in Iran made a rapid integration of these projects
extremely difficult. The sudden growth of the Point IV organization from a small technical cooperation program to a vast

scheme of national economic development within a short span of three years created such a momentum in the Mission operation that it could not be easily or suddenly turned back.

In the purely technical aspects of its activities, too, the Mission seems to have tried to do too much too soon. Instead of concentrating its efforts on one or two areas, attacking only one aspect of the problem, and choosing only one level of operation, the Mission was dragged into an all-or-nothing approach, thus ill affording both time and talent to prepare local people for an early take-over. In the areas of land reform, agricultural mechanization, curriculum revision, industrial relations, and village council formation, for example, where local circumstances widely differed from those prevailing in the United States, the Mission went too far without having sufficiently experienced and specialized staff. In the fields of American specialty (i.e., irrigation farming, agricultural extension, environmental sanitation and community development) on the other hand, the Mission could have prepared the ground for total integration if it had chosen a decisive and unwavering approach.

In deciding upon the level of implementation, the Mission seemed to have been over-anxious or ill-advised in adopting, again, an all-or-nothing policy. Mission advisors were scattered from the Prime Minister's office down to the small government agencies. Geographically, too, they were placed from the capital city of Tehran to some remote villages, with no coordinated pattern.

In a country like Iran with a highly centralized administration and a myriad of distant, oasis-like population centers taking their cue from the capital, it was extremely difficult for a foreign technical assistance mission to operate at the village or grass-roots level. Even if activities such as agricultural extension or environmental sanitation at the village level did, under proper preparation and great care, lend themselves to a direct reception of foreign technical assistance, other centralized activities such as public administration or education did not.

The Mission seems to have treated every field alike. Mission technicians were spread out in many fields, and at many levels, trying to advise a variety of people from the cabinet ministers down to the lowliest village leaders, in a variety of activities from the revision of the civil service code to the method of milking cows. None too seldom the advisors who dealt with cabinet members were in their language, tact and techniques similar to those who worked at the village level. And, not too infrequently did the Mission send its advisors to work in places where Iran's own technicians would not go (and would not be effective if they did) due to significant differences in outlook and motivations between the aid givers and the recipients. Thus, when integration came, this sprawling apparatus could not be easily brought under control.

In the arrangements made between the U.S. and the Iranian governments, the Mission Director was matched by a high-ranking Iranian cabinet minister, and the two together had responsibility for the joint operations. In an obvious attempt to upgrade the prestige of the Division Chiefs, they were also matched by cabinet ministers or agency chiefs in their respective fields. But this move proved to be ineffective in facilitating the Mission's work. Since in almost all cases, the ministers were too busy with their overloaded schedule, Mission officials could never spend enough time with them to plan things together. And in the post-integration period when the latter lost their power of the purse, they invariably found themselves in the uncomfortable position of having to act like a man who was not there.

Deficiencies in Tactics

In its tactics of operation such as employment of local personnel, selection of participants to be sent abroad, specific techniques of demonstration, there were also strong impediments to a rapid and effective integration.

The majority of the Mission's local employees were recruited outside of the Iranian civil service and in early years at a higher pay scale and altogether under better working conditions. The salary differentials for employees in the same position (e.g., typists, drivers, translators, etc.) were large enough to make the transfer of Mission employees to Iranian agencies impossible without demoralizing pay cuts. Consequently, even after integration, Iranian employees of the Mission were kept in a separate category and paid out of a separate fund, called the Special Activities Account.

The selection of participants, too, had not necessarily been made for a pre-planned integration. The total number of

Iranian technicians and specialists sent abroad under the Point IV program from 1951 through 1964 as participants is esti- mated to be around 1400. Of these trainees, some 1230 men and women were sent to the United States, and 170 to other countries. [12]

Participants were all nominated by the Iranian government agencies and they were generally higher echelon officials with better than average connections. For the selection of a majority, the knowledge of the English language had often been the deciding factor. Almost half of the trainees were over 40 years of age which made them unsuitable for lower-level positions. Some were on the verge of retirement; many could expect only a few years of active service. Furthermore, their placement in the Iranian agencies after return from abroad was not made in any way with a view to their potential role in the post-integration period. When integration came, they were also caught by surprise and were largely unpre- pared.

The lessons learned in the 1951-1955 period were used in the post-integration years, as selection of trainees was made with a greater degree of professional qualification. Aptitude gradually became the main basis of success, and English language deficiencies were made up in a series of pre- departure courses given by the Mission. Yet as late as June of 1964, the Mission's chief training officer still finds that:

> The greatest difficulty in the Participant Training Program continues to be weakness in the selection of participants. Too frequently selec- tions have been made on the basis of language proficiency or as an offering to win support of some other activity or as a reward for long service. [13]

As discussed in Part IV, in its attempt to demonstrate ad- vanced technological methods of operation, the Mission relied heavily on American techniques and American equipment, often neglecting to take early local absorbability into account. Many of the Mission devices and instruments were too delicate or too complicated to be of much use in Iran. In many cases, the training and demonstration that were provided with the aid of the new tools and equipment were only good as long as these devices lasted; once the equipment wore out, the training received was of little use elsewhere without this particular equipment.

The elaborate and expensive organization of many Mission projects was also beyond the financial and manpower capacity of local units.   Elementary and secondary demonstration schools established in Tehran, for example, were truly models of fine U.S. public schools, but they could not be started or kept in Iran without continuous outside aid.   These schools were thoroughly equipped with American school gadgetry, had selected staffs with salaries subsidized by the Mission, located in compounds rented at six or seven times the price of regular schools, and had classes of only 25 students -- one third the number of ordinary classes.

Most of the agricultural machinery introduced to Iranian farmers (apart from those that were not suitable to Iran for technical reasons) were, as mentioned before, too expensive for average farmers to afford, too complicated for many to handle, and impossible to repair in the area.   They served their purpose of demonstrating the new technique, but the technique itself could not take root because it was too radical, costly or unfamiliar.   Some of the tractors provided by the Mission, for example, reportedly stopped operating after only 20 hours of handling by the farmers.   The same lack of permanence was evident in the case of a large number of animals brought into the country for the purpose of cross-breeding demonstration.

Apart from the inevitable mistakes made in program planning, the Mission "planners" also seemed to have no time to prepare the ground before undertaking their new schemes.   Innocently oblivious to some of the local sensitivities, for example, the Mission flew a number of jackasses from Cyprus to Iran for the purpose of cross-breeding.   In itself and in an American environment, this would have been a routine and innocuous operation.   But, in a country where more than seventy-five percent of the population had not seen an airplane on the ground (much less been aboard one), and where donkeys were a traditional symbol of wretchedness and stupidity, the importation of so many jackasses by plane caused such a furor in the country, and gave rise to such derision of the Mission, that many a good and solid Mission achievement was overshadowed by this for many years after.

The Mission's lack of groundwork preparation also provided good opportunity for the program's foes to mobilize resistance against, or belittle the results of, its good work. Under hostile machinations, for example, some illiterate villagers reportedly refused for some time to allow artificial insemination of their livestock because they did not want to have "bastard" offspring. In the areas where villagers had only fat-tail sheep there was strong resistance against cross-breeding with the American variety because the latter resembled hogs -- an animal whose breeding and consumption were forbidden by the villagers' religion.

In providing foreign technicians and specialists to lead or advise joint projects, the Mission also missed one of the psychological points of successful operation under local cir-cumstances: the Iranians' admiration for academic stature. In Iran as in many underdeveloped countries, a man's prestige depends to an unusual extent on the academic degrees or titles he holds. Not being able independently to test the worth of a man's knowledge or experience in a new or unfamiliar field, most developing nations tend to measure foreign experts by the degree they possess or the international reputation they hold -- a sort of "brand name" confidence that consumers feel for a new or unfamiliar product. The higher the title, the bigger is considered the name, and the bigger the name, the more respect there is for the man's recommendations. The list of the "big names" invited to Iran in the post war period to advise the Iranian government on some thorny problems of national economy are a vivid testimony of the respect in which these men were held in the public opinion, regardless of what they recommended.

The Mission seems to have missed this fundamental point by not providing the Iranian agencies with enough inter-nationally–known personalities who could supply the needed prestige; and more significantly, by not publicizing the aca-demic degrees and experience of its degree-holding technicians.

From 1951 through 1965 an estimated 550 men and women [14] were sent by the United States to Iran as technicians, ad-visors and specialists under the Point IV program. [15] The widespread impression in Iran concerning the qualifications of Mission technicians was that they were too "ordinary," and that they lacked advanced degrees for solving Iranian problems. A review of the educational background and professional experience of the Mission assistants by the author gives a clue to the reason underlying such an unfavorable local impression. Of the 330 technical assistants whose curriculum vitae were readily available, some 30 had their doctorates (e.g., Ph.D., M.D., or Ed.D.) and 85 had M.A., M.S., or M.P.H. Against this, 175 of the technicians and advisors had a bachelor degree (e.g., B.A., B.S., or PH.B). The record for the remaining 40 technicians failed to show university graduation; a good many may have had a year or two of college studies, but there were perhaps some who might not have finished high school. [16]

Contrary to widespread belief, therefore, the majority of the technicians were not "ordinary" people, even in their home base, as they had above-average education and experience. One reason they did not command their counterparts' admiration was the fact that the majority had not reached to what the Iranians consider the pinnacle of education, namely having a doctorate degree. Another reason was that even those who had reached this pinnacle never deemed it necessary to publicize their academic standing. Few of them used their academic title before their name because, in the tradition of American organizations, they did not think that a man's academic degree could be of any real significance once he got his first job. The lesson learned was not inexpensive. When integration came, and these men and women lost their fiscal and operational authority, they were not accepted in their own right by the Iranian agencies, and with the prestige due to them.

REPARATION EFFORTS

In general, the opinion of the Iranian officials interviewed about integration was that it came at just about the time that people were beginning to get used to, and appreciate, Mission activities. In the words of a former official of the Public Health Cooperative, integration dealt a damaging blow to the public health program. As the Cooperative became a department of the Ministry of Health immediately after integration, public health activities became subject to the old Ministry regulations: salaries were low and employee morale declined; medicine and equipment brought in by the Mission were not regularly replaced, and exhausted supplies not renewed due to the lack of funds; operations in the provinces became again encumbered by too much centralization and a good deal of Tehran politics; many good people left the program and the whole thing began to revert back into the usual government routine until 1964 when again a partial revival got under way.

The post-integration period up to 1961, when the United States was still footing part of the program's bill, marked a less dynamic and perhaps a less productive phase of the Mission's operations.   Too many U.S. advisors, no longer enjoying direct authority and power over technical assistance activities, became apathetic observers; some became cynical defeatists, losing hope for the Mission's success; others left the Mission or were gradually transferred to other posts. The whole period was thus devoted to the gradual transforma- tion of the Point IV program into a series of piece-meal efforts to save what was left of the previous projects and activities.

From 1961 onward the financial costs of the completion, use, and maintenance of the projects were borne entirely by the GOI, and the Mission took an essentially advisory role. The activities were pared down to narrower geographical and functional areas. "Joint" operation outside or around the Iranian regular ministries was no longer considered necessary. Modernization of existing ministries and agencies under American technical guidance became the order of the day. More importance was placed on the Iranians themselves doing the jobs and getting the credit (or the blame) for them. Greater cooperation was achieved with other foreign agencies in the country, particularly with the United Nations team.

* * *

At the time of this writing, the U.S. technical cooperation program in Iran is still active; but it displays neither its original glamour nor its early years' vitality. According to a U.S. official document, the scale of the program has been re- duced "as a result of the progress achieved in 1953-62." The present fields of activity are limited to rural development, public administration and higher education. [17]

With fewer and more limited responsibilities on its shoul- ders the program seems altogether to be faring much better. But with the leverage of U.S. financial aid gone, and a sort of anti-climactic disillusionment about the whole cooperative effort having emerged, newer and more vexing problems have

come to the fore.   And the very problem of Iran's needs
for technical assistance (and priority among aid efforts)
still stubbornly remains to be adequately answered.

References

1. The process of foreign technical assistance, as an exchange of advanced ideas and techniques, is a continuing
   international economic relation and may indeed never end.
   But any one idea, or technique, should be able to be imparted and absorbed.

2. See supra, Ch. 2.

3. Norman Armour, op. cit., p. 1219.

4. D. S. Reid, CTR, April 16, 1959, pp. 3-4.

5. Hans Gaidies, CTR, November 4, 1958, p. 16.

6. G. G. Browning, CTR, June 5, 1957, p. 5. For "problems
   concerned with the shift from the Public Health Cooperative to the advisory status of American personnel" see
   Emma Torchia, CTR, July 7, 1961, p. 1.

7. J. S. Sullivan, CTR, May 28, 1957, p. 4.

8. H. A. Beck, CTR, November 26, 1957, p. 2.

9. See Completion of Tour Report of G. W. McDonald, Au-
   gust 7, 1958; W. G. Sundin, February 5, 1959; C. E. Kohler,
   September 13, 1960; M. V. Webb, September 27, 1960; and
   W. H. Larkin, March 18, 1965

10. P. W. Weiser, CTR, December 13, 1958, pp. 10-11.

11. A. D. Swisher, CTR, September 20, 1960, p. 4.

12. Approximately 21 per cent of these were in the field of
    agriculture; 14 per cent in public administration; 12 per
    cent in transportation; 11 per cent in health and sanitation;
    10 per cent in education; 8 per cent in public safety; 6 per
    cent in labor; 5 per cent in community development; and the
    rest in miscellaneous fields. According to a Mission study,
    almost 80 per cent of the trainees in the years 1951-1955
    came from Tehran and only 20 per cent from all other ten
    Ostans.

13. G. D. Bryson, CTR, June 24, 1964, p. 4.

14. The figure excludes the Mission's own administrative and clerical staff as well as "technical support" and "provincial office" personnel in charge of administration.

15. Approximately 26 per cent of these assistants were in the field of agriculture; 18 per cent in health and sanitation; 17 per cent in education; 15 per cent in public administration and safety; 7 per cent in industry; 6 per cent in community development; 5 per cent in transportation; 3 per cent in labor; and the rest in miscellaneous fields.

16. No comprehensive list of the Mission assistants who served in Iran, nor their curriculum vitae, can be found in the Mission publications. The Mission and the Agency for International Development have supplied the author with a partial list of names. The information on the background presented here is based mostly on the U. S. Department of State's Biographical Register which, however, omits a large number of non-career and non-professional staff.

17. See Proposed Mutual Defense and Development Program, FY 1966 (Washington: GPO, 1965), pp. 83-84.

CHAPTER

13

LESSONS LEARNED

In the last ten chapters, successive attempts were made to examine the objectives, activities and accomplishments of the U.S. bilateral technical assistance program in Iran against the background of the ten related assumptions or hypotheses established at the beginning of this study.

It was pointed out that for its optimum effectiveness, the Point IV program had to be established and carried out in such a way as to be able to: diagnose the host country's developmental problems; find compromise techniques to cope with these problems; make sure that the host country appreciates the significance of the diagnosed problems well enough to accept and carry out suggested solutions; and, finally, prepare the ground for the gradual absorption of its projects into the local developmental and administrative machinery.

It was found that the Point IV program solved a number of immediate problems and had a series of accomplishments during the 1950-65 period. These accomplishments in themselves were useful, important and often enduring. Yet in the perspective of the new problems created and the multitude of those emerging in the years ahead, their significance was limited.

Some of the impediments to the optimal effectiveness of the program were found to be inherent in the nature of the program itself; others were due to the limited absorptive capacity in the host country; the rest reflected the existence of a cultural gap between the two nations.

The program's objectives were not always internally consistent; its policies were not always mutually reinforcing; its organization grew in an unplanned fashion; domestic readiness for the absorption of technical aid was not widespread; local appreciation of the program's philosophy and objectives was not strong; and the program's technicians, techniques and technology were not always ideally suited to Iranian conditions.

As a result, few new problems were discovered; the solutions offered were mostly known and familiar solutions which for the most part did not require foreign technical assistance; and there was not a real machinery or procedure to insure the continuity of projects after they became integrated.

A good deal of the program's trials and tribulations have undoubtedly been unavoidable. A large part of the difficulties were probably unpredictable. The findings of this study, too, are based on some fifteen years of experience not available to the program planners and its agents at the outset. For these reasons, the purpose of this study has not been to attribute program difficulties and deficiencies to any one person, policy or party but to search for instruments of effective performance everywhere and in the entire undertaking. The intention of this chapter is to do the same.

This chapter seeks to present the highlights of the Iranian experience in a generalized form under the rubric of Lessons Learned. These lessons include, on the one hand, the Mission's positive accomplishments in both the physical and institutional fields. On the other hand, they refer to what a Mission advisor calls Point IV's "misdirected efforts, overzealous attacks on established customs, lack of sympathy and understanding for local and cultural practices, and other mistakes which have retarded or impaired the development of the Program." [1]   The theoretical and practical lessons learned from past experience can serve as a guide on how to, or how not to, offer foreign technical assistance. In this sense, the biggest success of Point IV in Iran may indeed prove to lie in its most conspicuous failures.

MAJOR FINDINGS IN A NUTSHELL

The following sketch of the conclusions reached in the last ten chapters is intended to show how the program fared in the Iranian case. The first observation is that the universal identification of Point IV with a cold war scheme, designed, financed and administered by a Big Power, made the program unacceptable to some, suspect to many, and insufficiently appreciated by most people in Iran. The program succeeded in

achieving some definite quick, visible, politically attractive
results.   But, harassed by the pressure of its incompatible
objectives, its ability to build a progressive program that
could produce favorable results routinely and without further
foreign assistance was significantly reduced. Foreign advice
that was locally accepted as "disinterested" had an inverse
correlation with the political composition of technical assistance staff. Also, the more politically-tinted the program was,
the more emphasis was naturally placed on publicity. And
as the program got more into the public eye, it got more of
the blame for the unpopular results.

Second, the real technical assistance that Point IV offered
to Iran was composed of: (a) introducing or emphasizing a
number of relatively new or insufficiently-recognized concepts
of rational social action (such as agriculture extension, fundamental education, preventive public hygiene); (b) establishing
or supporting some new or insufficiently-accepted socio-
economic institutions (such as the village council, rural cooperative, 4-H Clubs, program budgeting, staff-meeting); and
(c) encouraging and propagating a number of new or insufficiently—held values and attitudes (such as elevating the dignity
of shirt-sleeve work; informality in employer-employee relations; fact-finding as a basis of reaching conclusions; public
administration to be regarded as a field to be studied and not
practiced intuitively; learning as a continuing and integral part
of man's existence, and not limited to certain years and certain
limited knowledge). These were important contributions. Yet
to the extent that these activities were largely unrelated to
each other, their effectiveness was limited.   As a Mission
thinker puts it, "there is no virtue in helping people to do
better things they should not be doing at all." [2]   And as the
saying goes, something which is not worth doing at all is
certainly not worth doing well.   The Mission at times seems
to have missed both of these points.

Third, an effective implementation of Point IV assistance
required careful long-term planning so as to prevent new and
brittle techniques from crumbling under the weight of the old.
But the program's "shopping list" and "cafeteria" approach,
and its cold-war oriented, annual appropriations were not
compatible with long-range planning.   Putting too many resources in too many projects in too short a time not only resulted in a good deal of waste and inefficiency but also damaged
the chance of a steady and gradual assimilation of the projects.

The damage was particularly heavy in the case of intangible, institution-building projects which required a relatively longer period of incubation, development and out-phasing. Had the program been a long-term venture from the beginning, the Mission could have spent some of its appropriation in getting a few first-rate experts just to find out what and how many advisors and assistants were needed and where to get them.

The fourth big handicap to the Mission's success was a significant lack of correspondence, coordination and functional relationships between Point IV activities and Iran's other development efforts. The need, almost palpable from the start, was for a joint top-level coordinating committee to oversee all the various foreign grants, loans, equipment, commodities, technicians and participant fellowships in order to minimize the dangers of duplication. The Joint U.S.-Iranian Commission never really performed this task. In the absence of such an effective watchdog committee, not only did a good part of the outside help go into waste, but it also gave some vested local interests a chance to play one agency against another and to develop a wasteful competition among various aid-giving entities.

Fifth, the program's purpose, role, and limitations received little sympathetic understanding from the host country. Even to the end, the Mission was still expected to act as another dispenser of U.S. financial aid. Local authorities often asked for, or responded favorably to, technical assistance projects that were of a splinter or bailing-out nature involving physical structures and tangible results. Local counterparts often did not agree on what they wanted, what was best for their country, or how much of the aid they asked could be profitably absorbed.

Sixth, many Point IV projects were established under situations and in areas that were unfavorably disposed to their reception. Suspicion of Point IV motives, apathy toward slow-moving or intangible projects, the existence of political "pork-barreling", resistance for fear of the unknown, counterpart difficulties, and others made certain projects highly prone to failure from the beginning. The risks involved in undertaking these projects were not always calculable beforehand. But greater effort to gain local confidence, more suitable counterparts, and more emphasis on real local participation still might have saved many of these projects.

Seventh, vastly different cultural backgrounds and widely divergent techniques of production and distribution, often made the transmission of U.S. technology to Iran difficult and short-lived. American techniques and technicians adapted to the United States' highly advanced, minutely specialized, and intricately interwoven economy were not always appropriate, without modifications and adjustments, to the industrializing economy of Iran. The sad fate of the industrial projects in the early period showed that some of the American techniques and equipment, even if properly demonstrated and locally learned, could not gain widespread acceptance in the country due to their generally high costs. The slow progress of many other projects demonstrated that too many American technicians, even when thoroughly competent in their professions, could not be effective in their teaching or demonstration without their special tools, props, and environment. The dictate of economic efficiency and local absorbability required that in most instances the Mission provide Iran with different and less expensive equipment, and with less narrowly specialized technicians from countries more culturally, socially and industrially akin to Iran.

Eighth, while a good Point IV organization could have been by far the best and the most effective "public relations" for the Mission, the hurried and somewhat disorganized pace of operation in the early period, and the static and uncertain existence of the Mission after integration, reduced the organization's internal efficiency and hurt the Mission's prestige in the public eye. What was needed most was an effective joint planning and coordinating group at the top of the Mission's organization to translate mutually agreed-upon objectives into specific programs and see to it that both the administrative staff and operating personnel properly carried out specific projects. Even if the Point IV program in Iran were to terminate after a year, the Mission would have lost little by having this group at work. There was also a need for constant supervision and regular evaluation of technicians' work in order to keep a check on the projects' direction. As it turned out, however, often the only real evaluation made of an individual technician's achievement was his completion-of-tour report after it was handed in, i.e. after the milk was spilled. A good deal of precious time was wasted and some irreparable damage done to the program's prestige by failing to sift out the "failures and the misfits" before it was too late.

Ninth, contrary to the "Ugly American" publicity by the unfriendly elements about the character and temperament of U.S. technicians, the cross-section, character-wise, of the Mission personnel in Iran was probably as good as that of most communities and organizations in the United States.   Professionally, too, the hard working, the conscientious and the adjustable among the Mission staff were not few. The difficulty was mostly their insufficient suitability for their assignments. The assistants that Iranian agencies asked for, or the Mission offered, were not all nor always needed in Iran. The assistants Iran needed were not all nor always available in the United States. Sometimes, the needed assistants could not easily be found at the salaries and the terms the Mission offered. Sometimes, also, the assistants that were well-trained, acquainted with comparably underdeveloped areas of the United States itself, and suitable for operational tasks, were temperamentally ill-prepared to teach or to advise in Iran. [3]

Tenth, many sound projects did not always take root, or did not produce lasting results, because they were too advanced or too expensive for the country, or not continued long enough to be firmly established. In most cases, teaching was unsuccessful without demonstration; but demonstration often required authority in addition to responsibility.   When the authority was suddenly withdrawn from the Mission assistants after the integration, and was not effectively vested elsewhere, the assistants became a mere sounding board for the ideas of their counterparts. And this lack of authority worked against their playing an active role in fitting Point IV projects into Iran's own development schemes smoothly and gradually.

GAINS FROM THE EXPERIMENT

The lessons learned from the foregoing observations, and from the Iranian experience, point to the following conclusions:

(1) It is easiest, both to offer and to receive, technical assistance in the tangible, concrete projects dealing with physical, structural improvements; it is relatively more difficult in the case of intangible, institutional projects dealing with organization behavior and attitudes.

(2) In the realm of intangibles, it is relatively easier to succeed in new institutions where the adverse influence of

inadequate foundations, traditional misconceptions, or vested interest is at a minimum, thus allowing significant flexibility for setting up everything from "scratch."

And (3), in the old and already established institutions, the success is still relatively easier when: (a) the projects are non-controversial in the context of internal politics; (b) there is a "tradition" of international cooperation in solving extra-national problems; and (c) the techniques and tools of training, demonstration or operation are internationally standardized or agreed upon. [4]

In the Iranian case, easy success was achieved in building or equipping schools and constructing laboratories, factories or roads; but the more difficult tasks of changing the school discipline, imparting the importance of accuracy in laboratory work, instilling management efficiency, or demonstrating the need for real maintenance were not sufficiently taken care of.

In intangible projects, it was easier to introduce and expand agricultural extension, audio-visual instruction, public health, and office management which were relatively new to Iran. More difficult was the task of changing the systems of ownership and operation in State factories. And the hardest goal to reach was the improvement in the substance of education, the system of taxation, and the fundamentals of public administration.

The success through established organizations still was closer at hand in projects like malaria eradication or locust control (where the methods were universally accepted and the Ministries of Health and Agriculture had a tradition of cooperating with foreign governments or international agencies). And, the most difficult areas were community development and local governments where there were: domestic political sensitivities, no tradition of foreign cooperation, and significant divergence of views as to the best and most effective methods.

On a "rule of thumb" basis, these lessons point to the following (non-categorical) imperatives in the offer of technical aid. First, separate the lambs from the lions and call a spade a spade; do not mix technical assistance for economic development with military or other types of aid. Second, make sure the country really wants technical assistance (i.e., is willing otherwise to pay to get it). Third, determine the particular aspect, process, and level of development needing assistance; do not send technical assistants without knowing where they are needed, for what, and how long. Fourth, look for technical assistants familiar with the country's living, working and decision-making conditions; make use of third-country specialists if the right ones cannot be found at home. Fifth, do not insist on an all-or-nothing approach; offer aid, if necessary to a limited area; but make sure the aid is an integral part of a broader development process. Sixth, plan for the establishment, evolution, adoption, adaptation, and termination of any phase of technical aid in advance; avoid stop-go method.

These "lessons" are at best tentative. The experience on which they are based are taken from only one country in a relatively short span of time, and may not be conclusive enough for the provision of a standard recipe. There will also be questions as to the applicability of the Iranian experience in countries where environmental conditions provide a totally different background for aid operations. Yet, tentative as they are, the lessons learned in the Iranian case reach beyond the Iranian boundaries and, it is hoped, provide more than a mere casual empiricism.

References

1. W. A. Cram, CTR, January 4, 1958, p. 12.

2. E. F. Overend, CTR, July 26, 1960, p. 10.

3. Some Mission advisors believed that with a more solid program, stronger leadership in Washington, and a more serious appeal to dedicated individuals, many more first-rate people could have been induced to join the program.

4. Cf. G. W. McDonald, CTR, August 7, 1958, regarding the reasons for the relatively greater success of the public health program in Iran.

APPENDIXES

APPENDIX A

EXCERPTS FROM THE TEXT OF THE
MEMORANDUM OF UNDERSTANDING
FOR TECHNICAL COOPERATION ON

RURAL IMPROVEMENT

The Government of Iran having requested the cooperation of the Government of the United States in a program for the exchange of technical knowledge and skills designed to promote the economic development of Iran, and the Government of the United States having indicated that it is prepared to cooperate in accordance with the provisions of Public Law 535, 81st Congress, the following understanding has been reached regarding the principles and procedures for governing such a program:

The primary objective of the cooperative program shall be an improvement in the living conditions and productivity of the residents of the rural areas. In achieving this objective, special attention shall be given to a coordinated approach, at the village level, to problems of education, sanitation, and agricultural practices.

The program for rural improvement shall be based on a series of demonstration and training centers to be established gradually throughout the country at points near the principal centers of population. Effort should be made to extend, as rapidly as competent Iranians are available, the approved practices and procedures developed at the demonstration centers to those public and private landholdings where the necessary facilities are made available.

The Government of Iran shall provide such Iranian personnel, including rural school teachers, agricultural experts, and health and sanitation experts and such land, buildings, and equipment from local sources as may be required by the demonstration and training centers and it shall provide the Commission established /hereunder/ adequate cash funds amounting per annum to not less than 3,200,000 rials for meeting operating expenses.

The Government of the United States shall provide (a) the services of technicians in the fields of education, agriculture and health to supply technical and administrative direction of the work of the individual demonstration centers, and (b) equipment and apparatus not produced or manufactured in Iran.

In order to provide joint supervision over the cooperative aspects of the program for rural improvement and in order to furnish a ready means for consultation between the two Governments in regard thereto, there shall be established an Iranian-United States Joint Commission for Rural Improvement composed of four representatives of the Government of Iran and three representatives of the Government of the United States.   One of the representatives of Iran shall be elected Chairman of the Commission.   The Commission shall select a technical director to carry out its policies.

The duties of the Commission shall be: (a) to establish policies and procedures for the operation of demonstration and training centers, (b) to approve the places at which demonstration and training centers shall be established, (c) to submit for the approval of the Governments of Iran and the United States recommendations in respect of land, buildings, equipment, and personnel required, and (d) to harmonize the operations of this Commission with the work that is being carried out by the other Government and private agencies in each area.

The Commission shall publish periodic reports on the progress of its work and both Governments will give the Commission's work full publicity.

This Memorandum of Understanding shall remain in effect until terminated by either Government upon ninety days' written notice.

TEHRAN, ABYAZ PALACE, October 19, 1950

Henry F. Grady,   Ali Razmara,
Ambassador Extraordinary   Prime Minister
and Plenipotentiary
United States of America

APPENDIX B

EXCERPTS FROM THE TEXTS OF

NOTES EXCHANGED

between

TECHNICAL COOPERATION MISSION TO IRAN

and

THE IRANIAN PRIME MINISTER

AMERICAN EMBASSY
Tehran, Iran, January 19, 1952.

His Excellency
   Dr. Mohammad Mosadeq, Prime Minister,
     Imperial Government of Iran,
      Teheran.

Excellency:

With reference to the program of Technical Cooperation for Economic Development of Iran through the individual efforts of the Government of Iran and through the joint efforts of the Government of Iran and the Government of the United States of America previously discussed between the two Governments, I desire to set forth the proposed program and method of operation for the consideration of the Government of Iran.

The Government of the United States of America is prepared to make available a maximum of twenty three million dollars during the current year ending June 30, 1952, for such technical cooperation programs as may be requested by the Government of Iran and agreed to by the Government of the United States of America. The Government of Iran will, as its fair share of the cost of such programs, contribute such facilities, funds, and services in Iran as it determines that it can make available for such purposes. This contribution by the Government of Iran shall include the net proceeds or revenue realized from the joint projects undertaken pursuant hereto.

It is understood that the agreements subsidiary hereto embodying the projects requested by the Government of Iran and approved by the Government of the United States of America hereunder shall be negotiated between the appropriate minister or other representative or organization designated by the Prime Minister of the Government of Iran and the Chief of the Technical Cooperation Mission of the Government of the United States of America in Iran. These project agreements shall include description of the scope and duration of the proposed technical cooperation project, its method of operation, its means of financing, and the respective contributions of the two Governments.

. The Governments of the United States of America and Iran will endeavor to give full publicity to the objectives and progress of the Technical Cooperation Program carried on pursuant hereto and no less frequently than once a year the Governments of Iran and the United States of America will make public in their respective countries periodic reports on the Technical Cooperation Program carried on pursuant hereto which shall include information as to the use of funds, materials, equipment, and services.

The proposed Program shall enter into force on the date on which the Government of Iran indicates its concurrence in the proposed Program and shall continue until three months after either Government shall have given notice in writing to the other of its intention to terminate such Program.

If the proposed Technical Cooperation Program and the method of operation under it proposed herein are acceptable to Your Excellency's Government, it is requested that you notify me of Your Excellency's concurrence herein on behalf of the Government of Iran.

Accept, Excellency, the renewed assurances of my highest consideration.

(Signed) William E. Warne,
Director, Technical Cooperation Mission
of the United States of America.

(Office of) The Prime Minister

29/10/30   (January 20, 1952)

No. 28842

Mr. William E. Warne,
   Director of the Technical Cooperation Mission
     of the United States of America:

Your Excellency's proposal dated January 19 has been received and has been presented and agreed to by the Council of Ministers. For the carrying out of the Technical Cooperation Plan, their Excellencies Dr. Maleki, Minister of Health; Dr. Hesabi, Minister of Education; Engineer Taleghani, Minister of Agriculture; and Engineer Zanganeh, Managing Director of the Plan Organization, have been appointed by the Government. His Excellency, Dr. Maleki, the Minister of Health, will be the Chairman of this committee.

With highest consideration,

Dr. Mohammad Mosadeq
Prime Minister

APPENDIX C

EXCERPTS FROM

GENERAL AGREEMENT FOR ECONOMIC COOPERATION

BETWEEN

THE GOVERNMENT OF THE UNITED STATES

OF AMERICA AND THE IMPERIAL GOVERNMENT OF IRAN

<u>Whereas</u> the Imperial Government of Iran desires to raise the standard of living of the people of Iran by promoting economic and social development of the country, and,

<u>Whereas</u> the Government of the United States of America is willing to extend economic, technical and related assistance to Iran, and the Government of the United States of America and the Imperial Government of Iran, desiring to strengthen the traditional ties of friendship between the two countries, have agreed as follows:

The Government of the United States of America will furnish such economic, technical and related assistance hereunder as may be requested by representatives of the agency designated by the Imperial Government of Iran to cooperate in the planning and implementation of such assistance and approved by representatives of the agency designated by the Government of the United States of America to administer its responsibilities hereunder, or as may be requested and approved by other representatives designated by the Government of the United States of America and the Imperial Government of Iran. The furnishing of such assistance shall be subject to the applicable laws and regulations of the Government of the United States of America; the utilization of such assistance shall similarly be subject to the constitution, laws and regulations of Iran. It shall be made available in accordance with written arrangements agreed upon between the above-mentioned representatives.

The Imperial Government of Iran agrees to make the full contribution permitted by its manpower, resources, facilities and general economic condition in furtherance of the purposes for which assistance is made available hereunder; to bear a fair share of the costs of such assistance and to give the people of Iran full publicity concerning programs and operations hereunder. The Imperial Government of Iran will take appropriate steps to insure the effective use of assistance furnished pursuant to this Agreement and will afford every opportunity and facility to representatives of the Government of the United States of America to observe and review programs and operations conducted under this Agreement and will furnish whatever information they may need to determine the nature and scope of operations planned or carried out and to evaluate results.

All or any part of the program of assistance provided hereunder may, except as may otherwise be provided in arrangements agreed upon pursuant to Article I hereof, be terminated by either government if that government determines that because of changed conditions the continuation of such assistance is unnecessary or undesirable. The termination of such assistance under this provision may include the termination of deliveries of any commodities hereunder not yet delivered.

This Agreement supersedes the Agreement relating to the program of Technical Cooperation and Economic Development effected by an exchange of notes signed at Tehran on January 19 and 20, 1952. Arrangements or agreements implementing the above-mentioned Agreement and concluded prior to the entry into force of this Agreement shall hereafter be subject to this Agreement.

Done in Tehran on December 21, 1961, in the Persian and English languages.

FOR THE GOVERNMENT OF THE   FOR THE IMPERIAL
UNITED STATES OF AMERICA   GOVERNMENT OF IRAN
J. C. Holmes   H. Ghods Nakhai

APPENDIX D

LIST OF USAID IRAN PROJECTS
1950 -- 1965

Project Number	Project Title
1	Completion of Fars Cement Plant [a]
2	Construction of Ferric Chloride Plant for Tehran Water Treatment Plant [a]
3	Control of Insect Pests and Plant Diseases [a]
4	Construction of Fassa Sugar Refinery [a]
5	Installation of Air Navigation and Meteorological Equipment
6	Construction of Community Centers [a]
7	Improvement of Shiraz Municipal Power System [a]
8	Expanding Tchitsazi Cotton Mill [a]
9	Technical Assistance to Karaj Agriculture College
10	Agriculture Project Under Rural Improvement Program [b]
11	Health Project Under Rural Improvement Program b
12	Educational Project Under Rural Improvement Program [b]
13	Completion of Bandar-Abbas Water System [a]
14	Completion of Golpayegan Dam [a]
15	Malaria Control in Iran [a]
16	Expanding Rey Cement Plant [a]
17	Completion of Tehran Slaughterhouse [a]
18	Completion of Dizful Sanitation Project [a]
19	Initiating an Agriculture Census [a]
20	Preparation of Mineral Resources Development Plan [d]
21	Completion of Shaikh Ali Dam and Kuhrang Irrigation Tunnel [a]
22	Development of Land and Water Use Plans [a]
23	Drilling and Development of Twenty Deep Water Wells [a]
24	Improvement of Post and Telecommunications Service [a]
25	Completion of Karkheh Dam [a]
26	Improving Operations of Hormoz Salt Mine [b]

Project Number	Project Title
27	Development of Deep Water Wells [a]
28	Demonstration of Ghanat Construction [a]
29	Development and Improvement of Highways [a]
30	Crown Land Distribution Program [c]
31	Demonstration in Processing of Dried Fruits and Nuts [c]
32	Livestock Improvement and Management [a]
33	Improvement of Law Enforcement Services
35	Improvement of Cotton Production [c]
36	River Basins Surveys [a]
37	Establishment of Wool Sorting and Scouring Plant [a]
38	Establishment of a Bureau of Standards [a]
39	Agriculture Extension Service
40	Community Services [d]
41	Labor Training and Relations
42	Improvement of Plant Science [c]
43	Forestry and Conservation [a]
44	Public Statistics [a]
45	Training Iranian Nationals [1]
46	Providing Buildings and Facilities for Improving Educational System in Iran [a]
47	Establishing Demonstration Schools [c]
48	Establishing an Administrative and Supervisory Program in Education [c]
49	Providing Books, Magazines, Pamphlets and Audio-Visual for Schools of Iran [c]
50	Training and Demonstration of Rural Public Health [c]
51	National Iranian Railroad [c]
52	Development of Deep Wells and Distribution Systems [c]
53	Demonstration of Modern Automatic Looms and Weaving Practice in Tchitsazi Cotton Mill [a]
54	Kerman Demonstration Street Pavement a
55	Extension of Project Agreement for Construction of Community Centers [a]
56	Development and Completion of Canning Factory in the Bandar-Abbas Region [a]
57	Establishment of Farm Machinery Repair Shop and Agriculture Machinery Demonstration Training Centers [c]
58	Training and Demonstration of Laboratory Techniques in the Pasteur Institute [c]

Project Number	Project Title
59	Improvement of Farm Irrigation System and Irrigation Practice [a]
60	Training and Demonstration of Laboratory Procedures, Animal Disease Diagnostic Procedure and Vaccine Production [c]
61	Improvement of Hand-Loom Industry [a]
62	Demonstration and Training in Use of Highway Maintenance Equipment [c]
63	Urban and Rural Low-Cost Housing [a]
64	Rural Community Development [2]
65	Construction of Two Sugar Refineries [a]
66	Gendarmerie Literacy Training Program [a]
67	Establishment of Experimental Farm Machinery Cooperatives in Iran [a]
68	Erection of a Demonstration Community Canning Plant and Training Center [c]
69	Demonstration of Date Curing [c]
70	Radio Production Training [a]
71	Tehran University Soils Laboratory [a]
72	Training and Demonstration of Rural Public Health [3]
73	Construction of Karaj Dam [a]
74	Development of Zayandeh Rud Basin [d]
75	Development of Crop Production and Range Management [4]
76	Establishment of Audio-Visual Training [a]
77	Tehran Municipal Demonstration Children's Home [a]
78	Improvement in Selection and Placement of Personnel (Position Classification Surveys) [a]
79	Providing for Professional Services [a]
80	Improvement of Shirgah Wool Treatment Plant [a]
81	Cotton Classing and Ginning Improvement [a]
82	Lumbering Operations in the Caspian Region [a]
83	Bonded Warehouse [d]
84	Cooperative Specialists Training [c]
85	Demonstration Tea Processing Plant [a]
86	Introduction of Automatic Bottle-Making in Iran [a]
87	Rehabilitation of Deep Wells in Yazd Area [a]
88	Establishment of an Institute for Administrative Affairs [c]
90	Improvement of Banking Operations [a]
91	Shiraz Medical Center
92	Food Processing Services

Project Number	Project Title
93	Consultant Services to the Office of Port Management [c]
94	Community Development in Varamin Plains District [c]
95	Project Fund Agreement No. 7 Purchase of Heavy Construction Equipment and Materials [a]
96	Project Fund Agreement No. 8 Purchase of Heavy Construction Equipment [a]
97	Purchase and Installation of Heating and Humidification for Tchitsazi Tehran [a]
98	Purchase of Equipment and Services [a]
99	Architectural Services [a]
100	Development of Khuzistan Plains [c]
101	Agrarian Development Block [c]
102	Rural Development Council [c]
104	Regional Range Management Training [a]
105	Reclamation and Irrigation Development
107	Development of Agricultural Economic Services [a]
109	Industrial Institute
110	GOI Public Administration [a]
113	Study of Municipal Management [a]
115	Improving Teacher Education [a]
116	Technical Assistance to the Seven Year Plan Organization [a]
118	Engineering and Industrial Advisory Services
119	Transportation Facilities [b]
123	Completion and Expansion of Agricultural Facilities at Karaj
124	Highway Equipment Maintenance and Repair Shops
126	Demonstration Vocational Education Facilities [a]
127	Communication and Workshop Equipment for Airport Facilities
128	Development of Lake Rezaieh Navigation
129	Trans-Iran Telecommunications Link
130	Project for Contribution to the Completion of Forest Surveys in Iran [a]
131	Financial Statistics
132	Technical Assistance to Tehran University [a]
133	Technical Assistance to Agricultural Bank
137	Improvement of Mehrabad Airport [a]
204	Training Iranian Students [a]
206	Special Training Program [a]

Project Number	Project Title
207	General Nursing Services
208	Health Administration [a]
209	Environmental Sanitation
210	Quarantine and Vessel Sanitation [a]
211	Medical Education [a]
212	Jorjani School of Nursing
213	Malaria Eradication
214	Hospital Administration and Medical Care
215	Health Education
216	Maritime Legal Services [a]
217	Feeder Road Program
218	Equipment for National Police [a]
219	Radio Research and Evaluation [a]
220	Family Apartment House [a]
221	Civil Service Agency
222	Economic Mineral Survey
223	Armed Forces Vocational Training
224	Gendarmerie Training Administration [a]
226	Feasibility Study of Khuzistan [a]
228	Agricultural Credit and Cooperatives
229	Health Programming
230	General Education
231	Vocational Education
232	Agricultural Production and Marketing
233	Administrative Reforms and Training
235	Educational Plan [a]
236	Electrical Study for the Third Plan
237	Nuclear Reactor Training
238	Field Support for Agricultural Development
239	Village, Town and Provincial Development
240	Private Sector Industrial Development
243	Industrial Management Institute
254	Bandar-Abbas Port
261	General Health Services
262	General Mining Engineering Services
267	Development Bank
268	Highway Construction
270	Economic Development
501	Extended Special Aid [a]

Project
Number   Project Title

References

a)   Completed.
b)   Terminated and Transferred.
c)   Merged with other Projects.
d)   Never activated.

1)   Incorporating Projects 47, 48 and 49.
2)   Incorporating Projects 30, 84, 94, 100, 101 and 102.
3)   Incorporating Projects 50, 52, 58, and 60.
4)   Incorporating Projects 35 and 42.
5)   Incorporating Projects 51, 62, 88 and 93.